The secret of health for both mind and body is not to mourn for the past, not to worry about the future, not to anticipate troubles, but to live in the present moment wisely and earnestly.

—Buddha

THE QUEST FOR PERSONAL POWER

TRANSFORMING STRESS INTO STRENGTH

PHIL NUERNBERGER, PH.D.

G. P. PUTNAM'S SONS • NEW YORK

Excerpt from "The Waste Land" in *Collected Poems 1909–1962* by T. S. Eliot, copyright 1936 by Harcourt Brace & Company, copyright © 1963, 1964 by T. S. Eliot, reprinted by permission of the publisher.

Excerpts from "Burnt Norton" and "Little Gidding" in *Four Quartets*, copyright 1943 by T. S. Eliot and renewed 1971 by Esme Valerie Eliot, reprinted by permission of Harcourt Brace & Company.

Excerpts from Chart 1: "Factors Involved in Coronary Heart Disease" (p. 15); Table 2: "Stress Symptoms Check List" (pp. 25–26); Figure 1: "Muscular and Vascular Response Patterns" (p. 105); Diagrams on pages 182 and 183 in *Freedom from Stress* by Phil Nuernberger, Ph.D., copyright © 1981 by Himalayan International Institute of Yoga Science and Philosophy of the U.S.A.

"61 Points" figure from *Hatha Manual II* by Samskrpi and Judith Franks, copyright © 1978 by Himalayan International Institute of Yoga Science and Philosophy of the U.S.A.

Excerpts from "Switching On"—Dennison, P. E., *Switching On*, 1981, Edu-Kinesthetics, Inc., Ventura, CA, used with the permission of the author.

G. P. Putnam's Sons
Publishers Since 1838
200 Madison Avenue
New York, NY 10016

Library of Congress Cataloging-in-Publication Data
Nuernberger, Phil, date.
The quest for personal power : transforming stress into strength /
by Phil Nuernberger.
p. cm.
Includes index.
ISBN 0-399-14165-0
1. Self-control. 2. Self-perception. 3. Mind and body.
4. Stress (Psychology) I. Title.
BFBF632.N84 1996 95-33633 CIP
158'.1—dc20

Printed in the United States of America
1 2 3 4 5 6 7 8 9 10
Book design by Fritz Metsch
Illustrations by Kit Wray
This book is printed on acid-free paper. ∞

This book is dedicated to my parents, Irvin and Dolores, my first teachers. Your love became my strength, giving me the freedom to make my journey.

ACKNOWLEDGMENTS

I would like to acknowledge my debt to the ancient tradition of Tantra Yoga, from which my knowledge derives. While my experience is my own, without the loving guidance of my spiritual Master over the past twenty-six years, I would have little to say. He has been, and continues to be, the embodiment of the tradition, the unerring guide who continues to lead me deeper into the mysteries of the inner source. Whatever is of value in this book is a result of his love. Whatever mistakes have been made are my own.

I would like to thank an old friend who taught me much about writing, Anne Mazer. I value the feedback and suggestions from Diane Bemel and Bob Bostrom, good friends and wonderful human beings. I would also like to thank my editor, John Duff, publisher of Perigee Books, for his direction, knowledge, and support. I am grateful for his vision for the book. Credit also goes to my literary agent, Sally Wofford Girand, for her guidance in bringing this book to the right publisher. Kit Wray, a friend and sparring partner, provided the artwork and was always willing to go another step to meet unexpected deadlines.

I also owe a great deal to my brothers and sisters in the tradition who have nourished and supported me on the journey. Last, but certainly first in my heart, I wish to honor my wife and children for their continuing love and support.

CONTENTS

SELF-MASTERY: THE WISDOM PATH TO FEARLESSNESS

Introduction

||||||||||| I went to my first meditation class because a friend coerced me into going. I thought yoga was a fermented dairy product that health nuts ate, and wasn't interested in meditation. I had successfully completed my Ph.D. coursework in psychology, but was very disillusioned by the superficiality of the knowledge, the egocentric theory, and the preoccupation with trivia that characterized my chosen profession. Psychology seemed to offer few practical tools, and even less wisdom. And the professors were more interested in getting their next publication than in exploring the depth of human functioning.

But the meditation class quickly captured my attention. The instructor, a Brahmin priest who taught Indian philosophy at the university, presented a completely different perspective on personal psychology, one that I had never even heard mentioned before. One evening before class, the meditation teacher announced with great pleasure that his newly found guru, a great tantric spiritual Master from the Himalayan Mountains, had arrived and would talk to the class.

At six feet, two inches tall, with a powerful physique, the tantric Master certainly didn't look like any stereotype of a sage that I ever saw or imagined. Throughout the entire lecture that evening, my attention was riveted to him. After what was to me one of the most insightful discussions of human nature I had ever heard, he opened the discussion to the audience. I jumped to my feet and asked if yoga was ever used as a therapy. "Of course," he replied. "But perhaps you had better heal yourself first!"

As difficult as it was to hear, his instruction to heal myself was right on the money. I was suffering from bleeding ulcers and had labile hypertension. I was an expert at creating stress for myself and others. I knew all the answers, I could tell you all the theories and research, even which books to read. But I couldn't help myself. I had no idea how to stay calm and balanced or how to stop worrying so much. In short, even with all my credentials and accomplishments, I was just like the professors, full of intellectual knowledge but powerless, unable to take control of my life.

That lecture was the beginning of a long search that has taken me to India, Nepal, and the Himalayan Mountains. It has been a journey of synthesis, integrating my Western scientific background with a tradition of Tantra Yoga, a 4,000-year-old science of physical, mental, and spiritual self-mastery. This ancient discipline has proven to be a powerful antidote for the pervasive stress, disease, and unhappiness that are so endemic in this modern, fast-paced age. But above all, it has provided me and others with the knowledge and techniques of self-mastery, giving us the power to transform stress and unhappiness into wellness, self-confidence, and joy.

The Tantric Tradition: Science in Mythic Form

||||||||||| Nothing could have seemed stranger than this ancient tantric tradition with its gods and goddesses, demons and saints. But the dramatic and colorful symbolism of the Tantra Yoga tradition is necessary where knowledge has been passed as an oral tradition from Master to disciple, from teacher to student, without the aid of computers, books, and tape recorders. The stories and myths, heroes and villains, are remembered far more easily than facts and figures. However, my rigorous scientific and academic background with its overwhelming emphasis on logic and empiricism left me ill-prepared to listen from my own experience and heart, to discern the subtle meanings hidden within the symbolism. As I struggled to understand the mythology, I began to see that underneath the images and stories lies a powerful, systematic, and scientific approach to understanding the entire person, the details of how body, mind, and spirit all successfully come together in human form. As I discovered, Tantra Yoga is nothing less than the science of inner life, a prescription for personal power and excellence.

As I became more skilled in breathing and meditation, I began to realize that the demons and dragons of tantric mythology represented the powerful creative force of my own mind that had become distorted. I hadn't realized that I was such an active participant in creating my own misery. I wasn't consciously malicious to myself, but my unconscious habits were creating chronic problems. My mind and its habits had control of me, and I really didn't know how to help myself. I had no idea that I could control my physical self, take command of my thoughts and emotions, and use my mind more effectively. I didn't know that I could create a life of happiness and joy.

Like most people, I grew up learning to look outside myself to find answers to my problems. Doctors and medicines would cure my disease, friends and lovers would end my loneliness, attaining status, position, and power would bring me self-esteem and fulfillment, and money and all the things it could buy would bring me happiness. The kid who had it all, or at least as much as he or she could grab from life, would win.

You and I both know that this doesn't work. But we don't know what else to do. We are so externally oriented that we know very little about what happens within our inner world. It is an unknown region, a scary place filled with the terrible things the psychiatrists talk about, all the things we struggle to forget, all the powerful desires and fears that we work desperately to suppress.

Tantra: The Science of Self-Mastery

‖‖‖‖‖‖‖ Suddenly, I was face-to-face with an alternative, a tradition of inner mastery that told me that I had the inner strength and resources to change the misery I experienced. I did have the power to live joyfully, create balance between body, mind, and spirit, and live in harmony with myself and with others. But the catch was that I had to become responsible for myself, that I had to become a skilled human being. In other words, I had to become master of myself.

Under the guidance of my tantric Master I learned to pay attention to what was happening in my mind and inside my body. I began to see how my own habits distorted the creative force of my mind and created two very powerful dragons, fear and self-hatred. The real source of my stress was not the problems I faced or the people I knew, but these two dragons. It wasn't life that created my stress and unhappiness, it was me. Rather, it was my inability to manage my own powerful inner resources. I also discovered that loneliness had nothing to do with whether or not I had friends, family, or lovers. It was another dragon in my mind, only more sneaky and subtle. It would hide in the smoke and mirrors of my mind as I would focus on having friends and lovers, never recognizing the real source of loneliness.

As I practiced the breathing and relaxation exercises, my body began to heal. And as I learned to calm and quiet my mind through concentration and meditation techniques, I discovered an inner strength that dissipated my anger and reduced my fears. As I reached deeper into myself, I discovered a source of unlimited strength and wholeness, a spiritual core or Self that illuminated the dragon of loneliness and gave me the power to put an end to it.

The more I became aware of the source of my discomfort, my own thoughts, feelings, and habits, the easier it was to take charge of them. As I became more and more skilled, my inner balance returned and my stress began to diminish. I felt better, and so I was easier to get along with. My relationships deepened. I was more effective at my work. I was much less aggressive and hostile.

The more inner awareness and skill I gained, the greater was my ability to live without unhappiness and disease, to create a life filled with health, joy, and love. As my knowledge and power unfolded, I began to see just how connected I was to the world around me. My sense of isolation began to disappear, and I experienced a deep sense of commitment to and compassion for those around me. Sure, there are still tough times just as there are great times. But underneath, there lies a growing sense of ease, contentment, and strength.

As I became more skilled, I began to teach others the tools and techniques my Master had taught me. It wasn't long before they, too, began to access their inner strength. It wasn't necessary for them to travel to the Himalayan Mountains, or even know that what they had learned had its foundation in Tantra Yoga. What *was* important was that they too discovered their inner strength and became strong human beings, free from the stress and unhappiness created by their own inner dragons.

Returning to the Source

||||||||||| The way that most of us deal with the problems of life is more than a little misdirected. We basically ignore our inner resources. We are so caught up in the world around us that we don't see that both the cause and the cure of our suffering lie within ourselves. Because we look in the wrong direction, we have a distorted view of ourselves, and very little ability to use our powerful resources. As a consequence, our human skills have not kept pace with our technological skills. We have become so enamored of the power and speed of our technology that we increasingly ignore the nearly infinite power of our minds. In doing so, we become dependent on external means to solve internal problems. We overuse drugs, blame others for our own choices, and become victims of circumstance. The more things we have, the more disturbed we seem to become. With all our technical and scientific knowledge we still feel powerless, alienated from each other and fearful of the world around us. Instead of understanding and mastering the source, our own self, we keep dancing round and round with the endless things outside of ourselves.

Fortunately, the yogic tradition doesn't demand that you believe in a certain way or in a certain individual. It asks only that you approach yourself with a healthy, curious skepticism and a willingness to experiment and practice. Contrary to what most people believe, genuine Tantra Yoga Masters (like Zen, Sufi, and Taoist Masters) have no interest in collecting large gatherings of followers. The whole thrust of the tradition is to become free — of self-doubt, of neuroses, of self-imposed suffering of all sorts. But this freedom is not something that can be given by the Master or teacher. Having done the research and practice themselves, they serve as guides, helping you navigate through the labyrinth of your mind. Through example and methods, they bring you face-to-face with your greatest resource, yourself. But they can't make it work for you; only you can become master of yourself.

The Marriage of East and West

|||||||||| Over a hundred years ago Rudyard Kipling wrote in "The Ballad of East and West" that "East is East, and West is West, and never the twain shall meet." Rudyard Kipling was wrong. Two great traditions, the material science and advanced technology of the West and the wisdom and inner science of self-mastery of the East, *must* come together if we are to achieve the promise of our own humanity.

That doesn't mean that we must wear ocher robes, shave our heads, or burn incense in our homes. There is absolutely no reason to become mock Indian, mock Chinese, or mock Japanese. We may be intrigued, shocked, or amused by Eastern cultures, but we cannot afford to dismiss their knowledge of and tools for self-mastery, inner strength, and wisdom.

It doesn't matter what culture we live in, which religion we practice, or which political party we endorse; nor does it matter what calling in life — doctor, lawyer, or Indian chief. We all want to live without worrying and being fearful, we all want to feel self-respect and self-confident, and we all want to share joy and life with others. In other words, we all want to be successful human beings.

We can accomplish this if we understand the fundamental truth that lies at the heart of our humanity: self-knowledge and self-discipline (skill) lead to self-mastery; self-mastery alone leads to freedom, to happiness, to success in life.

Self-mastery has two essential elements: self-knowledge and skill. Like two sides of a coin, we cannot have one without the other. When we have self-knowledge but no skill, we become paper tigers — we know all the answers, but we can't live any of them. Self-knowledge without self-discipline is an empty bag. Many think that making more money, hearing an enlightened sage, or wearing the right crystal will somehow magically eliminate the misery of their lives. But nothing can save us but ourselves. In the tantric tradition, there is a saying: "You must light thine own lamp." We are provided with unlimited resources, but unless we become skilled in their use, they are of little benefit. Freedom is built on personal responsibility, which means developing our personal skill to act, to respond to a situation rather than react out of our emotional habits. The more skilled I am at using my inner resources, the greater my ability to respond successfully to any situation without creating stress, disease, and unhappiness.

On the other hand, self-discipline without self-knowledge leads to fanaticism. We become rigid, inflexible, unable to adapt to the rapidly changing circumstances that characterize modern life. Belief systems become rigid and inflexible, stifling creativity and the ability to understand ourselves and others. We begin to believe that our way is the only way, which eventually leads only to intolerance and fear. Our world becomes smaller and smaller as our habits make us slaves to unproductive and unhealthy reactions, and life passes us by. As we age we find fear instead of wisdom, loneliness instead of family and friends, and disease instead of health and comfort.

The Book

|||||||||| The structure of this book reflects the two elements of self-mastery. The first four chapters are concerned with self-knowledge, exploring and understanding the different dimensions of our human experience. Here you will find a road map of your inner realities, and the powerful inner resources available to you. You will also see how these resources are mismanaged and how the dragons of the mind—fear, self-hatred, and loneliness—are created. But it isn't enough to only *think* about the different dimensions. It is important that as you read the material you also do the exercises that allow you to experience the different levels. True self-knowledge comes from direct experience, not belief or intellectual analysis. These two tools of the mind are very limited if used without direct experience.

The five chapters of Part II focus on self-discipline, or skill, and provide the techniques and tools necessary to explore and take command of your inner resources. The exercises are basically of two different kinds. The first type is designed to illustrate a point, to help you become aware of a certain inner experience so that you understand it more completely. These exercises and techniques are integrated into the text, and four are found in Part I. They will provide you with insight, and make reading the book far more interesting and engaging.

The other exercises are designed to create specific skills. Several of them, such as Diaphragmatic Breathing, Meditation, and Centering, must be practiced on a consistent basis in order to build the skills necessary for self-mastery. Others, such as the Insight Exercise (Chapter 8) to make better decisions or the Sleep Exercise (Chapter 6) to help you fall asleep, can be used on a day-to-day basis or as needed. As you come across these exercises in your reading, go ahead and try them.

The purpose of the book is to provide you with the knowledge and skills you need to achieve true self-mastery. Simply reading the book, however, will not accomplish this. Unless you actually use these tools and techniques, unless you practice what you learn, nothing happens. But even if you take only one small technique, and practice that technique every day until it becomes your habit, you will gain the benefits in greater strength, less stress and unhappiness, and more joy and self-confidence. The addendum will help you develop a practical self-training program that will fit your own unique needs, and Appendix A will make it easy for you to find a specific exercise in the book.

I know that whatever effort you put into your own development will bring you great rewards. Don't hesitate, but don't overdo. Remember, the key is balance, practice, and patience. From the very beginning I was taught to experiment, to discover who I really am, and to develop my inner strength. Without asking a single thing from me except that I practice what I was taught, the Master led me step by step into the tradition, step by step into my own inner strength and wisdom. I can never repay him for his love and guidance, or the Tantra Yoga tradition for the knowledge and freedom that I have gained. But I can share what I have learned, and pass on to you the practical knowledge and tools that will lead you to your own wisdom, self-mastery, and joy.

PART I

THE KNOWLEDGE OF SELF-MASTERY

CHAPTER 1

THE POWER WITHIN

Self-reverence, self-knowledge, self-control,
These three alone lead life to sovereign power.
—Alfred, Lord Tennyson

||||||||||| More than twenty-five years ago, I was unexpectedly catapulted into a journey of inner exploration. In a Minneapolis church I came face-to-face with a Tantra Yoga Master from the Himalayan Mountains. Under his close, personal guidance, I began a lifetime of research that has been as intriguing as it has been rewarding. Along the way, I discovered resources that I only suspected might exist and an inner strength that I had only dreamed of. What I discovered was myself.

This was far more than self-analysis. I'd already had plenty of that with my Ph.D. in psychology. Instead, I discovered an inner strength that allowed me to face life without the nagging fears and worries that so commonly plague us. As I became more skilled in using my inner resources, I brought this knowledge into my clinical work. I initiated a biofeedback program in a chronic-pain clinic, and was soon teaching the same breathing and relaxation exercises that I had learned from the tantric Master. I found that my patients not only got rid of their headaches, but also began to do much better in all other aspects of their lives.

I soon realized that the clinical problems I worked with—headaches, chronic pain, phobic anxiety, high blood pressure—were only end-point symptoms of a much greater problem. People were generally stressed out about life. They were troubled and worried, had a variety of physical symptoms that made life more miserable, felt bad about themselves—and in general they just didn't find life satisfying and fulfilling. I also noticed something that the Master had pointed out. People were lonely, they felt isolated from each other, and they felt that no one understood them.

About that time I was invited to join a group of professionals who were working with young executives. My task was to teach them how to manage stress so they could think more clearly and work without having heart attacks. This was one of the first stress-management programs for executives in the country. As I became more familiar with the executives, it was clear that they suffered from the same kinds of problems that my biofeedback clients had. They endured headaches and high blood pressure, and felt anxious about their lives. They confronted the same problems of frustration and worry and they were insecure about their own abilities. By all external standards, these were very successful people. But most found life not very satisfying or fulfilling. They were burned out on life.

But as they became more sensitive to their inner resources, they began to use them more effectively. Like the biofeedback patients, they began to feel better and their symptoms went away. But they also began to think more clearly and make decisions more effectively. As we continued to develop their program in self-mastery, their concentration improved and they were less distracted by interruptions. The more skilled they became with themselves, the more effective they became at work, and they found more satisfaction in both work and their family life.

Solving the Dis-Ease of Modern Life

|||||||||| Since that time in the mid-1970s, "stress" has become a household word, a catch-all term for what troubles us. Many of us think we know all about stress and how to cope with it. Unfortunately, this is far from the truth. Over the past twenty years our efforts have been palliative at best. On April 18, 1988, *Business Week* ran a cover story entitled "Stress: The Test Americans Are Failing." For all the experts, articles, books, and seminars, we have yet to solve the problem. If anything, life is even more complicated, with greater pressures and higher levels of stress. And our ability to reduce these pressures has diminished, not increased.

The problem is that we approach stress like we approach any other disease— find out what is going wrong and fix it. But stress is uniquely different from what we normally think of as a disease. It isn't a biological entity like a bacterium or a virus, nor does it lurk in dank sewers or contaminated water. It is a *dis*-ease, an inner imbalance that we constantly create and maintain within the body and mind. Stress is *psychosomatic* in the true sense of the word—involving both mind and body. Its source is in the patterns and habits of our lives, a consequence of how we regulate, or, rather, how we do *not* regulate, the mind and body. *We create stress when we mismanage our own inner resources.*

My scientific, academic training taught me to look for causes, to identify the variables and control them. But the problems I faced, the ulcers and high blood pressure, were only the physical consequences of the chaos of my inner world—my emotional reactions, my thoughts and attitudes, my diet and lack of exercise. It wasn't the dragons in the world—the competitive graduate school, the pressure to earn high grades and to succeed, the contrariness of my girl-friend—that caused my unhappiness and stress, it was the dragons inside my head. My biofeedback patients also tried to find dragons to blame—the cause of their pain and suffering was family problems, too much responsibility, diffi-culties with the kids, the wrong medication. If only the world were different, then all would be fine. The executives did the same. For them it was time deadlines, poor profit margins, competition, family pressures. Again, if only the world were different. . . .

We can't fix life. Life is always going to present challenges and difficulties. As long as we look for causes and solutions outside of ourselves, we won't solve this problem called stress. Life will provide us with endless opportunities to be unhappy, to feel stressed, to experience pain. The problem is that when you slay one dragon in the world, it grows two heads and comes back to haunt you. No matter how many times we solve a problem, the very next day there is a new one to solve, or the same old problem reappears, dressed in different clothes.

We feel powerless because we are. We can't control the world, so we are stuck with whatever happens to us. In the face of this, we create myths about stress. These myths become gospel even though they do not fit the facts of our experience. Unfortunately, they cloud our understanding and limit our ability to deal with life and all its challenges effectively.

MYTH NUMBER 1: STRESS IS SOMETHING THAT HAPPENS TO US

|||||||||| We look for a cause, some "thing" that causes stress—a germ, poor work-ing conditions, difficult economic times. If we could only identify it, we could reduce our stress. But stress isn't some "thing." It cannot be put under a micro-scope, or bottled, or separated into categories and counted. We focus our atten-tion outward in a futile attempt to come to grips with whatever is giving us stress.

When we blame outside circumstances for our own stress, we become vic-tims. We go along in life, minding our own business, and then this stress mon-ster in the guise of our boss, time pressures, traffic, or our children's demands suddenly leaps out of the bushes and attacks us.

Nothing could be further from the truth. We cannot point to another per-son, a situation, a "thing" in our environment and say, "That is stress." Contrary to what we may wish to believe about our work, the time pressures we face, or even our spouse, they are not stress. They may act as stimuli to our stress, but our stress exists in only one place in the world, inside ourselves.

The bad news is: *We are the source of our own stress.* Stress never "happens" to us; stress is our *reaction* to the things that happen to us. We can't control the world around us. Goodness knows we try. We buy insurance, sign contracts, invest, and become union members. But does all this really protect us from stress? No matter how hard we try, we cannot protect ourselves from change.

The good news is: *We are the source of our own stress.* If we have the power to create stress and unhappiness, we also have the power *not* to create stress and unhappiness. We don't have to become victims of change or anything else. We can do something to help ourselves. Knowing about stress doesn't stop us from having high blood pressure, from feeling fatigued, irritable, or depressed. We don't need more analysis and statistics. The solution to the problem is self-knowledge and skill, being aware of our inner strength and knowing how to use it.

MYTH NUMBER 2: THERE IS GOOD STRESS AND BAD STRESS

|||||||||| One of the most popular and misleading myths is that there is both good stress and bad stress. This myth confuses stress and arousal, and it stems from an overemphasis on laboratory research and the all too common error of over-generalizing. Not all arousal is stressful, and not all stress is created through arousal.

Stress experts talk about good stress and bad stress, yet not one of them can define the difference between good stress and bad stress except in terms of the consequences. When we are excited about something, and motivated to accomplish a task, that is called "good stress." When we have a headache, or suffer from an ulcer or a heart attack, then it's called "bad stress." Saying that there is good stress and bad stress is like saying there are good heart attacks and bad heart attacks. Bad heart attacks are fatal, while good heart attacks only damage your heart, giving you the opportunity to have another.

Let's say that you go jogging. You exercise your body, increasing your heart rate and making your muscles work. You come home feeling refreshed and alive. Then someone says to you, "See, you have good stress." The next day you go jogging and suffer a heart attack. While you are lying in the grass, that same person comes up to you and says, "Now you suffer from bad stress."

You have good stress when good things happen, and bad stress when bad things happen. Unfortunately, you can't tell the difference until after the heart attack, the ulcer, the headache, or the consequence of poor decisions. Some people say that it's a matter of too much or too little stress. But how do you distinguish between enough stress and too much?

You end up with a game of stress roulette. If you win, and have good stress, you get to play the game again. If you lose, and suffer bad stress, you end up in a coronary care unit. Not a very useful way of understanding stress.

The experts rely on laboratory research. But laboratory research is a highly defined, very narrow, and constricted piece of behavior. It doesn't even mimic one-hundredth of one percent of human behavior. If we limit our understanding to scientific research, we limit our understanding of our inner reality. If we look to our own experience, when we explore our inner reality we find a very different story: *Whenever we create stress, we have changes in our body that are destructive and lead to disease, we interfere with our ability to think clearly, and we limit our creative abilities. No one ever benefits from stress.*

MYTH NUMBER 3: WE NEED STRESS
TO ACHIEVE OPTIMUM PERFORMANCE

|||||||||| We often hear this myth repeated right after Myth Number 2, and it is particularly prevalent among supervisors, managers, and people who feel they must control someone else's behavior. Far too many bosses use fear as a management tool. They think that if they "put the fear of God" in their employees, they get more work from them.

This is partially true. If you motivate people with fear they increase their activities. But what happens tomorrow? The vast body of research literature in behavior and productivity leads to the same conclusion. Fear causes an immediate increase in productivity quickly followed by an even greater decrease. Fearful employees soon become hostile, angry, and resentful, all of which damage morale and interfere with productivity. The rapid increase in productivity is short-lived, but hostility, fear, and resentment continue for long periods of time, reducing overall productivity.

It's amazing how many managers, parents, and other authorities have no awareness of the long-term negative consequences of fear. When I hear bosses or managers talk about putting their people under pressure to get better performance, I know that the long-term prospects for their departments or businesses are very bleak. *No one wins through intimidation.*

Still others think that if they put themselves under pressure, they will do better. They confuse being stressed with being challenged. The arousal or excitement we feel when challenged does not lead to stress. We need challenge in life to excel, to reach heights of performance that we would not normally reach. This is very healthy for us. When we don't have challenge, life becomes rather dull and meaningless. In fact, lack of challenge is a significant source of stress for those who feel regimented in their work.

On the other hand, when we are fearful, which is emotionally and physically different from feeling challenged, the arousal we experience is stressful. Our bodies tense, and our minds become clouded. We don't feel well or think clearly, and life becomes more and more miserable. The more fearful we are, the more unbalanced we become, and the more stress we experience.

MYTH NUMBER 4: I DON'T HAVE STRESS

||||||||| I never thought I had stress either. I had pressure, I had a few minor health problems, but I didn't have any stress. After all, I was a Ph.D. in psychology; I certainly wouldn't have stress. And I'm not the only one who thinks this way. Many of us deny stress because:

1. Real men don't have stress.
2. I am superwoman, I can (have to) do it all.
3. Only weak people can't cope with pressure.
4. We are unconscious of the reality of our lives.

There are few people in our society who are really free from stress. It doesn't matter how many degrees you have, or how much money you have, stress is in all probability a significant part of your life. The most dangerous part of stress is that often you don't even know you have it. You become accustomed to a certain level of chronic stress, and it begins to feel normal, a part of everyday life. You even believe that some stress is good for you. In reality, this unconscious and constant level of unrelieved "normal" stress often leads to disease.

TAKING BACK THE POWER

||||||||| These myths reflect our ignorance and our inability to deal with life from a position of inner strength. Instead of responding effectively and confidently to the pressures and challenges of modern life, we find ourselves playing the role of victim. Chased by one dragon after another, we feel powerless and ineffectual. As soon as we slay one dragon, another appears. Not realizing that these dragons are only reflections of our inner dragons, we become more and more cynical about ourselves and our ability to make a real difference in life.

This is a book for dragon slayers. It is for those who are tired of being chased, cornered, and disturbed by the destructive patterns and habits of their own minds. It is a manual for self-mastery. Based on the path of Tantra Yoga, it is the way to access inner strength and wisdom and become free of the terrible dragons of fear, self-hatred, and loneliness. And while they exist only in the mind, they are the source of our stress, real enough to create disease and unhappiness for ourselves and others.

Only through self-mastery can you use the power of your inner resources to create a loving, fearless, and joyful life. You will not find any magic incantations that make the dragons disappear. You won't need them. The dragons of the mind are powerful and persistent, but you are stronger and more powerful. You will discover the knowledge and tools of inner strength that will give you the confidence to face whatever life brings, fearlessly and joyfully, using your own wisdom to make the right decisions.

Awareness and Skill: Distilling the Power of Self-Mastery

IIIIIIIIII Like two sides of a coin, self-mastery has two aspects that cannot be separated: self-awareness and skill (self-discipline). It is the dynamic interaction of these two elements that gives us the power to live life the way we choose. Having one without the other is like trying to eat milk with a fork. Self-awareness without the ability to act on our knowledge leads to frustration and neurotic impotency. We know what we should do, but we have no power to do it. On the other hand, when we have all the discipline and skill in the world but no self-awareness, we become fanatics or egomaniacs, our skills driven by fears and desires.

SELF-AWARENESS: THE EXPERIENCE OF POWER

IIIIIIIIII Self-awareness is not what we *think* about ourselves, it is what we are *aware of* about ourselves. Often what we think about ourselves is quite different from who we really are and what our experience really is. I may think that I am relaxed, cool under pressure, even have a wonderful sense of humor, but what I experience is the pain from the chronic tension in my shoulder and neck muscles, frustration and anger from the deadlines I face, and a rigidity that prevents me from being playful and laughing at myself and the situations I find myself in.

Self-awareness is an ongoing process where we learn to be a witness, an observer of ourselves as well as the world around us. This is not self-analysis, where you constantly ask yourself, "Why did I do that?" As most of us know, this quickly leads to depression or leaves us feeling crazy and incompetent. Nor is it a self-centeredness where everything revolves around the ego, and we inflate our egos to make ourselves the most important person. This is an ego problem that has its roots in self-condemnation and fears of being unimportant.

To see myself clearly, I must give up being judgmental about myself as well as being overly impressed with myself. Self-awareness means becoming an observer, simply watching the mind and body work together. The more I judge myself or the more I try to impress myself and others, the less able I am to see myself clearly. I don't want to be distracted by all the dumb things I might do, or by all the wonderful things that I might accomplish. In order to see myself clearly, I must look beyond all the colors of the ego and see past the fear, judgment, or pride.

In fact, genuine self-awareness has nothing at all to do with the ego. Self-awareness is an open, observational process that allows us to watch the ego perform its functions. Through awareness we see (hear, feel, sense) just what the mind and body are doing. Being an observer, we witness both strengths and weaknesses with equanimity. It is like being a court reporter, the individual in the courtroom who must listen and record everything said without making any interpretation. We must become court reporters to our personalities, witnesses who listen without making judgments or interpretations.

This act of awareness (called *mindfulness* in Zen) has power in and of itself. If someone pinches you on the arm, you quickly feel the pain and pull your arm back. Identifying with your body, you experience the pain directly and sharply. But if you relax, become an observer, you find that when your arm is pinched the pain begins to diminish and has little effect on you. The impact on the body is the same, but by being a witness or observer, you break your identity with the pain. This gives you greater ability to understand and control the pain. You can use this principle to eliminate or control any kind of pain.

As self-awareness deepens, we become more aware of the power and beauty of our personalities. As we grow in our ability to observe, we discover the hidden relationship between body, mind, and spirit. We begin to see that the mind is already creative. We find that we do have the wisdom to choose the right course for ourselves. We discover an inner strength that is unaffected by the circumstances in which we find ourselves. And we experience a power within us that goes beyond the limits of mind and body. Self-awareness means to consciously experience the different dimensions of our finest instruments, our minds and bodies, and experience at the deepest level their relationship to our true Self, the spiritual core of our being.

SKILL: THE ABILITY TO CHOOSE

||||||||||| All of our awareness is useless without the skill to use it. Self-discipline is the other half of self-mastery. We often use the concept of self-discipline to beat up on ourselves. But in truth, self-discipline is simply the ability to do what you choose to do. Each one of us has skill, and every day we use self-discipline. But because we aren't aware of what we do, we become skilled in ways that create problems for us.

Let's take a simple example. For many of us, flossing our teeth is a habit that we learned in childhood. For those who didn't learn that habit, flossing the teeth every day is a chore. They have been told by a dentist, and they know intellectually that they must floss to prevent gum disease, but they have trouble remembering to do it. It simply hasn't become a daily habit. When they meet you at a party, and naturally the discussion eventually turns to the ins and outs of gingivitis, they look at you in amazement when they hear that you floss every day. "My, how disciplined you are!" they remark. As you realize that this conversation has become very strange, and begin to edge away, you still don't see yourself as disciplined. After all, you know all the things you would accomplish if only you had more self-discipline.

Every day we act with discipline. We do the same things, day in and day out. Only the disciplines we practice aren't always ones that we consciously choose for ourselves. They simply arise out of our unconscious habits. If I have the habit of slouching when I sit in front of my computer, then every day I practice slouching. I have become self-disciplined in the art of slouching. When I begin to realize that sitting in this way doesn't feel good, then I begin sitting up straight. Every day I practice sitting up straight until that becomes an unconscious habit. Now I have a discipline that helps me physically and mentally.

To be skilled means that we practice a particular set of behaviors until it becomes a habit. The key word is *practice*, but practice what? If you want to be a skilled tennis player, you practice tennis. If you want to become a skilled accountant, you practice accounting. But what do you practice when you want to become a skilled human being? Unfortunately, we seldom think in these terms. Formal education fills our heads with facts, figures, and systems, but it doesn't teach us how to use the most important tools that we have, the powerful inner resources of our own minds.

We need a systematic, practical approach to help us develop our inner skills. This is the essence of the tantric tradition. It provides us with the concepts and tools that allow us to live our daily lives with awareness and discipline, with skill and power. It is the practical science of self-responsibility.

Personal Responsibility:
Creating Power Through Self-Mastery

|||||||||| Because we aren't skilled human beings, we feel powerless and ineffectual, and become more dissatisfied and cynical about ourselves and our ability to make a real difference in life. Instead of responding effectively and confidently to the pressures and challenges we face, we all too often find ourselves playing the role of victim. To compensate, we turn even more aggressively to external resources—technology, therapists, medicines, laws. And when these disappoint us, we turn to magic crystals, subliminal tapes, herbal teas, and New Age brain machines.

There is an untapped resource of power and abilities, but it doesn't come in a pill, it isn't dispensed by a therapist, and it isn't activated by crystals hung around the neck. We, ourselves, already have this resource. But we must develop the knowledge and discipline to use it. This is what it means to be responsible. It does not mean just accepting "blame" or finding fault. Think of responsibility as two concepts: "response" and "ability." One obvious dimension of response ability is the capacity to respond rather than react. When we *react* to something, we are not making a conscious choice, but acting out of habit. Imagine that you had one of those workdays when nothing seemed to go right. No matter what you tried to do, something or somebody would come along and throw a monkey wrench into your plans and frustrate your efforts. Finally, you leave for home. You get into your car, pull out on the highway, and some jerk pulls out right in front of you. You crowd up behind him, lay on the horn, scream obscenities, and give hand signals expressing your anger. It's only then you notice that there are several antennae on the car and a license plate that says "State Police" in small letters before the numbers.

If you hadn't been in reaction, you probably would have chosen a different set of behaviors. Your emotional state not only inhibited your perceptual abilities (you didn't notice rather critical information) but led you right into reacting in ways that might very well prove to be troublesome. The stronger the emotional reaction, the more rigid and predictable our behavior becomes, the less creative we are, and the less freedom we experience. To have *response ability* means that we have both the awareness and the skill to take effective action, that we have the freedom to consciously determine our behavior. The more knowledgeable and skilled we become, the greater our response ability.

Emotional reactivity is an important dimension and an easy example to illustrate. But response ability refers to our capacity to use *all* the resources at our command. Self-mastery means that we grow in our capacity to use all dimensions of our personhood—physical, mental/emotional, social, and spiritual—in a conscious, skillful way.

TAKING CONTROL OF OUR HEALTH

||||||||||| Not too many years ago, Western medical science insisted that we had little control over what happened in our bodies, and even less control over disease. When we became sick, we went to a doctor, the "expert" who assumed total responsibility for our illness. We took our pills, underwent our operations, and hoped for the best. This abdication of response ability has been a serious and costly mistake for many.

Fortunately, in the early 1960s we found that by using biofeedback we could control and change physical events in our bodies that, according to the experts, were uncontrollable. Suddenly, we were learning how to consciously regulate blood flow, control the firing of muscle neurons, even change brain-wave patterns. Almost overnight, everything science had told us about the "involuntary" nervous system was being questioned.

The recognition that we do have control over what happens in our bodies (something the yogis have known and demonstrated for more than 4,000 years) is just beginning to have its impact in Western society. We find a new philosophy and practice of medicine emerging called "holistic health," which involves the whole person—mind, body, and spirit—in creating health and wellness. Prevention, participation of the patient, self-awareness, and skill are key elements. Instead of just prescribing medication to reduce hypertension, cardiologists such as Dr. Dean Ornish involve the patient in a complete program of education and training in deep relaxation, aerobic exercise, proper breathing and diet, and techniques of emotional management, all based on yoga. Using the same approach, patients in chronic-pain clinics overcome headaches, insomnia, and phobic anxiety by becoming skilled in relaxation, breathing, and meditation.

What greater magic is there than to discover that you have the power and knowledge to become free of arteriosclerosis or high blood pressure, or eliminate headaches that you have had for years, or live your life without anxiety or depression? Let's look at some of the health problems we face from the viewpoint of self-mastery and see how much control we really have.

PSYCHOSOMATIC DISEASE: MIND/BODY DISHARMONY

|||||||||| Medical researchers are finally recognizing the fact that our minds and lifestyles have a great deal to do with whether or not we stay healthy. Consider the following research facts:

- Of those patients who visit a physician with one of the ten most common symptoms, only 16 percent have symptoms with clear organic causes. That means that over 80 percent are seeing a doctor for psychosocial reasons that medicines and drugs cannot resolve.
- Researchers find that daily small pleasurable events, such as a pleasant family celebration or having friends over, strengthen the immune system for the next one or two days. On the other hand, unpleasant daily experiences, such as work pressures or an argument with your spouse, weaken the immune system on the day of the event.
- When you are unable to let go of your daily grind, your health suffers. Researchers report that men who are incapable of relaxing after work have an increased risk of heart attack nearly three times greater than those who say they can relax and forget about their work. Even for those with slower-paced jobs, the inability to relax was associated with increased risk of heart disease.
- Health is grounded in an optimistic, joyful approach to life. Research shows that those who are able to create a strong sense of belonging and connection with others have fewer diseases and less stress. Those who have altruistic beliefs and behavior are more resistant to stress and chronic disease.

Physicians and health-care experts generally agree that a high percentage (perhaps as high as 70 to 80 percent) of our diseases are psychosomatic. This does not mean that our symptoms (such as ulcer pain or a headache) are imaginary; they are certainly real enough, and real physiological changes do occur. Nor does it mean that we are neurotic. The term *psychosomatic* means that our emotional, mental, and behavioral habits play a subtle but critical role in creating the conditions which allow disease to develop. In other words, our personalities and lifestyles lead to actual physiological changes which either evolve into disease or allow disease conditions to exist.

A new area of research called psychoneuroimmunology, the study of the influence of the mind and emotions on the immune system, is just beginning. Researchers examine how depression inhibits the immune system and opens the way to cancer, and how anger and cynicism play a key role in the development of heart disease.

But then, the opposite is also true. If we become aware of how the mind and body work together, and become skilled in using the mind to direct our emotions, we can heal or minimize many of the diseases from which we suffer, and even prevent many of them from developing.

My own experience of developing bleeding ulcers by the time I was twenty-five is a classic example. I was highly competitive, tended to worry a lot, and found it difficult to express my feelings openly. Added to this was the quart of cola I drank every day and a diet rich in fried foods eaten on the run. The stress created by my personality traits and my habits resulted in high blood pressure and ulcers. When I finally took charge of my resources, altered my diet, became skilled in relaxation, breathing, and meditation, my ulcers disappeared and have never returned.

If I hadn't learned to use my own resources properly, medication, a rigid diet, and even surgery would have become necessary. And if I had attended to the early symptoms, I could have prevented the ulcers from ever developing. A disease doesn't just happen to us. It is the end result of a series of events that eventually culminate in the disease. But we often overlook the early stages of the disease process. Consequently, the final stage is seen as an entity unto itself, having little relationship to our living habits and patterns. We miss the opportunity to prevent the disease and the suffering and expense that go along with it.

AN AFFAIR OF THE HEART

||||||||||| One out of every two deaths in the United States is caused by some form of heart or vascular disease. The costs of these diseases in medical and personal terms are enormous.

Heart and vascular diseases are classic psychosomatic diseases. We may inherit a genetic weakness, but that inherited weakness does not automatically mean an early death. Whether or not we develop heart disease is most often a consequence of the unconscious choices (behaviors) that we make. We have known for years that our personality characteristics (worrying, inability to communicate, hostility, anger, cynicism, and impatience) and our lifestyle choices (diet, being a workaholic, lack of exercise) are the primary causes of heart disease. In the late 1950s, Mayer Friedman and Ray Rosenman made us aware of the Type A and Type B personalities. In the 1980s, researchers at the National Institutes of Health found that the necessary element for heart disease to develop was "emotional toxicity," or how we react emotionally to the events in our lives. More recently, in *Is It Worth Dying For,* Dr. Robert Eliot talks about the "hot reactor," the individual who reacts to stressful situations with extreme cardiovascular responses. Under pressured situations, the hot reactor's body produces large amounts of stress chemicals which create changes in the cardio-vascular system, including drastic increases in blood pressure. Eliot estimates that one out of every five people, regardless of whether they are a Type A or Type B personality, is a hot reactor, and most don't know it.

Some commentators take issue with the fact that we are "responsible" for our disease. They confuse the word "responsibility" with "blame." This is clearly not what is meant here, nor is that the message of Eliot or other re-searchers. People do not knowingly create disease for themselves. The problem is that we do so unknowingly because we are not aware of what we are doing or of the consequences of our reactions. We don't pay attention to the subtle pres-sures, tensions, and feelings that tell us we are out of balance with ourselves, nor do we have the skills to correct those imbalances and live life without them. The problem is not one of blame, but of limited awareness and skill.

Take hypertension (high blood pressure), for example. This pervasive cardio-vascular disease is especially dangerous because ordinarily there are no warn-ings or symptoms. The experience of high blood pressure is so subtle that you usually don't realize that you have it unless a doctor checks it for you. Hyper-tension often leads to tragic consequences—the higher the blood pressure, the higher the risk of developing hardening of the arteries, which in turn leads to heart attacks and strokes. According to the American Heart Association, more than 25 percent of the American public suffers from essential hypertension.

In *The Relaxation Response*, Dr. Herb Benson points out that the mechani-cal or physiological causes for hypertension are few. A constricted artery to a kidney is the cause of about 2 to 5 percent of high blood pressure problems. Other physical causes can be pregnancy, tumors of the brain or adrenal glands, or a malfunction of the thyroid gland. *However, 90 to 95 percent of all cases of hypertension are known as "essential hypertension" for which there is no known physiological reason.*

High blood pressure is almost always a stress reaction of the vascular system and not caused by an organic disease. Because we don't know how to control our emotional reactions or maintain inner balance, we can't control our blood pressure. A doctor treats us with medication to lower our blood pressure, but that doesn't eliminate the disease or solve the problem, it only manages the symptom. If this is the only course of action you take, you are engaging in a dis-ease maintenance program, not becoming healthy.

THE CHEMICAL QUICK-FIX DISASTER

||||||||||| Because we don't know how to use our inner resources to solve prob-lems, we must depend on external resources. We take aspirins (consuming as

much as thirty-two tons a day) to get rid of headaches, tranquilizers (used by 11 percent of the population) to ease anxiety, and alcohol (10 percent of the population is either alcoholic or a problem drinker) to ease stress and psychological pain. Yet, like blood pressure medication, these drugs only manage or alleviate symptoms. Not a single one gives us the power to resolve our problems or become skilled, joyful human beings.

The internal biochemistry created by alcohol or by tranquilizers is not the same biochemistry created by balancing and relaxation exercises. Nor do chemicals provide us with insight, awareness, or skill. Needless to say, the consequences of taking drugs are not the same consequences achieved through self-mastery techniques. Aspirin and other painkillers do not cure a headache, nor do tranquilizers cure chronic anxiety. At best, they allow you a little relief, a little time to do something to solve your problems. When the medicine wears off, the symptoms eventually return. After all, if taking pills "cures" the disease, then why do we have to take them over and over again? Symptoms are actually warning signs that the system is out of balance. It can be dangerous to make them disappear and not deal with the cause.

It's not the use of medications or even the glass of wine that is the problem. It is the increasing reliance on drugs to solve our problems that leads to abuse and even greater problems. Far more dangerous, they often suppress the awareness and inner strength we need to alter the situations and personal tendencies which cause the problems in the first place. Instead of using drugs carefully as part of an overall program that involves training and education, we turn to drugs as a quick fix to solve every problem that comes along.

We aren't helpless. We simply aren't aware of the power we have within ourselves to be free of disease. What if we didn't react with anger and stress, but instead responded to situations with confidence, calmness, and clarity? What if we became sensitive to how our diet and our exercise, or lack of it, affect us? We *can* eliminate and prevent high blood pressure, we can live without tension headaches, we can heal our ulcers, and we can even eliminate cancer. And we can certainly live without alcoholism and other drug-abuse problems.

A better example of the power of self-mastery can't be found than the programs of Dr. Dean Ornish. He has proven with research as well as clinical practice that even arteriosclerosis, hardening of the arteries, can be reversed with the proper diet, exercise, and self-management techniques without the use of cholesterol-lowering drugs. By taking control of their own inner resources, developing new habits and new ways to respond instead of react, his patients increase both the quality and the length of their lives.

But where is it written that we must wait until we have heart disease or some other problem to help ourselves? Although we might not have learned these skills growing up, no one prevents us from learning them now. Why not teach ourselves and our children how to use the power and resources that we have available to us? Now is the time to become skilled, not after the heart attack.

To become skillful with our health, we must understand even more subtle dimensions of our being than the body. Tantrics look upon the body as an extension of the mind, a semi-solid expression of our thoughts and feelings. The condition of the body—whether or not we exercise, the type of diet we follow, the body's reaction to the environment—can certainly affect the mind, but the real power for health and happiness, as well as for social and environmental health and well-being, lies within the mind. When the mind is disturbed, that disturbance is reflected in our environment, in our social relationships, and in our bodies. A balanced, healthy mind, in charge of its power and resources, creates a healthy body and a healthy environment. On the other hand, an unbalanced, disturbed mind creates disturbance at all levels. To create a healthy body, a healthy environment, and a healthy culture, we must become masters of the subtle thoughts and emotions of our own minds.

The Three Dragons: The Displacement of Power

||||||||||| There are three destructive conditions of the mind: fear, self-hatred, and loneliness. They are like fire-breathing dragons that usurp the creative force of the mind and corrupt our resources, creating disease, unhappiness, and suffering. They seem to be so powerful that we feel helpless before them. We don't realize that we ourselves are the source of their power, and that we can take it away from them.

FEAR

||||||||||| The most dramatic consequence of self-mastery is the ability to live without fear. Fear, the most destructive of the three dragons, is the cause of much of our suffering and stress. While we may be familiar with fear, we often don't realize just how pervasive this monster is. Much of our anger and resentment are rooted in fear. Greed most often begins with the fear of not having enough or of not being important. Then when we accumulate wealth, we become obsessed with protecting what we have. Fear drives us to acquire political and military power, feeling that if we can dominate, we will be secure. But this kind of power can become perverse and feed our insecurities. The more powerful we become, the more we worry about someone else becoming powerful. The cold

war between America and the Soviet Union was a classic example of how fear drives entire cultures: so much power and intellect dedicated to servicing both individual and national egos leading only to an unending sense of insecurity, of not having enough, of not being "the best."

There are many faces of fear but the most terrible is violence. Whether it is the homelessness and street violence in American cities, the horrors of conflict in Bosnia and Rwanda, sectarian violence in India or Ireland, or political murders in Haiti, all have their roots in fear. Terrorists operate in a culture of fear, intentionally using it to gain power and control.

Many of our fears are less dramatic, but not the less destructive. Some people spend their entire lives fearful that they will not meet someone else's standards. Even gossip has its roots in fear. If we can make others look small, and by so doing make ourselves look better, we compensate for the fear of being unimportant. Religions, governments, and communities use fear to control others, and parents use fear to control their children.

We usually don't like to think of ourselves as being fearful. We use softer words, such as "worried" and "anxious," which seem a little more acceptable. But worry is a form of fear, and being anxious is how we feel when we succumb to fear. Since we do it often, we get pretty good at it. Most of us become so skilled at worrying that it becomes part of our lives. And yet the only thing we accomplish by worrying is misery for ourselves and others.

What would life be like for you if you lost all your fear? What if you didn't worry about what might happen to this or that, or you weren't afraid of what others might think of you, or you didn't have to worry about losing your job or paying your bills? Most of us think that if we were only richer, prettier, stronger, better-looking, more charming, safer, taller, slimmer—or if we had a better job, newer car, bigger house, more friends, better-looking lovers, more respect (the adjectives are almost endless)—then we wouldn't worry, and we would be happy.

Worry and fear aren't created by a lack of things, they are created by how we think. If you have the habit of worrying, it doesn't matter who you are, what you have, or what you do, you will worry because that is the habit of your mind. This useless habit is one of the biggest causes of disease and unhappiness. And yet it has become so much a part of our lives that we even think that a little fear is helpful, and that fear is a natural part of being human.

There are people who live life without being afraid. They realize that fear is *not* a natural part of their being, but rather a product of the mind, a fantasy that grips and destroys, but a fantasy nonetheless. Through knowledge and practice, they conquer the mind's habit of creating fear. This is one of the first goals of Tantra Yoga, as well as the martial arts. Tantra Yoga Masters are called "Masters" because they have mastered their own minds and have conquered their fear. The same is true of the samurai. the great sword and martial arts masters of Japan, or the great Taoist Masters of China.

You can do the same. You can live life without the petty fears and worries that dog us from day to day, and without the great fears that every so often rattle our cages. Even the most desperate of situations can be faced without fear. As a young man, my Master often walked through the mountains of northern India. The mountains were, and still are, rugged, forested, and untamed. Once, while crossing a very narrow footbridge across a deep ravine, a tiger started crossing the same bridge from the other side. The bridge was so small that only one creature could pass at a time. My Master knew that if he retreated, the tiger would attack. Instead, he raised his arms and rushed toward the tiger, giving a powerful shout. The tiger immediately backed off the bridge, turned tail and ran. Through self-mastery, you mobilize your powerful innate drive for self-preservation and create both the energy and the focus to find a solution to any problem. But once you allow fear to paralyze the mind, you lose your ability to make choices and become locked into reaction. The greater our self-mastery, the greater our ability to face any situation without fear and to live our lives without worry.

SELF-HATRED: THE OTHER SIDE OF MISERY

|||||||||| At times it seems that we are masters of creating misery. When we aren't worrying about whether or not something awful is going to happen to us, we remember all the hurts, mistakes, and failures in our past. In other words, when we aren't preoccupied with someone or something attacking us, we turn around and attack ourselves. We seldom live up to expectations, we are never quite good enough no matter how good we get, and we keep making the same old mistakes. We suffer from guilt, continually find fault with ourselves, condemn ourselves for not living up to our own or someone else's expectations. These are all part of the dragon of self-hatred. After so many failures, mistakes, and broken dreams we begin to give up on ourselves and on life. Some of us become depressed, withdrawn, and passive, accepting whatever life gives as a cruel joke that we must endure. Others, angry at themselves, become angry at the world. They become cranky and hostile, taking out their own misery on others.

Like fear, self-hatred is a habit of the mind, an arbitrary way of looking at life and at oneself that leads only to further mistakes, poor performance, and unhappiness. When someone else attacks you, at least you have the opportunity to conquer your adversary by mobilizing the body's defenses. But when you attack yourself, there is no outcome but defeat. You cannot win in a battle against yourself; you only create conflict and suffering. Instead of mobilizing your body's systems to defend yourself, you become depressed, passive, and withdrawn.

Attacking ourselves is only a habit of the mind, a consequence of the way we learned to see ourselves as we grew up. We can always find many reasons to punish ourselves for the mistakes we make and the expectations we fail to realize. Like fear, the dragon of self-hatred feeds on our lack of self-awareness and skill. We strengthen the dragon by constantly reminding ourselves of our weaknesses and mistakes. But as long as we continue to feed this dragon of self-hatred by paying attention to it, it continues to breathe fire and create misery for us.

The secret is to stop feeding the dragon by experiencing your own inner strength and beauty. You can't create self-esteem by constantly telling yourself that you are a wonderful person. Self-esteem and self-respect grow out of the experience of committed effort. Whether or not you succeed is not as important to your self-respect as when you know that you tried your best. And if you continue to make the effort, if you continue to work with your resources, you will eventually succeed. Self-mastery arises out of effort, the underpinning of success.

The tantrics have long known that depression and apathy damage the immune system and lead to serious disease. They also know that when you give up on yourself and become a victim, you deny yourself the power to grow and change. You stay stuck in your own ignorance. That's why the tantrics believe that the only true sin is sloth, the unwillingness to make an effort. Mistakes are seen as a necessary part of learning, not reasons for punishment. But without effort, personal power remains undeveloped and unused, and the outcome is self-hatred.

LONELINESS: IN IGNORANCE OF SPIRIT

|||||||||| The third dragon is loneliness, the most subtle of all the dragons. It is the most difficult to defeat in part because it hides in our misunderstanding of its nature. Most of us think of loneliness as being apart from loved ones, having no one with whom to share our feelings, hopes, and dreams, our fears and concerns, and our experiences. The more unable we are to communicate our inner thoughts and feelings, the more lonely we feel. To solve this problem, we gather loved ones, build friendships, even join clubs and organizations. We think that if we have friends and family, people around us who love and care for us, we will never be lonely.

But it doesn't work. As rewarding as family and friends are, they do not keep us from being lonely, they only distract us from our loneliness. In fact, the more we depend on our loved ones to keep us from being lonely, the more lonely we become. Think about it for a moment. Are you ever lonely for your enemies? Do you miss having unpleasant people around you? No, we are lonely for our friends and family, for those people to whom we feel close. It is the absence of our loved ones that makes us lonely.

We think that loneliness involves our relationship with others, but it really involves our relationship with ourselves. It arises out of our sense of individuality. Our life experiences seem to confirm that we are truly alone. We are born into this world alone, we die alone. No one feels our pain or our joy, nor do they digest our food, breathe for us, or feel what we feel. Even though we may communicate and share these experiences, it is still "me," the ego-sense of individuality, that tells me I am alone. We don't experience any "self" that is connected to, or a part of, any other self. As a consequence, we fail to understand the fundamental connection we have with each other and with the universe at large.

Yet there are times when we experience a sense of wholeness, of completeness, of kinship with the universe at large. It may happen when we look up at the starry heavens, or watch the birth of a child, or participate with others in working through a crisis situation. It doesn't happen because we have expectations or make demands, we simply experience a strong sense of belonging to something greater than ourselves. At this moment, we lose our ego-sense of self, and experience being part of a greater identity, a greater "Self," and all loneliness vanishes. Unfortunately, these experiences are fleeting, easily lost in the shuffle of our day-to-day distractions, pressures, and reactions.

When we are genuinely loving, we also break free from our ego-sense of self. But we confuse "loving" with "being loved." Most of us engage in a desperate search for someone to love us, but we confuse the issue by saying that we need someone to love. We *say* we want someone to share with, someone we can love, but what we are really saying is that we need someone to love us, someone who will make us feel important and keep us from feeling lonely. This is not love, but emotional attachment which leads us into dependency. We believe that we need this person to be happy, to be content, to be fulfilled. So our loving becomes distorted by our emotional needs. When they don't love us back, we feel miserable and unloved. When they aren't around, we feel lonely.

We all have a remarkable, unlimited capacity to love one another. There is a wide range of expression of our love, from brotherly and sisterly love to romantic, sexual love. But as long as we continue to confuse love and emotional attachment, we will continue to be lonely, even when we have someone to love.

We can conquer this dragon of loneliness, but we must turn to our deepest resource to do so, our core spiritual Self. The great spiritual sages of all traditions say that our loneliness lies in the ignorance of our spirit, the core of our being. When we become aware of this Self, we experience the mystery of life, the unbroken and unending connection we have with each other and with the universe. We become fully conscious of the universal Spirit that flows within and through us. Picture life like a large oak tree filled with leaves, twigs, and branches. Our ego-sense of self makes us feel like we are a leaf on this tree. When the winds blow, the leaves rub against each other. Sometimes this is a pleasant experience and sometimes it is very unpleasant. As leaves, we feel isolated and apart from one another, even though we can see that we all belong to the same tree. When we become conscious of our spiritual Self, we realize that we are far more than just the expression of a single leaf. We are more than even the branch and the trunk. We are the life force within the tree.

We cannot realize the power of this experience by analyzing it. Intellectual understanding is not the experience of wholeness, nor does it put an end to loneliness. Those experiences of wholeness gained by watching a birth or gazing at the stars are not intellectual, logical events. We must go beyond the intellect and become conscious of the human spirit directly. This is the heart of the meditative traditions of self-mastery—to calm the mind so completely, to be so focused, that we experience this spiritual Self directly. In Tantra, this experience is called *samadhi*, while in Western meditative/spiritual traditions it is referred to as a "mystical experience" because it takes us beyond our thoughts and emotions, beyond even our beliefs.

The mystical experience is powerful and undeniable. In just one experience, our loneliness, our fear, and our self-hatred are diminished by half. As we become more skilled in our ability to have this awareness, we gradually lose all sense of loneliness, all fears are vanquished, and all self-hatred is eliminated. Our ego-sense of individuality now becomes an instrument by which we express in our unique way our thoughts, our love, our joy, and our strength. We do not lose our identity, we polish and refine our identity until our spiritual Self shines through like a bright light, and we experience the real joy and freedom that are our true heritage.

Living with Strength:
The Practical Application of Mastery

|||||||||| This mystical experience is not an empty promise, but the consequence of the systematic development of self-mastery. It is, in essence, the unleashing of our inner strength, joy, and love. It is the culmination of our self-mastery into Self-realization. We don't accomplish this by trying to change ourselves,

but by consciously developing our inner awareness and strengths. Instead of change we create transformation, becoming all of what we truly are—an expression of light, love, and power. As we progress in this transformation, our minds become more and more free of disturbance and we become more effective, joyful, and loving human beings. Instead of using the force of the mind to create fears and worries, we use it to solve problems and bring greater beauty into the world. As we experience our inner strength and confidence, we become more flexible, unlocking rigid belief systems, losing our fear of making mistakes and what others may think of us. As we free ourselves from emotional distortions, and enhance our perceptual abilities and our thinking, instinct and intuition become sharp and clear. As we lose our self-hatred, we discover unlimited self-confidence, will, and decisiveness and begin to use them as *conscious* skills. In other words, we become skilled human beings.

As we discover the strength and wisdom within ourselves, others begin to discover the strength and wisdom within themselves. The way we relate to others—our close personal relationships, our sense of community, our capacity to give, to belong, and to relate to other human beings—depends on who we are as individuals. If we teach ourselves and our children how to live without fear, we would have a culture free of violence. If we teach ourselves and our children how to love and respect ourselves and others, we would have a culture free of hatred and condemnation.

We cannot have a society free of fear, violence, and hatred until we have a citizenry free of fear, violence, and hatred. The key is education and training in self-mastery, not slogans, guns, and prisons.

A CULTURE OF MASTERY

||||||||| Even though the quality of our entire lives is dictated by our state of mind, most of us spend incredibly little time enhancing, or even maintaining, sound mental health. In fact, very little effort is made in modern society toward training the whole mind. Reflecting this deep-felt need, many are turning to religion, self-help books, and pop psychology to find some relief for the mental dissatisfaction so prevalent in our society.

But what is it we are looking for? Are we really searching for knowledge and mastery, or is it just another search for an easy, quick answer—a psychic "pill," a magical crystal, a new religion to lead us into the promised land and remove all our unhappiness, and leave us free from loneliness and disease?

If we invested in self-mastery we would create a different culture. Our hospitals would become health learning centers, teaching the basic skills of diet, exercise, and stress management as well as healing arts. Prevention would be the primary thrust instead of disease maintenance. With the proper focus on education, our children would learn early in life how to use their internal controls to maintain balance and direct their emotional energy. They would have the self-respect as well as the self-discipline to resist drugs and teen pregnancies. Then we might find that we don't need to spend 14 percent of our gross national product on health care, or struggle to build more and more prisons. Our cities might become true cultural centers rather then ghettos of violence, drugs, and hopelessness.

It isn't money or external resources that we need—we need to refocus our energies. What would be the consequences, for instance, if we turned on the TV and, instead of someone hawking the latest drug or diet gimmick, there was a celebrity saying, "Don't forget to practice your relaxation tonight. Don't forget to work with your mind tonight. Don't forget to tell someone you love them. Most of all, don't forget that you have all the strength and resources you need to be happy and healthy." What if we started to sell self-mastery instead of drugs, providing insights and simple techniques that people could practice? What if we made stories showing self-confidence, compassion, and common sense the focus of our television shows instead of stories about infantile greed, petty jealousies, and violence?

Awareness and Skill: Passageway to Freedom

||||||||| The way to freedom lies in self-awareness and skill. Through our own efforts we can create a life of health and wellness, of joy and love. But just as important, this path unlocks our inner creative potential and determination, which we badly need to solve the tremendous social and economic problems we face. To establish balance and harmony in our society we must establish balance and harmony within ourselves. Like my initial lesson from the Yoga Master: first, we must heal ourselves.

For this, we need the right attitude in daily life—and for the right attitude, we need to access our innate inner strength. Unless we become skilled in the use of our inner resources and create a bridge between them and our external lives, our efforts will be futile.

The solutions to our suffering are amazingly simple. This is not to say that they are easy. But they are available. We need to experiment personally and see which ones work for us. The first step is to develop a road map, a practical way of understanding ourselves and the resources we have available to us. After all, if we are the source of our own unhappiness, we are also the source of our own salvation.

CHAPTER 2

SELF-KNOWLEDGE: THE DIMENSIONS OF IDENTITY

Know then thyself, presume not God to scan;
The proper study of mankind is man.
—Alexander Pope

|||||||||| You don't have to be an intellectual genius to develop your power as a human being. Anyone can learn to use all of their inner resources—physical, mental, and spiritual. Nor does it matter what kind of work you do, whether or not you have a college degree, whether you are single, married, divorced, or widowed. Becoming a skilled human being doesn't depend on external things, but what we do with ourselves. There are senior executives as well as plumbers, chefs, and housewives who have become skilled human beings. How we choose to use the skills that we develop is a matter of individual choice and opportunity. But anyone can become skilled, anyone can develop their strength.

When I first met Jerry, he was forty-two years old, and had been out of prison for only a short time. Growing up poor, Jerry learned to steal at an early age as a way to provide food for the family. Over the years, he stole millions of dollars, but he also spent sixteen years in prison. With each new prison term, he would immediately do something that would land him in solitary confinement. He found that this was the safest way to do the time. The biggest problem for him in solitary was never having enough to eat. Since he was in solitary, his food was brought to him as he wasn't allowed to pass through a cafeteria line with other prisoners where he could help himself. During his last time in prison, he began to read books on yoga that talked about eating as a way of discipline. He read that if you chew your food thoroughly, you will eat far less and digest your food more completely.

Intrigued, Jerry began to follow this small discipline. Soon, he was leaving food on his plate, no longer requiring the large amounts he was used to. Through this one small act of discipline, Jerry realized that he had the power to make choices. If he could control his appetite, he certainly could control the choices he made for himself. He didn't have to continue being a thief and spending his life in prison. He began to use the relaxation and breathing exercises to help him gain greater self-awareness and self-control. When he finished serving his time, he returned to Minneapolis and continued to practice his exercises and develop his inner balance and self-discipline. He married, fathered a beautiful child who is now a teenager, and is a loving, supportive husband and father. The past twenty years have not always been easy, and Jerry is certainly not wealthy. But he continues to develop his self-awareness and discipline, and his life is free of worry and crime. My friend's power is in the kind of person he has become.

Prison didn't change Jerry. He did that for himself. Instead of reacting like he always did, Jerry decided to do something differently. The more he learned about himself, the more choices he realized he had. The more he practiced the exercises, the more able he was to make those choices. Like Jerry, we must look within ourselves to discover our strengths. To take charge of our lives, we must take charge of ourselves. But what is this "self"? This question has as many answers as there are people who ask it.

Being Human: The Whole Picture

|||||||||| As human beings, we are complex organizations of physical events, energy, perceptions, thoughts, feelings, and emotions, and something more that we will simply call for now the spirit. What others see in us, and how we see ourselves, is what we often refer to as the personality. But there is far more to us than meets the eye.

We tend to define ourselves in many different ways: we are rich or poor, male or female, liberal or conservative. These economic, biological, or political labels often limit our self-awareness and keep us from overcoming our fear, self-hatred, and loneliness. We can analyze ourselves in biochemical and/or genetic terms, but that doesn't help us understand our thoughts. We could use psychiatric concepts, but most psychiatrists focus on pathology, not strengths, and we end up with one-sided, distorted pictures of ourselves.

Enchanted with technology, we often think of ourselves as biocomputers, sophisticated biological machines. But machines are closed systems. We can take them apart and put them back together again. We can switch parts from one machine to another. We can build a computer piece by piece, adding up parts to create a system. If we don't like the system we build, we change it around and create a new system.

But we can never add up the parts and pieces to get a human being. Human beings are more than the physical parts of the body. While some scientists would have us believe that we are only the body, our experience tells us another story. If we lose a finger, an arm, or a leg, we don't think of ourselves as being less of a human being. We may see ourselves as less capable, even less lovable, but inside there is something that still insists that we are a person, a complete human being. We can think, we can dream about the future and take actions based on those dreams. We can live in the past, totally ignoring the present reality. Human beings have other dimensions that go far beyond the physical body. Even without having a mystical experience, most of us believe there is a spiritual dimension, a soul or consciousness that transcends both the mind and body.

We are living "open systems." We constantly interact with our environment, change it, and in turn are changed by it. Open systems are characterized by options and creative expression. Human beings have the capacity to create chaos or harmony, to be self-destructive or create wellness and fulfillment. We can choose to eat to excess, to drive too fast, to work too hard, or to lose control of our emotions. Or we can eat properly, drive carefully, balance our work with leisure time, and take control of our emotional lives. We may cure disease by altering our emotional condition, by stimulating our immune system through imagery, by taking herbs and natural medicines, or by using synthetic medicines. Similarly, we can solve problems in a variety of ways. We may draw upon our past experience, base our decisions on instinct, use intuitive knowledge, rely on logic and intellect, or combine these methods. The mind has unlimited capacity to structure knowledge, insights, and creative expression. No technology comes even close to matching human creativity, adaptability, and flexibility. We have infinite opportunities, ways and means to achieve what we want, *if we develop the knowledge and skill to use them.*

Open systems are also characterized by *harmonization,* the ability to achieve and maintain harmony of energy and effort. We have an innate ability to maintain inner balance, or harmony, which allows us to function efficiently and effectively. A good example is the resting heartbeat when our heart pumps blood and performs its duties, but does so in a state of balance. No one dies from a resting heartbeat. But if we do something to disrupt the system—bad diet, improper breathing, lack of exercise, inappropriate emotional reactions—we destabilize it and our heart becomes unstable. Instead of a balanced heart rhythm, we end up with irregular heartbeats or high blood pressure.

We find that same harmony of energy and effort when we are focused on our task and work seems effortless. At this time we aren't creating excess tension, worrying about something else, or doubting ourselves. The mind is calm and thoughts are clear. But if we destabilize the system—start doubting ourselves, worrying about what someone will think of our efforts, remember all the times when we failed—then we create a chaotic situation and our work suffers and we finish the day with a headache or feeling worn out.

We are not simply biochemical reactions, but *living* systems. We are sustained by a life force that cannot be flipped on and off. A computer "comes alive" when you plug it in and run an electric current through it. You can switch the computer, or any machine, on and off without doing any harm. It's very difficult to do that with a human being. Our life force is an essential part of who we are, and plays a vital function in our ability to live without stress. On still another level, we think, we feel, we dream—our rich mental and emotional life plays a crucial role in determining our health and well-being.

When we act as if the different elements of our lives are separate from one another, we lose our human power. For example, when a cardiologist treats high blood pressure with medication and ignores the role of diet, exercise, emotions, family, and work life, he treats the patient as a machine. When we ignore our intuitive knowledge, deny our emotions, and rely solely on so-called logic, we act as if we are machines. We must look to all aspects of our personality system if we want to achieve self-mastery.

We come as a complete package. Any action we take involves all aspects of the personality. We do not make decisions without our memory playing a role, nor do we play handball without our liver functioning. Just as teamwork makes a world-class team, it's teamwork within the personality that makes a world-class human being.

The Six Dimensions of Identity

||||||||||| Instead of labels, we need a simple, practical way of seeing ourselves, one that allows us to recognize and explore all the different aspects and resources at our disposal. The tantrics use a concept of six dimensions to define the relational structure of body, mind, and spirit. These are illustrated and briefly described in Figure 2.1. The outer five dimensions are like sheaths that fit over the core sixth dimension, the spiritual Self. This spiritual Self is the core identity while the other dimensions constitute the expressive vehicle, the instrument through which the spiritual Self expresses itself in the world around it. While each dimension has unique functions, one cannot be separated from the others. Each is a necessary part of being human. We always function as a whole person, not as individual, mechanical pieces. Whenever we think, or talk, or act, all parts of our body, mind, and spirit are involved. By exploring these dimensions, we can see where our resources lie and how to use them to create magic.

We begin our journey with the physical dimension, the body, and then travel inward through increasingly more subtle levels of energy that make up

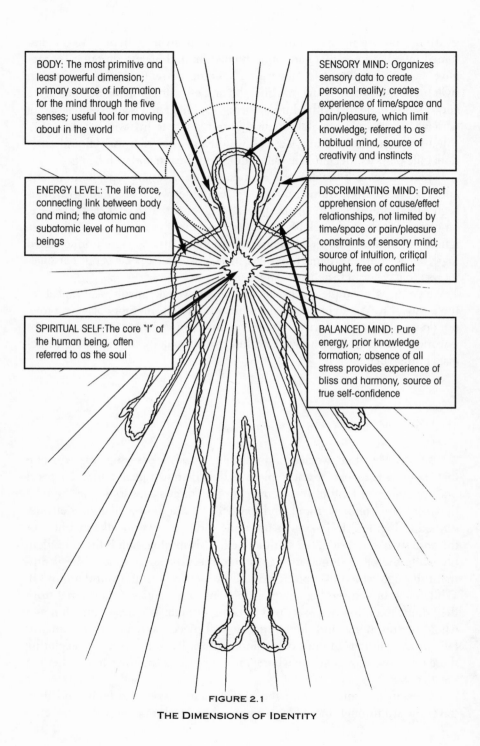

BODY: The most primitive and least powerful dimension; primary source of information for the mind through the five senses; useful tool for moving about in the world

SENSORY MIND: Organizes sensory data to create personal reality; creates experience of time/space and pain/pleasure, which limit knowledge; referred to as habitual mind, source of creativity and instincts

ENERGY LEVEL: The life force, connecting link between body and mind; the atomic and subatomic level of human beings

DISCRIMINATING MIND: Direct apprehension of cause/effect relationships, not limited by time/space or pain/pleasure constraints of sensory mind; source of intuition, critical thought, free of conflict

SPIRITUAL SELF: The core "I" of the human being, often referred to as the soul

BALANCED MIND: Pure energy, prior knowledge formation; absence of all stress provides experience of bliss and harmony, source of true self-confidence

FIGURE 2.1
THE DIMENSIONS OF IDENTITY

the life force and mind. We end with the sixth dimension of pure awareness, the spiritual Self. Each succeeding dimension is more subtle and contains more powerful resources than the previous one. The more subtle the dimension, the greater the potential for personal power and freedom.

The Power Functions: Tools for Self-Mastery

||||||||||| Once we know where to look, we can find the tools we need to achieve self-mastery. Each dimension contains different functions which combine to create knowledge and action. These "power functions" create and direct our thoughts and behavior. Used skillfully, they help us become successful, healthy, and happy. But when we mismanage them, we become stressed, unhappy, and diseased. For instance, emotional energy is a power function of the sensory level of the mind. Our emotions can inspire and motivate, or they can create fear and rigidity. We can react to a situation, become angry and blow up, or we can take control and channel our anger into determination and will. The difference lies in our ability to direct our emotional energy, to choose our response instead of reacting out of habit.

As we mature, there are periods in our lives when our emotions are strong and developing. Teenagers have a notorious reputation for emotional ups and downs. Whenever you mention that you have children who are entering their teens, most people roll their eyes and extend their condolences. Certainly the teenage years can be a time of surging emotions. But that doesn't mean that self-control isn't possible. If teenagers understand how to manage the powerful emotional energies that develop during these years, they have the means for great learning and accomplishment.

Raka was just becoming a teenager when she decided to develop her inner strength. Raka has a mercurial personality. Usually good-natured and easily generous, when pushed she can also explode in a fit of temper. Raka loves to play basketball, and is very good at it. When she first started playing, she would get angry whenever someone would play rough against her. She took every competitive knock personally. Before long, she would be so angry she couldn't focus on the game, and would make mistake after mistake. The more angry she got, the worse her playing became.

Finally, she saw that her anger was preventing her from playing effectively, and would often result in her being benched. Then one day she realized that if she could channel her angry energy into jumping higher and moving faster instead of directing it toward an opponent, she would be able to outplay the others. With practice Raka taught herself to focus on her performance instead of the other player. It took time and effort, but the payoff was well worth it to Raka, and to the team. Now when she begins a game, she is cool, calm, and in control. Instead of getting angry during a game, Raka becomes more intense and focused, and doubles the intensity of her play. Like any good athlete, she focuses her energy on out-rebounding, out-shooting, and out-playing her opponent. Raka takes control of her mind and uses her emotional energy to motivate herself for even better performance.

It doesn't matter what age we are. If we don't take control, it's all too easy to be victimized by our thoughts and emotions and trapped by the tension in our bodies. The starting point is inner awareness. Our ability to use our resources skillfully develops to the degree that we become aware of them within ourselves.

The first step in self-mastery is self-knowledge. That means more than just having ideas about who we are. It is based solely on direct experience. As we learn about the different dimensions of personality, we will have a map of the territory we want to explore. But like all maps, it can't substitute for being there. Let's start by first being there, and begin with an experiential journey through the six dimensions of the personality. First read through the Traveling Exercise a few times until you feel comfortable about the sequence, and then do it as completely as you can by memory. After a few times, you will easily remember the sequence. You can also record the exercise on a cassette tape and listen to it, or have a friend guide you through the exercise. If you wear contact lenses, take them off before doing this or any exercise, such as deep relaxation, concentration or meditation, that requires you to close your eyes for more than a few moments.

Notice how quiet you feel after doing this exercise. Do you feel any difference in the tension levels of your muscles? Did your breathing become more quiet and stable? Almost always, simply directing your attention inward toward the center of your mind creates a calm, restful state.

As you explore the different dimensions, you will have different experiences—body feelings, the movement of breath, thoughts, objectivity about your thoughts, and quietness. The first time you do this, you may experience only the most obvious events—chronic tension in your shoulders; the insistent demand of immediate problems; old, familiar patterns of guilt and regret. But as you become more experienced and sensitive, it becomes easier to identify the different functions of each dimension, and see how experiences are being created. As you do this, you slowly gain greater control over these power functions, and they become more helpful. This means that you have more choices, a greater freedom to act and think.

To help understand each dimension, we can compare them with a sophisticated computer system. Each dimension is analogous to a different function

(When doing an exercise, a series of periods (. . .) indicates a pause.)

Sit back in your chair, close your eyes, and relax as well as you can . . . Let your breath become very smooth and even . . . Breathe without any effort on your part . . . Now direct your awareness to your body . . . Where do you feel tension in the body? . . . Can you feel your heart beat? What else do you feel in your body? . . . What do you feel or sense, what do you hear, what do you smell? . . . Now bring your attention to your breath . . . What does the air feel like as you breathe in and breathe out? . . . Be aware of the lungs as they expand and contract . . . Be aware of your feelings of energy . . . Is your energy level low or high? . . . Is the quality of the energy calm or tense? . . . Now be aware of your thoughts . . . Don't try to think them, just be aware of your mind thinking them for you . . . Notice how they jump from one topic to another . . . Be aware of how some thoughts grab your attention more than others . . . Do you notice any relationship between your thoughts and your level of energy? . . . What happens when a worry comes to your mind? . . . Do you notice any relationship between your thoughts and tension in the body? . . . Now go to what seems to be the center of your mind and allow yourself to think of a problem you must solve . . . Don't allow your emotions to pull you into the problem, just look at the problem as if it were quite separate from you . . . Examine the problem as if it had nothing at all to do with you . . . Do you notice anything different about the problem? . . . Is there any greater clarity, and do you notice any details that you may have passed over before? . . . Now imagine yourself going further into the center of your mind where it is very quiet and still . . . Allow yourself to experience this stillness and quietness for a few moments . . . Notice what happens to the thoughts . . . Now visualize a pure flame . . . Let the flame be as small, as perfect, and as clear as your mind will allow . . . After a few moments, be aware of the stillness in the very center of your mind . . . Now become aware of the thoughts of your mind . . . Now become aware of your breathing . . . Are you breathing differently than when you first started this exercise? . . . Now be aware of how your body feels . . . Now gently open your eyes.

within the system. Remember, however, that this is just an analogy. Even the most powerful computer cannot begin to match the flexibility, power, and wisdom of the human body, mind, and spirit.

THE FIRST DIMENSION: OUR PHYSICAL BODY

||||||||||| The first and most familiar dimension of the personality is the body. The body is analogous to the hardware of the computer system—screen, keyboard, hard disk, logic chips, all the physical elements of a computer. Our health and wellness depend a great deal on how skillfully we care for the body. The relationship between the body and our happiness is simple and direct: when you aren't healthy, you don't enjoy life and you don't function well.

The body is an extremely sensitive barometer to both the mind and the world around us. A valuable source of information and knowledge, it tells us immediately when something is not quite right, both in our environment and within ourselves. If we pay attention to the body's signals, we gain insight into both our environment and our inner reality—the condition of our health, emotional states, and even our instincts and intuition. These physical responses can be quite dramatic, such as a pounding heart when we get up to give a speech, or a tensing of our shoulder muscles as we hear about a new work assignment. But often they are subtle—a feeling of unease in a social situation when there is no obvious reason to be uneasy, or a slight tightening of the tiny muscles around the corners of the mouth when we become angry.

The more sensitive we are to the body's messages, the easier it is for us to stay healthy. The body always lets us know when we are out of balance. The most common signal is muscle tension, but it can just as easily be a change in sleep patterns, the way we breathe, or an elevated blood pressure. These early signals warn us that something is wrong, and if we ignore them, we may develop a disease. For example, high blood pressure is most often a clear signal that we are not handling pressure well. If we don't know that we have high blood pressure, it can lead to a disaster, such as a stroke or heart attack. Once aware of the problem, we can easily take steps—deep relaxation, proper breathing, the right kind of exercise, greater emotional control—to correct it.

When we ignore the signs or symptoms of our bodies—or, worse, eliminate the symptoms without dealing with the cause—we only create a bigger problem. Taking pain medication for a tension headache relieves the symptom, but it doesn't change the underlying cause, the chronic tension in our muscles. As a consequence, we end up taking the pills over and over again because we didn't solve the real problem of chronic tension.

The Anatomy of Self-Mastery

In many ways, we can consider the body to be a very sophisticated biocomputer. The control system for this biocomputer is the brain and nervous system. If we understand how to take control of this system, we have the means to take control of the body. We will need to rely less and less on external resources to control our well-being. Of course, the details of this sophisticated biocomputer are quite complex, but the operating principles are rather simple.

The main controls are the brain and its extension, the spinal cord. Together these two are called the *central nervous system*. The brain is the central processing unit (CPU) of our biocomputer where we store information and run our programs. All other nerves in the body are part of two powerful nervous systems that carry out the directions of the brain and send information back to the brain for processing. The first of these two systems is the sensorimotor nervous system, which controls our sense organs and our muscles. It is often called the *voluntary nervous system* because we can easily and consciously choose to use our senses or muscles. Our sensorimotor system is both a powerful data collection system and an action system. As key elements of our perceptual process, our senses provide us with information about both our inner realities and the world around us. The sensorimotor system also controls muscle tension and relaxation, providing us with the ability to move and be active.

The other system is called the *autonomic nervous system* and regulates our internal organ systems, such as cardiovascular functioning and digestion. It is called "autonomic" because it can function automatically to regulate our internal organs without us having to pay attention to it. The autonomic system is particularly important to us because it controls our stress reactions. If we know how to control this powerful system, we can control stress and free ourselves from the diseases and problems created by stress.

The Balancing Act

The autonomic nervous system is made up of two distinct nervous systems called the *sympathetic* and *parasympathetic*. Together these two systems regulate the activities of our organs. In general, the organs are supplied with nerves from both systems, which is called reciprocal innervation. For example, both systems innervate the heart. Sympathetic stimulation speeds the heart up while parasympathetic stimulation via the vagus nerve slows the heartbeat. At rest, both systems discharge at a low level, and the resting heartbeat represents a balance of the two opposing influences. If we exert ourselves, or if we become anxious, the heart speeds up. This is first accomplished by a decrease in vagal (parasympathetic) activity and then by an increase in sympathetic activity.

We can picture these two systems as a complex and sophisticated balancing act. The sympathetic system creates arousal in the body. It does things like speed the heart up and cause the liver to release fuel for the muscles to burn. The parasympathetic does just the opposite. It creates inhibition or rest in the body. It slows the heart down and makes the liver store fuel. When we are healthy, these two systems work together like our right and left hands work together to accomplish a task. They balance each other, exchanging dominance as the need requires, and maintaining equilibrium (homeostasis) as dominance shifts.

Most of us are familiar with the term "fight or flight." This is the alarm reaction that provides us with the energy and arousal needed to defend against an attack. It is controlled by the sympathetic system, which allows us to have instant arousal throughout the entire body. Whenever something startles us, or we feel under attack, the whole body reacts. On the other hand, the parasympathetic controls each organ or organ system independently from all others. As a result, we can be uptight with too much tension, with almost all systems overproducing, and still have one or two organ systems underproducing because of specific parasympathetic influence. For instance, ulcers are a parasympathetic disease. But one of the characteristic patterns of people who suffer from ulcers is chronic anger and tension, the expression of sympathetic imbalance. Because these two systems are structured and function differently, we have an almost infinite number of possible combinations between arousal and inhibition. This great flexibility in the control system gives the body a variety of ways to carry out the directives coming from the mind.

How We Usually Think of Stress

Nearly everyone thinks of stress in terms of the fight-or-flight reaction. The concept of stress as fight or flight originated in the laboratory research of Hans Selye. In the 1950s, Selye, expanding on the work of an earlier psychologist, Walter Cannon, began to explore what happens to living organisms when they maintain a constant state of arousal.

The fight-or-flight alarm reaction depends on our perceptions and thoughts. Whenever we think something or someone is going to harm us in any way—physically, emotionally, socially, or financially—this alarm goes off. It also goes off whenever we think someone or something that we care about is going to be hurt, such as our children, our job, our income, our position in society, even our new car. If we don't see any danger, we don't have a fight-or-flight reaction even if the danger is really there. On the other hand, if we think there is danger even when there isn't any, we react as if there were. The intensity of our reaction depends on how great we think the danger is. Small threats, such as day-to-day worries, set off a small, limited reaction. Big threats, such as the possibility of being fired or a near-miss in an automobile, set off reactions that involve the endocrine system and last for several days, or even weeks.

The entire fight-or-flight alarm reaction consists of four stages:

|||||||||||*Alarm Stage—The Fight-or-Flight Reaction:* As you react to a threat, your body engages the fight-or-flight reaction and prepares to protect itself through confrontation or flight. Your muscles tense, your blood pressure and heart rate increase, your breath quickens, and your whole body is ready to do something. When you come close to having an accident in your car, you probably experience a fairly intense state of arousal. You can have this same response when you see your child in danger, to a lesser degree when you hear that your project is canceled, and to an even smaller degree when you hear someone talking about you in a negative way.

|||||||||||*Adaptation Stage:* After the intense arousal, your body must adapt to and compensate for all the physiological changes occurring from the alarm. This attempt to return to normal as quickly as possible is called homeostasis. The problem is that you usually don't get quite as balanced or relaxed as you were before the alarm. Even after a threat is resolved, a subtle residual alertness remains in your unconscious mind, keeping the body from becoming completely relaxed. This eventually leads to a chronic level of stress, and you become accustomed to gradually higher levels of arousal and tension in the body.

|||||||||||*Fatigue (Exhaustion) Stage:* If the arousal continues, or if new threats continue to arise, you eventually begin to deplete your body's reserves of fuel. You overutilize your resources, exhaust yourself, and become fatigued. You have to work harder and harder to get the same amount of work done and, often, you become so tired that all you can do is shuffle papers. The popular term for this is "burnout." At this stage your body begins to break down, setting the stage for disease.

|||||||||||*Termination ("Goodbye") Stage* If there is no relief from the arousal, if you continue to drive yourself, you suffer the consequences: your health breaks down, you suffer from disease, you can even die. When any organism remains in a state of constant arousal (or stress), it literally wears itself out. The resulting stress on the physiological systems leads to breakdown, disease, and death. This is a very accurate description of what causes an executive to have a heart attack at age fifty or even younger.

Most researchers believe that the same physiological arousal that characterizes the fight-or-flight alarm response is also necessary for a healthy life. Engaging in any challenging event results in physiological arousal, and it is obvious that these states are very healthy and productive. Hard work and exercise are healthy for both body and mind. Without arousal we could never achieve, gain any knowledge, or meet any challenges.

As a result, most stress researchers follow Selye's approach and generalize the term "stress" to mean any and all arousal. Selye defined "stress" as "the non-specific response of the body to any demand made upon it." The problem with this definition is that the only time we do not have a "non-specific response" is when we are dead. For Selye and many others, stress is an unavoidable condition, an unfortunate fact of life. How useful is a theory that tells us that we have no choice, that we will always be a victim to stress?

Stress as Fight or Flight: A Concept Too Narrow

Laboratory research is too narrow and confining to describe accurately what happens inside a human being. Selye based his theory strictly on his laboratory research on sympathetic arousal, ignoring the less dramatic but equally powerful role of parasympathetic inhibition. The stages of alarm, adaptation, and fatigue are described exclusively in terms of arousal, overutilization, and depletion of bodily resources. For Selye and most professionals, any arousal is stress. It doesn't matter whether that arousal is generated by exercise, by a challenge, or by an alarm response brought on by fear. But these states are different, and have vastly different consequences. We think differently, we feel differently, and we act differently when we are challenged than when we are fearful. Calling all of these states of arousal stress creates a great deal of confusion.

The Origin of the Myth of Good Stress

Defining stress as arousal (sympathetic dominance) ignores the very real and potentially harmful effects of parasympathetic activity. Consequently, Selye's theory cannot account for the stress created by depression, passivity, or withdrawal. Nor does it account for dietary or environmental stress. For example, the fatigue you feel when you are depressed isn't because of burnout. This low energy state is caused by a lack of activity, not by too much. Depression is extremely stressful, and can be easily as dangerous and as fatal as a prolonged state of fatigue created by too much fight-or-flight arousal.

The confusion of arousal and stress is the source of the myth of good and bad stress. Selye referred to any positive outcome—such as being more productive, having fun, strengthening a muscle group, or success in a task—as "Eustress." Any negative outcome—a heart attack, a headache, feelings of failure or anxiety, or a bad decision—was called "Distress." In other words, good consequences mean that you have good stress, and bad consequences mean that you have bad stress. Since the only difference is in terms of the consequences, Selye's theory has no predictive power, and is essentially useless as scientific theory. More important, it is useless as a practical guide since you don't know whether you have good stress or bad stress until after you have the heart attack. Simply creating new terms such as Eustress and Distress only adds to the confusion and does little to clarify the issue or provide you with the controls you need to prevent stress from happening.

The Key Role of the Mind

Nor can we ignore the key role of the mind in generating stress and unhappiness. The autonomic and other physiological responses are regulated primarily by the limbic system in the brain. The limbic system, in turn, is controlled and influenced by the higher cortical processes, that is, the thinking process. As the neurophysiologist Roger Sperry succinctly states in *Consciousness and the Brain,* mental events control physical events.

Until the advent of biofeedback, the scientific and medical community believed that the autonomic nervous system was really autonomous. We thought we were victims of the nervous system, but we were really victims of our beliefs. Now we realize what the adherents of self-mastery have always known, that the mind exerts absolute control over the autonomic system. We have all the control we need to regulate the autonomic nervous system. We need to understand what that control is and how to use it. In other words, we need to understand our inner resources.

The Other Half of Stress

No one doubts that the fight-or-flight reaction can lead to exhaustion, pathology, and even death. By the same token, though, what happens if there is sustained or intense parasympathetic activity? Does this also lead to difficulties and disease? When we examine human behavior, we find many problems that can only be described as an overreaction of the parasympathetic nervous system. Strangely enough, however, very little attention has been given to this neurological event.

Although the parasympathetic system has not had the same degree of attention as the sympathetic, it's clear that certain illnesses are associated with excessive parasympathetic activity. One is asthma, in which the airways in the lungs constrict abnormally and obstruct the smooth flow of air. Another is the duodenal ulcer, which results from an oversecretion of hydrochloric acid in the stomach. Both of these illnesses involve physical changes associated with increased right vagus nerve activity—the major parasympathetic nerve.

Other events also suggest possible negative effects of excessive parasympathetic activity. Fainting from pain or from the sight of blood happens because of a strong right vagus nerve discharge to the heart which slows the pulse so much that the brain does not receive enough blood to maintain alertness. Oddly enough, the initial response to the anticipation of pain (as when you face a dental procedure) often involves the heart rate's slowing down rather than speeding up, indicating increased parasympathetic activity and predominance—even in the face of an overall increase in sympathetic discharge.

It's common knowledge that too much tension leads to very serious conditions such as heart disease and high blood pressure. But did you know that too little tension, which is the situation when we feel depressed, can also be deadly? Medical research clearly shows that when you consistently inhibit your internal systems, they begin to lose their capacity to function properly over a period of time. This affects all your internal systems, including the immune system. Medical science also recognizes that the failure of the immune system can lead to cancer. Recent research clearly shows a definite and well-established relationship between depression and certain forms of cancer, as well as a variety of psychosomatic diseases. For instance, those who undergo severe trauma from loss (such as the death of a spouse, or even retirement) may become so depressed that their immune system is severely depleted, and death occurs within a relatively short period of time. The phrase "He died of a broken heart" may be trite, but it does reflect a general awareness of the impact of grief, loss, and depression on immune functioning and human behavior.

The Possum Reaction

It's clear from medical research that our concepts of stress must take account of the power of our parasympathetic nervous system. Our own experience confirms this. When we pay attention to what people actually do, we see another response to threats and danger that does not involve arousal or the fight-or-flight response. We've all known people who, when they become afraid, threatened, or worried, go home to bed or become quiet and withdrawn. These reactions involve a completely different neurological, biochemical, and psychological response, one that involves the parasympathetic nervous system instead of the sympathetic nervous system.

We *never* function with just half of our autonomic system. While many of us react with a fight-or-flight arousal response, many of us do just the opposite. Just as a possum rolls over and plays dead when threatened, some people, when faced with a threat, exhibit very similar kinds of behavior. Instead of getting uptight, these people engage the "possum reaction." They retreat, become withdrawn and depressed, and often feel tired and worn out. Their reaction to fear is not arousal, but inhibition. We also activate the possum reaction when we engage in self-criticism and relive our past mistakes. The more we attack and punish ourselves, the more depressed and withdrawn we become.

Whether or not the possum reaction has the same evolutionary value as fight-or-flight is debatable. Some of us may learn the possum response because we weren't successful in solving problems with the fight-or-flight reaction. In his book *Helplessness*, Dr. Martin Seligman shows how depression stems from learning the feeling of helplessness, and that this feeling can and often does lead to disease in the body and mind. What is more, it can ultimately result in death. More than likely, the possum response is a complex syndrome involving not only constitutional factors and socialization, but also learning. In any event, it is evident that a number of people react to a threat by parasympathetic dominance.

The possum reaction is far too complex and extensive to be explained merely as an extreme state of flight. Just as there are four stages involving the fight-or-flight reaction, we can differentiate four stages in the possum reaction. These stages are:

|||||||||*Alarm Stage—The Possum Reaction:* Your body reacts to a threat by inhibiting vital functions and closing down. It doesn't matter whether it is someone or something attacking us or we attack ourselves through self-criticism. In the possum reaction, we try to protect ourselves by withdrawing and avoiding confrontation. We feel hopeless, helpless, and out of control of our lives. Our physiological reactions include decreased heart rate, decreased muscle tone, and increased mental lassitude.

|||||||||*Activation Stage:* Possum reactors turn their systems on low as a way to protect themselves. To rebalance, they need to speed things up, to become more involved in activity, to get their systems back into gear and running up-to-speed. Solving the problems of a possum reaction requires an approach different from that for a fight-or-flight reaction. For example, if you have high blood pressure, a symptom of too much tension, part of the treatment process must include deep relaxation in order to reduce the tension and take the pressure off the vascular system. On the other hand, deep relaxation therapy for a "depressed" person can deepen the depression, increasing the potential for suicide. Depression calls for action, such as aerobic exercise and regulated sleep, as part of the treatment regime in order to shift the autonomic tone toward a more active state.

|||||||||*Atrophication Stage:* Overactivation of the fight-or-flight reaction leads to burnout. But it's difficult to suffer burnout when you sleep ten to twelve hours a day. Possum reactors feel chronic fatigue not because they overdo, but just the opposite. They underutilize their systems through inhibition, by constantly turning them on low. Eventually, these systems lose their capacity to function. The same thing happens when you break an arm or leg, and wear a

cast for six months. Your muscles aren't exercised, so they begin to atrophy. When we don't use our organ systems appropriately, they lose their ability to function. That's why aerobic exercise is so important for the heart muscle. And if you don't make a habit of urinating more than once a day, by the time you are sixty, the chances are good that you will lose the voluntary use of your bladder. If you don't use it, you lose it!

|||||||||| *Termination ("Goodbye") Stage:* The consequences of the possum reaction are just as deadly as those of the fight-or-flight response. When we consistently inhibit organ functioning, the end result may well be breakdown, disease, and/or death. Clear examples are an enlarged heart from lack of exercise and the close relationship between depression and certain forms of cancer, particularly breast cancer. Although some physicians still argue the point, clinical evidence and research point quite compellingly to the conclusion that chronic or severe depression contributes to the onset of cancer.

The Worst of Both Worlds

We don't limit ourselves to just one alarm reaction or the other. Because the sympathetic and parasympathetic systems are built and function differently (the sympathetic coordinates an overall response while the parasympathetic is site specific), we have an infinite variety of internal responses. We are quite capable of mixing our alarm reactions and, unfortunately, creating problems that involve imbalances in both systems. We create stress from either a fight-or-flight reaction, or the possum reaction, or a complicated mix of the two. For example, we can feel both depressed *and* tense and anxious. This mixture actually characterizes many, if not most, diseases, such as asthma, Crohn's disease, and ulcers.

|||||||||| *Stress: A Question of Balance* Popular as well as scientific thinking about stress is too narrowly focused on sympathetic arousal and the fight-or-flight alarm reaction. We are told that being challenged and being under stress are the same thing, although we know that they feel quite different. The great traditions of self-mastery understand that stress is always destructive, and that it involves both the sympathetic fight-or-flight alarm reaction and the parasympathetic possum response. The key to understanding stress is not whether we get too wound up or don't get wound up enough. The key is to understand autonomic balance.

We realize that a person can "worry himself to death," or "die of a broken heart," or even "die of boredom." But no one has ever been accused of dying from tranquillity or balance. We know that challenge, laughter, and happy surprises are necessary and beneficial to our mental and physical well-being. Yet

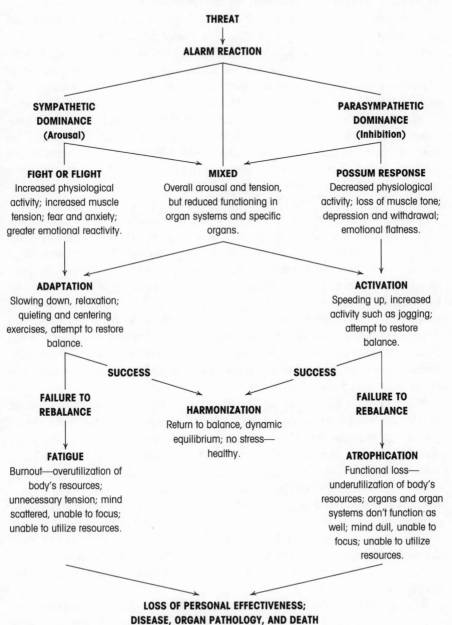

TABLE 2.1

STRESS REACTION STAGES
FIGHT OR FLIGHT AND THE POSSUM RESPONSE

THREAT

ALARM REACTION

SYMPATHETIC DOMINANCE (Arousal)

PARASYMPATHETIC DOMINANCE (Inhibition)

FIGHT OR FLIGHT
Increased physiological activity; increased muscle tension; fear and anxiety; greater emotional reactivity.

MIXED
Overall arousal and tension, but reduced functioning in organ systems and specific organs.

POSSUM RESPONSE
Decreased physiological activity; loss of muscle tone; depression and withdrawal; emotional flatness.

ADAPTATION
Slowing down, relaxation; quieting and centering exercises, attempt to restore balance.

ACTIVATION
Speeding up, increased activity such as jogging; attempt to restore balance.

SUCCESS   **SUCCESS**

FAILURE TO REBALANCE

HARMONIZATION
Return to balance, dynamic equilibrium; no stress—healthy.

FAILURE TO REBALANCE

FATIGUE
Burnout—overutilization of body's resources; unnecessary tension; mind scattered, unable to focus; unable to utilize resources.

ATROPHICATION
Functional loss—underutilization of body's resources; organs and organ systems don't function as well; mind dull, unable to focus; unable to utilize resources.

LOSS OF PERSONAL EFFECTIVENESS;
DISEASE, ORGAN PATHOLOGY, AND DEATH

all of these involve high states of arousal which, if unbalanced, become stressful and dangerous. It is also obvious that relaxation is not only very pleasant, but necessary and beneficial. Yet too much relaxation, such as in pathological depression, also becomes stressful and dangerous.

With this in mind, we can look at stress from a more comprehensive and more functionally useful viewpoint, as shown in Table 2.1. When we take the entire autonomic system into account, along with research *and* our experience, we can define stress in a very systematic and specific way: *stress is a state of autonomic imbalance, characterized by unrelieved or excessive dominance of either arousal or inhibition, or a complex unbalanced interaction of the two.*

Stress occurs when we are out of harmony within ourselves. And the moment we become unbalanced, we create changes in the body that lead to disease and inhibit the resources of the mind. Our organs and systems are interconnected. If an imbalance occurs within one organ, it will affect the rest of the system. Conversely, if the overall autonomic response is balanced, individual subsystems will begin to achieve balance.

We can experience two general types of balance. The first is *dynamic balance,* a shifting back and forth between activity (arousal) and rest (inhibition). We can work hard for periods of time, and if we balance this with periods of rest and relaxation, we avoid stress. As long as we remain sensitive and responsive to the needs and signals of the body, we can go through the day without creating stress. This kind of balance is like the child's game of teeter-totter. If both children are about equal in weight, they can teeter back and forth, and have a wonderful time taking turns at going up and down. But if one is too heavy, the game becomes unpleasant, and the purpose is defeated. If we tilt too much to one side, without allowing the other side to have its influence, we become unbalanced and create stress.

Many of us do this very thing. We like to work hard and play hard, meeting the demands of an active life, but forget that we also need times of quiet and relaxation to clear the mind and recharge our batteries. Or we constantly worry about things, become overly alert, and don't allow our systems to rest. By being action addicts and/or worrywarts, we put too much weight on the sympathetic (arousal) side of the teeter-totter and create chronic tension and strain for ourselves. On the other hand, some of us become couch potatoes and simply refuse to move, preferring out of choice or habit to stay passive and withdrawn. These individuals have the other side of the teeter-totter down, and don't allow the body and mind to get the action they need to stay healthy and alert. For both, it's a problem of flexibility, of not allowing a dynamic shift to create the proper balance.

The principle of dynamic balance is somewhat misleading, however, and oversimplifies an extremely complex system. Our autonomic nervous system doesn't work like a mechanical balance where increasing one side decreases the other as the analogy seems to indicate. Whether we have stress or balance is determined by a complex interactive process involving both the sympathetic and parasympathetic systems. The enormous flexibility of the autonomic system allows us to be very creative in the ways that we create imbalance and stress.

||||||||| *The Autonomic Nervous System: Sophisticated Energy* The more important form of balance is what we might simply call *harmony*—a dynamic equilibrium between sympathetic and parasympathetic activity. When we achieve this, work seems effortless. A physical example is the resting heartbeat, which is in perfect autonomic balance and yet still pumping blood and accomplishing its job. You also experience this balance when you become so focused on a task that you forget about everything else not relevant to it—even time seems to stop. In this state of concentration, body and mind are coordinated and work becomes effortless. We are totally relaxed as we work, using only the energy necessary to do the job.

The autonomic nervous system is an extremely sophisticated energy system that functions as a unit to maintain balance and harmony in the body. We find a far more accurate diagram in Figure 2.2, the familiar ancient Chinese Taoist symbol of yin and yang (a) which represents the wholeness that contains diversity. The whole is represented by the complete circle, while the interflowing black and white shapes symbolize the fundamental positive and negative forces of the universe. These forces are not in polar opposition but represent complementarity and diversity within wholeness. We can use this symbol to illustrate the sophisticated harmony that characterizes a healthy autonomic nervous system. Picture the circle as a crystal sphere representing the entire arena of autonomic influence and control. The sphere represents both the sympathetic and parasympathetic systems, separate systems which operate together to form a whole system. When the system is in harmony (b), and there is no stress, the crystal areas are clear. When a disharmony or imbalance occurs somewhere in the system (c), we have a state of stress, represented by shadings within the sphere. Intense or prolonged imbalance leads to dysfunction and disease. Just how the system breaks down and what diseases any one individual develops depend on a complex variety of factors—constitutional and genetic, psychological, environmental, dietary, even exercise. The variety of factors, and their complex interactions, makes it very difficult to predict just how any one individual will be affected. But the basic factor is the imbalance.

By defining stress as autonomic imbalance, we eliminate the confusion between "good stress" and "bad stress." Stress is *not*, and never has been, good for us. The fact that we can have either arousal or inhibition does not, in and of itself, mean that we have stress. *The essential element in determining whether or*

FIGURE 2.2
WHOLENESS AND DIVERSITY

A

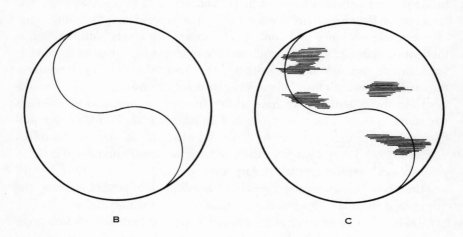

B   C

not we have stress is whether or not the autonomic nervous system is balanced. The principle is simple and clear: If you maintain neurological balance, you remain free of stress. On the other hand, anything you do can be stressful if you are out of balance.

Deep relaxation, diet, and exercise play vital roles in eliminating and preventing stress in the body. These activities also affect all other aspects of the personality. The more relaxed we are, the more creative and insightful we become. Proper diet helps maintain emotional stability and clarity of thought. Exercise not only strengthens the body, but helps reduce depression and allows us to be more excited about life in general. The more knowledge we have about the body, the more balanced we become, and the better we feel.

THE SECOND DIMENSION: ENERGY—THE MISSING LINK

||||||||||| When you turn this page, it feels substantial, a thing that you can touch and see, even smell, hear, and taste. That's because you are using your body's senses. From physics, we know that what appears to our senses as a solid object is really not solid at all, but a complex patterning of atomic and subatomic energy particles. As useful as our senses are, they are crude compared to sophisticated microscopes. If we put this page under an electron microscope, we would find nothing solid, only patterns of energy. The body is no different from any other physical object. If we could look at our own body beneath an electron microscope, we would find only patterns of energy. This energy substructure is the foundation of our material reality, and forms the second dimension of our personality.

The life force is a very subtle form of energy that flows through all living creatures. In our computer analogy, this second dimension represents the electricity that allows the computer to run. Our life force sustains the body and its systems. Western science and medicine approach the body on the physical level, as if the only reality is biochemical. When you go to a doctor, she doesn't talk about your energy, she prescribes medication to create a biochemical change. Even the physicist whose entire professional career involves studying energy forgets his knowledge when he is sick, and treats his body as if the chemical (physical) level were the only reality.

This life force has been the focus of intense study in Eastern meditative and self-mastery disciplines, such as Tantra Yoga, Zen, and the martial arts. In spite of all the cultural differences between the various traditions, they universally understand energy to be the connecting link between body and mind, and have detailed maps of its channels and various subfunctions. In Tantra Yoga, this energy dimension of the personality is referred to as the "pranic sheath." The term "prana" literally means "first unit of energy," or the most subtle form of energy. Just as the body has a vascular system to distribute blood, there are channels to distribute energy throughout the energy dimension. These energy channels are referred to as "nadis." In Chinese psychology and medicine this life force is "Chi," and the Japanese call it "Ki." The Japanese and Chinese refer to the various energy channels as meridians, and use them as the template for acupuncture points. The various traditions also substantially agree on major energy centers that are distributed throughout the energy dimension. These centers, called "chakras," represent powerful centers of control. At the most subtle level, chakras are the formatting templates for the mind. On the physical level, they control the activities of the body. A genuine Yoga Master has complete knowledge of these energy centers and, as a consequence, can demonstrate remarkable controls over both mind and body. A typical representation of the major chakras and their relationship to powerful neural plexuses, which are control centers for the body, is shown in Figure 2.3.

We get energy from a variety of sources—food, sleep, sunlight. But the most important source of energy is our breath. We can go without food for weeks, without water for days, but we can live only a few moments without breathing. This alone makes breathing the critical power function of this dimension. Because of its critical function, our breathing has become so much a part of us that as long as we aren't deprived, we pay little attention to it. We don't realize that the way we breathe plays a critical role in self-mastery.

All traditions of self-mastery spend significant effort in studying the breath. Each tradition has an extensive repertoire of breathing exercises which are used to develop a sophisticated control over the breathing process and, through these exercises, a high degree of control over what happens in the body.

Often this control seems miraculous. In *Beyond Biofeedback*, Elmer Green, formerly the director of the Voluntary Controls Laboratory at the Menninger Clinic in Topeka, Kansas, and his wife, Alice Green, reported on laboratory research on Swami Rama, a Tantra Yoga Master. Under laboratory conditions, he demonstrated remarkable control over his body. In different experiments, he

- consciously and intentionally stopped his heart from pumping blood by creating arterial fibrillation in which his heart fluttered at 300 beats per minute;
- lowered the temperature at one point on his hand by 5 degrees Fahrenheit while simultaneously raising the temperature by 5 degrees at another point on his hand only millimeters away;
- voluntarily controlled the production of different brain waves;

FIGURE 2.3

NEURAL PLEXUSES AND CHAKRAS

DIAGRAM OF NERVE PLEXUS
AUTONOMIC NERVOUS SYSTEM

DIAGRAM OF CHAKRAS

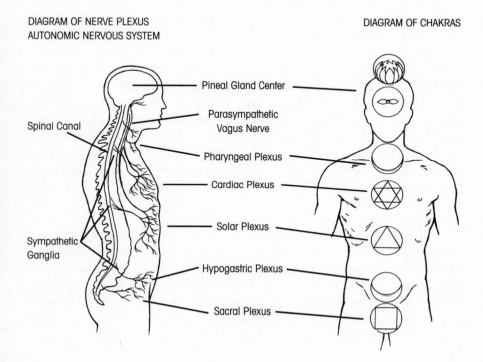

Pineal Gland Center

Spinal Canal

Parasympathetic
Vagus Nerve

Pharyngeal Plexus

Cardiac Plexus

Solar Plexus

Sympathetic
Ganglia

Hypogastric Plexus

Sacral Plexus

- was fully conscious of what was happening in the room while in deep sleep as evidenced by a slight gentle snoring and steady stream of delta brain-wave rhythms.

These and other experiments demonstrated absolute control of the entire nervous system achieved primarily through control of prana, the energy dimension. Yoga practitioners learn to use this underlying link between body and mind to help maintain a healthy body, as well as to help calm the mind and stabilize emotions. The Yoga Master uses this knowledge to eliminate cancer from his body, while the martial artist uses it to create such strength in the muscles that blows to her body have no effect.

Whether or not we learn the remarkable controls of this great Yoga Master is not the point. The critical issue is whether or not we learn how to use our breathing to gain greater self-mastery. While we may not reach the degree of skill demonstrated by a Yoga Master, we can certainly learn to use the subtle energy dimension to maintain physical and mental balance regardless of the situations in which we find ourselves. Unfortunately, most of us have a habit of breathing that creates more work for our heart, leads to chronic stress, and often causes hypertension.

In the body, we experience imbalance and disease as physical symptoms. Within the energy dimension, we experience them as unbalanced energy. Too much energy and we become hyper, "bouncing off the walls" and unable to focus. At other times, we feel low on energy, maybe even depressed, and barely able to function. When our energy is balanced, we feel energized, ready and able to take on the world. The more we understand about this level of our personality, the greater our skill and the more useful it becomes. In Chapter 6, we will see that we can balance our nervous systems, take the pressure off our hearts, and calm our minds by becoming skilled in breathing.

From Life-Force Energy to Mental Energy

As we move through the energy dimension, we enter the fascinating realm of the mind. Here we find the three most subtle dimensions of the personality. The mind is the instrument that we use to understand the world around us. The mind is also a field of energy that is modified or altered by its interaction with the world. We experience these modifications as the thoughts, images, and sensations that constitute our knowledge. Unfortunately, not everything we learn is helpful to us. In fact, some of these modifications are destructive.

Don't confuse the mind with the brain. These are two very different realities. The brain is a physical organ, part of the body, which serves as the control room for the mind. The brain acts as a transducer, changing the subtle energy of the mind into biochemical and neurological events that move the body. Of course, the quality of the mind's expression is greatly influenced by the condition of the brain. If the brain is damaged, the mind's capacity to express itself is diminished. It doesn't matter how sophisticated your software program is—if the circuits are damaged that program will not run properly in your computer. Although the body and energy dimensions influence the mind, the real power lies in the mind.

THE THIRD DIMENSION: THE SENSORY MIND—CREATING PERSONAL REALITY

|||||||||| We call the third dimension of the personality the sensory mind because it collects, organizes, and interprets sensory data. This dimension corresponds

to the software programs that run the computer. The sensory mind is a busy, noisy place filled with sensory stimulation, emotions, wants and desires, habits, and feelings. Its primary job is to interpret the world around us, and to create a personal sense of reality, the context through which we view the world. Just as the software program organizes meaningful patterns from data input, the sensory mind makes meaningful patterns of sensory input. It does this through four power functions:

1. Perception
2. Language
3. Emotions
4. Habits

The perceptual process is a reality generator. We collect information through our senses, and organize it into meaningful patterns. A single act of perception involves a complex mixture of many different events. Our memories, beliefs, and expectations as well as our constitution, genetic inheritance, state of health, and level of stress all act as filters which shape and color our perceptions and determine the quality of our experiences. More important, in order to structure sensory input, the sensory mind creates our experience of space and time. The sensory mind is also where we experience pain and pleasure. All these factors lead to a unique reality for each individual. Two people sitting in the same room, having the same experience, will see and interpret that experience in highly individual ways, and will not always agree as to what really happened.

As we organize sensory stimulation through the perceptual process, language plays a key role. The words we use actually define the personal reality in which we live. A favorite story of mine illustrates this point clearly:

In the clubhouse, three umpires were discussing the pending World Series game. The youngest, proud of being selected to participate in the World Series, bragged to his colleagues: "I never worry about mistakes. I call them as I see them."

The other two umpires started laughing, and the middle-aged umpire retorted: "Well, you're still a little wet behind the ears. I call them as they are!"

The old umpire smiled and looked out the window.

"What are you smiling at?" the middle-aged umpire finally asked his elder.

"Well," said the old wise one. "It seems as if there are two here who are still a little wet behind the ears. They are what I call them."

Life, too, is what we call it. A particular event in our lives can be either good or bad, exciting or dull, awful or wonderful. We are not really describing the actual event, but what that event *means* to us. Our personal reality is made up of the meanings we give to things, the values we assign. Language is the tool we use to create meaning. Once we use language, we are stuck with the consequences of our interpretations. Much of the unhappiness that we create for ourselves happens because we don't realize the impact that our language has, nor do we know how to use language as a tool to help ourselves.

The interpretations we make determine our emotional reactions. In turn, our emotional reactions distort our perceptions, interfere with thinking, lead to conflicts, and create disease. Many of us feel like victims of our emotions, and yet we alone create them. Our problem is a lack of awareness and skill. We aren't aware of our unconscious patterns until after we react. Once we react, it becomes increasingly difficult to redirect all this emotional energy into useful channels.

We need emotional energy to succeed and enjoy life. Our emotions stimulate, challenge, and motivate us to accomplish what we want. We become impassioned and inspired; we persist in difficult tasks until we reach our goals; we focus and become intensely involved—all because of emotional energy.

Whether we use our emotions to help or hurt ourselves depends a great deal on our habits, the fourth function of the sensory mind. Habits are one of the most deeply rooted and pervasive functions of the mind. We express our entire personalities through habits. Habits regulate every aspect of our lives, from the most trivial, like which part of the body we wash first when we shower, to the most profound, such as the skills of a neurosurgeon.

It's easy to see the enormous impact habits have in your life. Clasp your hands in front of you, on your lap or on the desk, wherever they are comfortable. Look at your hands. Notice the position of your thumbs. Now, switch your thumb position. Doesn't that feel a little odd? You can even shift the interlocking positions of your fingers. It still feels odd. The slight discomfort you feel isn't because the new position is damaging your hands or fingers, it's simply because you changed a habit of your body. Try shifting another habit when you get dressed tomorrow morning. As you put on your slacks, stop, and put the other leg in first. Most people fall over as they alter this simple, almost meaningless pattern of behavior.

Habits dominate the three outer levels of the personality—sensory mind, energy, and the body. We have habits of driving, eating, walking, and talking. The way our blood flows and whether or not we tense our muscles are controlled by habit. How we react, feel, even how we think are all regulated by the power of habit. Habits of posture, for example, influence our attitudes, and vice versa. Try this experiment. Some morning when you wake up feeling really good, walk to work as if you were carrying a large, heavy burden—shoulders slumped, head dropped, and eyes gazing at the gutter. In a very short time, you will find your mood down in the gutter with your gaze. Then try the opposite, particularly when you feel down. Walk with shoulders back, head held high, as if you were master of everything you see. Watch what happens to your mood.

All of our skills—typing, playing handball, managing, building a fire—are determined and controlled by habit. Sexual activity is controlled by habit. The friends we choose, the work we do, the clothes we wear are all controlled by habit. Of course there are other factors involved in behavior, such as the power functions of the mind, genetics, and the environment. But habits provide the structure of what we think, what we do, and how we react. Habits allow us to live skillfully and usefully. Habits can also kill us.

Some habits can have serious, even deadly consequences. Taking drugs, driving recklessly, and eating poorly are only a few of the more obvious ones. Psychotherapists work with attitudinal, emotional, and behavioral habits which lead to anxiety and depression. Dentists deal with the ravages of poor dental and dietary habits. Doctors attempt to alleviate the symptoms of poor health habits. All of us have habits which result in chronic stress. Knowing that habits may be either useful or damaging is not enough. We must also learn how to bring the power of conditioning under our control and eliminate those habits which create problems for us.

As we shall see later, habits are the power behind our skill. But we didn't consciously choose most of our habits, and many of them are destructive because they feed the three dragons of the mind. However, if we know how to take control of the powerful function of the mind, we can build habits that help us create a healthy body and mind instead of chronic conditions of stress, unhappiness, and disease.

The dragons of fear, self-hatred, and loneliness breathe their fire and manifest their suffering through the power functions of the three outer dimensions of body, energy, and sensory mind. Any time we worry, berate ourselves, or feel lonely, isolated, or abandoned, all three dimensions are affected. But these effects are like a storm at sea. When the wind blows, it creates waves and currents that can be dangerous to a ship on the surface of the sea. But below the surface, the water remains calm and undisturbed. The deeper you go, the more quiet and calm it becomes. The body, energy, and sensory mind are like the upper levels and surface of the sea called life. The dragons are the storms that create all sorts of dangerous conditions. The body, like the surface waves of the sea, is always dramatically affected. The sensory mind is like the great moving currents below the surface that give direction to the waves, and the energy level is that exchange between these powerful currents and the surface which allows waves to form. When we can only remain on the surface of the personality, we have no recourse but to weather whatever storms come.

The deeper we go into the personality, the greater the calm and quiet will be regardless of how stormy the sea of life becomes. The three deepest, most subtle levels of the personality are never disturbed no matter how intense the dragons become. If we can access the resources of these deeper levels, and use them skillfully, we maintain control of ourselves no matter what kind of crises we face.

THE FOURTH DIMENSION: DISCRIMINATION AND THE POWER OF INNER WISDOM

||||||||||| Deep within every mind is the capacity to know the truth, to understand reality as it is. This capacity is known as the discriminating mind. At this subtle level, the mind has the power to discern cause/effect relationships, to distinguish between what is real and what seems real. Discrimination is the quiet realization that, for all the promises and planning, the project you are working on is not going to get off the ground, or that illusive contract will be signed even though it appears unlikely now. This is the power of knowledge, our capacity to know the truth, to understand reality as it really is, not as we have learned to think it is. This dimension corresponds to the language dimension of a computer system. Just as computer language determines what the program will be, our power of discrimination tells us what reality is.

The discriminating mind allows us to think things out, to analyze situations effectively, and to make choices. When we don't use it, we act solely on habit. For instance, if we go to a movie every Saturday night, we don't really make a decision, we act out of habit. We use our discrimination only to pick the movie. However, if we make a conscious decision about where to go—visit friends, go dancing, or take in a movie—then we use our capacity for discrimination. It allows us to make decisions on the basis of information and reasoning rather than from habit.

On a deeper level, discrimination provides us with intuition: insight into the real consequences of our actions. Our inner wisdom allows us to make the right kinds of choices, avoiding regret and guilt often created through hasty action. We have all had the experience of taking an action that we were convinced was right. But before we did it, a small, quiet voice inside said, "Better not do that." We paused for just a moment, but then our desires, wants, wishes, or fears reasserted themselves and told us, "Of course this is the right thing to do. Isn't it all planned out? Come on, let's get on with it." We went ahead with the plan, and three days later everything fell apart, which led to the thought, "I knew I shouldn't have done that." And we did know. We just didn't know how to listen to our discriminating mind.

The dragons cannot directly affect the discriminating mind, but they certainly can distract us and prevent us from using it effectively. This dimension of the mind is very subtle and quiet. When the sensory mind is noisy and active, it can easily bury the subtle voice of our wisdom. Distracted by our desires and fears, and locked into our habits, it becomes difficult to access and listen to that still, quiet, inner voice. The more disturbance we have, the more difficult it is to think things through, to discern the subtle cause/effect relationships in our choices and actions.

The key to wisdom lies in the ability to create a deeply calm and quiet mind through concentration. In the tantric tradition, as in other traditions of self-mastery, we first learn to bring balance and flexibility to the body, stabilize our energy systems, and calm the noisy sensory mind. Then the emphasis of the training begins to shift as we learn to develop our insight into the nature of things. The discriminating mind is considered to be the pure intellect, unsullied by the distortions of emotions, and free from the space/time constraints of the sensory mind. In Tantra Yoga, a variety of techniques and approaches are used to develop the power of this pure intellect. As we become more aware of this power of discrimination, and more skilled in its use, we make better decisions and avoid many of the troubles that we would normally create for ourselves.

THE FIFTH DIMENSION: BALANCE AND CONFIDENCE

|||||||||| At the center of the mind lies the fifth and even more subtle dimension, the balanced state. Here, the mind's energy is in a state of pure harmony and balance, and not yet modified into patterns of thought and knowledge. In this condition of purity, it is beyond the influence of language, emotions, and habits, and totally unaffected by any external disturbance. This dimension corresponds to the potential of computer language before it is written into specific instructions.

When we become conscious of this dimension, we experience a profound peace and harmony that has nothing to do with pain or pleasure. We experience complete freedom from any and all conflicts, needs and desires, worry and anxiety. At this level of the personality, we are at peace with ourselves and the world. This center of tranquillity is the source of genuine self-confidence.

Much of the stress that we experience stems from fear and worry. In other words, stress is often the result of a failure of self-confidence. The less confident we are, the more we worry and berate ourselves. The more worry and failure we create, the less confident we feel. We become caught in a vicious circle of negative reinforcement. And yet, each of us has an inner resource of complete self-confidence that lies unaffected by failure and disaster. Every human being is born with this center of confidence and inner strength. However, distracted by the noisy sensory mind, we often don't recognize it, nor do we learn how to tap this enormous resource.

We do experience this pure confidence from time to time. Remember the time when you were out for a walk. You might have been strolling around the neighborhood, or along the beach, or in a forest. More than likely you were by yourself, but not necessarily. All of a sudden, you felt as if "God's in His heaven—All's right with the world," an overwhelming experience of complete contentment. The experience didn't last longer than a few moments, but for that brief time, you were completely free of any worry and self-doubt. You felt absolutely wonderful and content.

Now this didn't happen because you won the lottery, or were taking some kind of drug. In fact, very likely nothing at all had changed in your life. You still had the same job, the same bills, the same problems to resolve. All of the elements that constantly create stress in your life remained unchanged. But those few moments had a profound impact, and you went home refreshed, ready to tackle the world again.

The magic was all you. You did it by relaxing, quieting the noisy chatter in your mind, and allowing your mind to focus inwardly. You became conscious of your own calm center, which was always there. What if you could access this strength anytime you needed it? What if, right in the middle of a difficult situation, you could simply drop your gaze, focus inwardly for a moment, and experience this inner harmony? How would this ability affect your level of confidence and the amount of stress you experience? The balanced mind, the deepest, most subtle dimension of the mind, provides the inner strength we need to face life without disturbance, with unshakable self-confidence and fearlessness. It is a matter of awareness, access, and skill.

THE SIXTH DIMENSION:
THE SPIRITUAL CENTER OF CONTROL

|||||||||| The owner/operator of a computer is an independent force that decides how the computer is going to be used. The sixth dimension corresponds to the owner/operator of the computer. The human mind and body are complex instruments with a great many resources. But there is a spiritual core beyond the mind and body that we must acknowledge, experience, and learn to use. The mind/body complex has tremendous resources, but the final power lies in the Self, the spiritual force which uses the personality as a tool. Depending on your perspective and beliefs, you may call it the soul, higher power, or center of con-

sciousness. We will simply call this ultimate decision-maker the spiritual Self. Unless we access and experience this indomitable spiritual core, we cannot gain our final freedom from the dragons of the mind or achieve self-mastery.

In an address to the Congress of the United States, Václav Havel, the playwright who became the first president of a democratized Czechoslovakia, spoke eloquently about the power of the human heart. In speaking of what he learned from his struggles for freedom, Mr. Havel said that "the salvation of this human world lies nowhere else than in the human heart, in the human power to reflect, in human meekness and in human responsibility."

To paraphrase Mr. Havel, our ability to live without fear, self-hatred, and loneliness ultimately depends on developing the power of our human spirit, our innate ability to love, to be compassionate, to live fearlessly. This is the power of the human spirit. Whether we express this human spirit in religious or philosophical beliefs is a matter of choice. But to truly experience the power of our spiritual core, we need self-knowledge and skill.

When we act in ways that are counter to our own human spirit, we create the most subtle and pervasive kind of suffering. We seldom recognize the price we pay when our actions are inconsistent with our values and beliefs. This inconsistency affects not only the relationship we have with ourselves, but also with others. If we are distrustful, spiteful, egotistical, this not only creates problems in our relationships, but also creates weakness and stress within our own personalities. Our inner strengths depend on personal integrity, the ability to be consistent with our own values. When we stand up for what we believe, not only do we strengthen the will, but we experience self-respect and inner strength. On the other hand, if we act in ways inconsistent with our own humanity and beliefs, we create inconsistencies in the mind that lead to feelings of guilt and weakness.

We all have experiences that allow us to touch this spiritual core in some small way. We often refer to them as "peak experiences." They may happen when we witness the birth of a child, or when we watch a beautiful sunset or sunrise. A surprisingly large number of people have had a "mystical experience," an experience so powerful that it alters the way they look at and experience life. For some, it happens when they have a close brush with death, often referred to as a "near-death experience," and have actually experienced dying and being brought back to life. For others, it happens during a religious retreat after long days of silence and prayer. Still others seem to have them by accident, not knowing what precipitated the experience. Probably the most famous of these is the incident of Saul, the great menace to the early Christian community. As he rode his donkey to Damascus, Saul was struck by lightning (a poetic way of saying he had a profound mystical experience) and became Paul, the great Christian prophet and saint.

Even if we rent an ass and ride it on the back roads of Syria, it is highly un-likely that we will be hit by lightning and have a mystical experience. Fortu-nately, the meditative traditions provide the systematic methodology where anyone who makes the effort can develop the capacity for this experience and the knowledge it brings. The tantric Masters know that this powerful experi-ence can be the fulcrum for the achievement of self-mastery. The tantric tradi-tion is dedicated to the personal mastery of this spiritual core. Because it is the highest of our human experiences, there are no simple and quick exercises or techniques on the way to enlightenment. But as we gain in self-mastery, as we become more balanced, stronger, and achieve greater insight, we acquire the capacity to experience this powerful spiritual core. Because of the necessary preparation it takes, the specific exercises that will ultimately lead to this pow-erful spiritual experience are given in the final chapters.

Self-Mastery and the Whole Person

|||||||||| We cannot separate ourselves into parts. We come as a complete pack-age. Any action we take involves all dimensions of the personality—physical, mental, and spiritual. Turn back to the beginning of this chapter and go through the Traveling Exercise again. This time, be aware of the different power functions at each level. Don't try to change them, or use them in any particular way. Just pay attention and become more familiar with how they op-erate within your personality.

As you go through the exercise and become more relaxed and focused, feel-ings of loneliness, anxiety, or self-criticism will disappear. This is because we are most natural when we are relaxed and focused. And unlike the different power functions within each dimension, the dragons aren't a natural part of the personality. We weren't born fearful, self-critical, or lonely. These are products of the mind, not innate functions. When we simply observe the natural dimen-sions of the personality, the dragons are quieted, and remain hidden in our habits, striking out at the most inconvenient times. Before we can claim self-mastery and take charge of our power, we must find where these dragons hide and understand how they steal our inner strength. In confronting our dragons, we will see how to take their power away, and use it to create harmony, joy, and love in our lives.

CHAPTER 3

OUR ALL TOO HUMAN MIND: HOME OF THE DRAGONS

We have found the enemy and it is us.
—Pogo

|||||||||| We don't have to go far to find our dragons. They live inside the mind, we feel them in the body, and they mess up our energy. Whenever we feel attacked, when we worry or become afraid, the body reacts with alarm. The heart begins to beat faster, blood pressure goes up, muscles become tense, and we feel knots in the stomach. It doesn't matter what we worry about—finances, someone saying something bad about us, our children—the consequence is the same, we experience an alarm reaction. A little bit of worry or fear creates a small, almost unnoticeable reaction, while an intense fear, or sustained worry, creates changes in the body that may last as long as two or more weeks.

When we attack ourselves, remembering all our past mistakes and how we never seem to do anything right, the body reacts by shutting down. Instead of being alert and mindful, we become discouraged, depressed, wearied, and withdrawn.

When loneliness haunts us, the body seems to ache for comfort and touch. It's well known that infants suffer, even die, if they aren't physically held and cuddled. Young children need attention and love from their parents. If it's not forthcoming, it leads to psychological problems that can remain throughout a lifetime. As adults, we don't lose this need for contact comfort. We need to feel close both physically and emotionally. When these needs aren't satisfied, we may compensate with overeating, drug or alcohol abuse, promiscuity, or any number of neurotic symptoms.

It's much easier for our dragons to disturb us if we are physically worn out and unhealthy. When we take care of the body, when we are healthy and balanced, the dragons have a much more difficult time creating problems for us. Part of our power is our ability to create a healthy body, resistant to the stress and strain created by our fears and worries. In this way, the body becomes a tool we can use to help overcome our fears, worries, and loneliness.

The same is true for the energy dimension. The dragons can overenergize us, filling us with anxious, nervous energy, or they can zap our energy, leaving us feeling tired, worn, and depressed. If we know how to use our energy in a positive way, we can use it to weaken the dragons and take control of the mind.

But all the exercise and all the best food cannot compensate for the damage done by our fear and self-hatred. No matter how skilled we become with our bodies and energy, as long as we allow the mind to feed the dragons, we will be unhappy, stressed, and unhealthy. We must go to the source—the sensory mind that creates and feeds these dragons.

Your mind is the one tool you use no matter what you do. When trained properly and used skillfully, it is an endless source of power, creativity, and well-being. But when you don't know how to manage its power, your mind creates unhappiness, stress, and disease.

Mark Twain said, "I am an old man with many troubles. Most of which never happened." Most of the time, the things we worry about never take place. But even knowing that doesn't stop us from worrying and creating problems for ourselves. Even when our past experience tells us that everything will eventually work out, we spin our wheels, stress our bodies, and become irritable with our friends and family. All for very little reason.

But while you were worrying, it didn't seem that it was inappropriate. In fact, it probably seemed as if all hell was going to break loose and you were really going to have problems. Who was telling you to be frightened? Who was telling you that you wouldn't be able to handle whatever was coming at you?

The Chattering Mind

|||||||||| Pay attention to what is happening inside your head at this moment. Notice how you are constantly talking to yourself. We call this mental activity "thinking," but that's a very generous term. Most of what goes on inside your head isn't very "thoughtful" at all, just one idea setting off another, one image leading to another. This inner dialogue, or chatter, can become quite remarkable. Not only do you talk to yourself, you also answer yourself. You even talk to others, and they answer you. You can have complete conversations going on inside your head.

Mind chatter can be thoughtful, creative, and productive. We can use it to solve problems with critical thinking, to direct our emotional energy for motivation and determination, and to express our creativity and self-confidence. But left unmanaged, it can become an endless source of unhappiness, stress, and disease. How does this happen?

Remember that the sensory mind's purpose is to create some sense out of the world around us. Through its power functions of perception, language, habits, and emotions, it provides us with a personal sense of reality. Since this part of the mind creates our experience of space and time, it is not limited only to the present. In fact, one of the first things you will notice is that your mind moves easily in time and space. You can think about what you are going to do next week, or what you did last week, or pay attention to what you are doing now. You can imagine yourself in one place or another.

Close your eyes and imagine your favorite vacation. Where would you be? What would you do? How would you dress? Who would be with you? After a few moments, open your eyes. Notice that your body, including your brain, hasn't gone anywhere. Only your mind traveled. It has the freedom to play in time and space, but your brain (and the rest of your body) only functions in the present. The brain's job is to take the subtle movements of mind energy that we experience as thoughts, images, or sensations and translate them into biochemical and neurological events so the body takes the action involved in the thoughts or images.

The brain doesn't discriminate between thoughts or images of the past, the present, and the future. To the brain, every thought happens only in the present. Nor does it differentiate between thoughts about an actual physical reality, something real, and fantasies. To the brain, every thought, every image, is as real as the next one. So *every* thought is immediately translated into the body for action. When your mind anticipates the future or dwells on the past, your body responds as if the event were happening in the present. Mind and body are no longer coordinated, creating a state of imbalance.

This lack of coordination is insignificant if our thoughts are emotionally neutral. Let's say your attention wanders while you are reading this book, and you think about the quart of milk you must pick up before dinner tonight. The moment you have that thought, your body is being programmed to literally pick up the quart of milk. If you were hooked up to sensitive medical instruments, such as an EEG (electroencephalograph) to read your brain waves, an EKG (electrocardiograph) to measure your heart rate, and a GSR (galvanic skin response) detector (such as a lie detector) to read electrical changes on the surface of your skin, we would be able to measure the subtle changes in your body as it responds to the thought.

Since you probably aren't emotionally involved in picking up a quart of milk, you invest very little energy in that programming. The changes in your body are so subtle and slight that you will not even feel them. When your mind chatter does not have an emotional charge, it has very little impact on your body.

If, on the other hand, you started thinking about losing your job or being in an accident, the emotional energy of these thoughts would dramatically increase and set off an alarm reaction inside your body. Not only could we measure some rather dramatic changes going on inside your body but you would feel your shoulder or jaw muscles tighten, your stomach begin to churn, and even hear tension in your voice. The greater the threat is to you, the more intense the emotional response and the more dramatic are the changes in the body.

When we worry about things, or constantly judge ourselves and dwell on past mistakes, our emotions create energy problems and we become unbalanced. Remember Chicken Little, the archetype who made a career of worrying? Like Chicken Little, the chronic worrier lives from one crisis to the next, and every little thing seems to upset him. Much of his mental activity is useless—consisting of endless speculations on future events and reconstruction of past events. The impact on his body is very apparent. He is always tense and his movements are uncoordinated and jerky. He probably complains about headaches, and his breathing quickly becomes rapid and shallow. There is very little focus on the here and now, just a lot of "what if" kinds of statements. When we constantly program ourselves with fear and negativity, our poor bodies have no choice but to respond with tension and stress.

Words and images are powerful. They inspire, create insight, solve problems, hurt, and even destroy. In the sensory mind, words and images define our personal sense of reality. As the wise old umpire knew, our reality is what we call it. Not only do our words have an impact on others, they have an impact on ourselves. The words we use to describe our experiences and to interpret our perceptions also determine our feelings and emotional reactions. Whether we are happy, sad, angry, depressed, challenged, or fearful depends a great deal on the language and images we use. If I describe a situation as very difficult, and the people involved as hard-nosed and judgmental, I will probably feel insecure and not very comfortable. If I describe the same situation as a challenge, and the people as interesting and discriminating, my attitude toward the situation will be quite different.

Our mind chatter is actually the expression of our creative force. We can't escape thinking, nor should we. This creative force can be a powerful tool for us if we have the skill to choose words that are free of destructive emotional connections. Unfortunately, we don't always choose our words with care. In fact, most of the time the words we use are determined by our habits. Because we aren't sensitive to how these words affect us, we are stuck with the emotional reactions that they create. This emotional connection to the words we use is a large part of the dragons' power.

Take a moment to become aware of your chatter. Don't get involved with it, just be a witness and watch the different thoughts, images, and sensations that arise in your mind. Now try this short exercise in mind/body awareness. Read through the exercise first, and then close your eyes and go through the four steps.

1. Close your eyes and visualize your mind like a room, with thoughts and images coming in one door, passing through the room, and going out the other door. Notice how one thought leads to another in a seemingly endless progression of thoughts, images, and sensations. As you do this, be aware of how your body feels.
2. Close the door the thoughts are going out, and let the thoughts pile up in the room for a few moments. Then pay attention to your body. What differences do you notice?
3. Now open the door and let the thoughts clear from the room. How does your body react as the thoughts depart the room?
4. Then close both doors, and picture an empty room. What do you notice now in your body?

Which was most comfortable: watching the thoughts pass through, letting the thoughts pile up, or having just the image of the empty room? How did it feel when you let the thoughts pile up in the room? Isn't that very similar to how you feel on a busy, rushed day?

Thoughts and Images: Mind Magic

||||||||||| Until we begin to pay attention, we don't realize that every thought we have has an impact on the body. Mostly these changes are very subtle, far below our level of awareness. They may be as gentle as the slightly increased blood pressure and heart rate that take place when we think about engaging in exercise, or the increase of saliva in the mouth as we think about dinner or smell food cooking. More dramatic are the changes in physiology induced through hypnotic suggestion. Even more spectacular are the occasional reports of someone performing a dramatic physical feat during a crisis. Recently, the media reported that a man in his late fifties or early sixties saw a young girl pinned beneath a large concrete pipe. He had just recently recovered from a heart attack and was avoiding any strenuous activity, particularly lifting. But when he saw the little girl pinned beneath the pipe, he didn't waste a second. He ran over and single-handedly lifted the pipe off her, allowing others to pull her out. Later, he and his two grown sons tried to lift the pipe again and were unable to budge it. He figured the pipe must have weighed around 700

pounds. The actual weight of the pipe was over 2,000 pounds. This incident demonstrated the power of the mind and brain to initiate, direct, and alter physiological events through thoughts and images. The more emotional energy that is tapped and directed, the more powerful the impact.

THE BUTTERFLY IMAGE

|||||||||| To demonstrate it for yourself, try this small experiment. Put your thumb and forefinger together, forming a circle. Have a very strong friend put his two forefingers through the circle of your thumb and forefinger, hooking his fingers around yours. Then ask him to try to pull your thumb and finger apart. At the same time, try as hard as you can to keep him from pulling your thumb and finger apart. Of course, your friend will succeed.

Relax your hand a minute or two and try the experiment again. This time, close your eyes and picture, as clearly as you can, a large, beautiful monarch butterfly that you are holding between your thumb and forefinger. If you hold the butterfly too tightly, you will crush its wings and kill it. If you don't hold it tightly enough, the butterfly will flutter away. Keep your arm, wrist, and hand very relaxed, with just a slight separation between the thumb and forefinger. When the image is very clear, nod your head and have your friend again try to separate your thumb and finger. No matter what happens, concentrate on holding the butterfly. Don't let go of it.

If you can maintain the image clearly in your mind, you will find that your friend will not be able to open your fingers. It will help if another friend stands there and keeps saying, "Hold the butterfly, hold the butterfly!" This suggestion helps maintain and strengthen the image in your mind.

Think for a moment of the images and suggestions that you keep in your mind on a day-to-day basis. Be particularly aware of those which have a significant amount of emotional power. What happens inside the brain is complex. We don't have to know the details, but we must realize that every thought we think has an impact on the body. The greater the emotional content, the stronger the impact. We often talk as if thoughts and feelings were separate, but the truth is that they are both part of whatever we experience. Every thought has an emotional component, even though many of them are so slight that we don't feel the emotion in the thought.

The Dragons' Lair

|||||||||| Now you can see why you felt a little tense when you let the thoughts pile up inside the room of your mind. Each and every thought has some direct impact on the body. This is where the dragons live—in the uncontrolled thoughts and images of the sensory mind. Most of us pay little attention to mind chatter even though it easily dictates our happiness or unhappiness, whether we feel challenged or afraid, whether we experience joy or get locked into depression. We get caught up in our mind chatter and forget to be a witness. When we lose awareness of this creative force, we lose our ability to exercise choice and control over what we think.

If you have a fearful or self-critical thought, and then let it go, your reaction is usually very slight. But how often do you keep fretting about the same thing? What really creates emotional disturbance is that you constantly repeat the same worry. Going over and over fearful or negative thoughts feeds the dragons and makes them stronger.

But if you don't have the skill to take command of your chatter, you are helpless to defend yourself. The dragons become stronger and stronger and, after a while, seem to be a permanent part of your mind and personality. Even your body begins to change as chronic tension and disease reflect your inner conflicts. This in turn further weakens your will and a vicious cycle develops as your destructive thoughts lead to further destructive thoughts.

You can do something about this. You don't have to be a victim to the dragons in the mind. Let's confront the dragons and see just how they distort the creative force of the sensory mind.

Fear: The Destructive Use of Imagination

|||||||||| The most dramatic of the dragons is fear. It colors our perceptions, distorts our thinking, and destroys our bodies. Nothing is more dangerous, more destructive, and more useless than fear. Fear can destroy us as individuals as well as our families and neighborhoods, even our nation. It has become so much a part of our lives that we have come to believe that it is necessary and helpful, that it somehow protects us. Nothing is further from the truth.

The great irony is that fear doesn't even exist outside of our own fantasizing minds. It is born in the uncontrolled chatter of the sensory mind. In a very real sense, fear is nothing more than the creative force of the mind run amok.

We are not born with fear. We are born with a primitive biological drive for self-preservation. But this biological drive has expanded to include more than just our physical being. It also includes our ego-self, the characteristics of the personality that we identify as "me," such as a sense of humor, a reputation for fair play, even a position or status at work. The ego-self also includes anyone and anything that we emotionally identify with, such as children, a job, or even a new car. When we distort this powerful drive for self-preservation through uncontrolled chatter, we create the dragon called fear.

Many of us have experienced the difference between fear and self-preservation. If you have ever come within a paint job of having a very serious accident, you probably felt

- your heart beat faster;
- dramatic changes in your breathing patterns such as fast breathing or holding your breath;
- perspiration or sweaty palms;
- nausea, possibly spasms in your gastrointestinal tract;
- trembling, or shivers;
- emotional changes such as fear or anger;
- your whole body becoming tense;
- an intense concentration or focus on what was happening.

What you felt during this close call was an intense *fight-or-flight alarm reaction*. The fight-or-flight reaction mobilizes your body's resources to protect itself either by taking action to solve the problem (fight) or by running away (flight). This alarm reaction is your body's reaction to your fear. The greater your fear, the more intense the fight-or-flight reaction. The neurological, biochemical, and psychological changes created by this alarm reaction can be so intense that it's like a big thunderstorm going off in your body.

Unfortunately, you don't have to face a crisis to have a fear reaction and set off the fight-or-flight alarm. Every time you worry about something, anytime you feel threatened, you set off this fear reaction. It may be as innocuous as someone saying something bad about you, it may be deadlines that you face, worries and concerns about your children, even worries about the weather. It doesn't have to be a crisis. Yet we are so used to being apprehensive that it becomes part of our everyday lives and we are unaware of how much tension we carry.

But fear, and the fight-or-flight alarm reaction, isn't the only choice. It's possible to have a very different experience in the same situation. Have you ever had a close call in your automobile or faced some other danger or crisis, and suddenly everything began to happen in slow motion? If you recall an instance like this clearly, you will also recall that during the incident, *you did not feel any of the changes cited above as part of the fight-or-flight alarm reaction—at that moment, you weren't fearful or worried at all.* You were relaxed, clear-minded, and focused, and had the time to take the small actions necessary to protect yourself. This was an entirely different physical, mental, and emotional reaction than the fight-or-flight alarm reaction. Instead of fear controlling your mind and body, you were acting under the influence of self-preservation.

When self-preservation dominates your response, concentration alters the way your mind organizes sensory input, and you experience everything in slow motion. You feel relaxed, alert, and ready for action. You become even more focused, and more aware of your surroundings. This relaxed alertness allows you to see and think more clearly, and to move quickly and gracefully. You are fully prepared to take any necessary action to protect yourself. Your body and mind are completely coordinated, and there is no stress in the system. This is self-preservation, which occurs whenever you completely focus on what is happening at the moment.

It's not unusual that during a crisis you will act with self-preservation, staying calm, focused, and effective. Then once the crisis is over, all of sudden you feel weak, your heart races, and you become fearful as you realize *what might have happened.* There was no experience of fear until your mind began to chatter about what might have happened.

Two crucial elements determine whether we suffer from fear or use self-preservation. They are (1) the way we use time and (2) the ego. We create fear when we speculate about the future. We never fear what *is* happening, we only fear or worry about what *might* happen. Fear is a projection of "what if." We are dealing with a fantasy, an expectation of some future event, not an event that is happening at the moment. The mind perceives possible future harm; the body acts *as if* it is happening now; and *voilà*, we have a fear reaction. But when we focus on what *is happening* instead of what *might happen,* we utilize our primitive power for self-preservation. Body and mind focus on the same reality—the present—resulting in balance and coordination, and no fear!

Once we develop the habit of anticipating threats and creating fear, we set ourselves up for real problems. By paying attention to imaginary threats, we program these events into our lives. The more we fear, the more energy and attention we direct toward these possible events—and the more we create the conditions that bring about exactly what we wish to avoid. By worrying, we literally practice for disaster. A good example is what happens to many of us when we have to give a talk to a large audience. The mind begins to worry: What if I forget? What if I stumble when I walk up on the stage? What if they don't like what I say? The more we imagine all of these terrible possibilities, the more we are actually rehearsing them. By the time we begin the talk, we are so unnerved that we actually commit these very mistakes.

Look at the language of fear. Our thoughts are based on *what if,* and we create all sorts of terrible descriptions and images of what might happen to us. People skilled in manipulating others often use our own imaginations to control us. Instead of threatening us directly, they trick us into threatening ourselves. If we plan something they disapprove of, they tell us, "You better not do that. You *know* what will happen if you do." Of course, we have no idea what will happen, but the mind quickly begins to tell us about all the awful things that might happen if we don't toe the line. These sneaky people don't have to threaten us. They know that our own minds will do a much better job of it.

Simply thinking about future events doesn't create a problem between mind and body. We have a marvelous capacity to prepare for future events—plan meetings, anticipate problems—without any stress. The key is whether or not we think that we will be harmed.

Fear always involves the ego, our personal sense of identity, which expands to include the people and things with which we are emotionally identified. Instead of simply having a problem to solve, we have a problem that potentially will harm "me." Often, this happens so subtly that we don't even notice that we have just trapped ourselves. Suppose you get assigned a project at work. If you see the assignment as a challenge and feel confident about yourself, you focus on the problems to be solved, make decisions, take the necessary steps, and evaluate your outcomes. If you make mistakes along the way, you take corrective actions until you achieve your goal. But if you perceive this assignment as a threat, and worry about what your boss or someone else thinks about the quality of your work, you set off the fight-or-flight alarm reaction. Your mind begins to play in the future, anticipating what might happen if you fail. The resulting fear and worry upset your balance, your body becomes stressed, and your mind is too disturbed to focus properly. You inhibit your creative and intuitive abilities, and end up with a headache or stomach pain. All of this makes it increasingly difficult to do the job creatively and successfully, and life becomes difficult and unpleasant.

Listen to and compare the language of someone who worries about a certain event and someone who faces the same event with confidence. Along with pessimistic references to the future, the worrier will also have a number of self-references, all reflecting some kind of pending tragedy or harm that he will suffer. The individual with confidence will speak about the problem that must be solved, and will probably already be planning some action. Her ego is not on the line in any negative way.

We train ourselves to fail by the worries and fears we imagine. The greater the imagined threat, the more energy goes into the imbalance between mind and body, and the more diseased we become. Even a small worry brings about some activation of the fight-or-flight response. Whenever we create fear, we harm ourselves at all levels. Fear has no value other than to create stress and misery, cloud the intellect, inhibit memory, and close off access to intuitive and instinctual knowledge.

Self-Hatred: The Destructive Power of Selective History

||||||||||| It isn't difficult to create a chronic pattern of failure and misery. All you have to do is constantly remind yourself of how awful, weak, or incompetent you are, and brood on your past mistakes, hurts, and failures. Just as unmanaged chatter about the future creates fear, unmanaged chatter about the past creates self-hatred. But instead of the fight-or-flight reaction you have when you are fearful or worried, your body becomes passive and goes into retreat. Again, you lose touch with the present, and cannot deal with it effectively and joyfully. The consequences are that you become withdrawn, weaken the immune system, make more mistakes, and feel even more incompetent.

The attacks we make on ourselves through self-hatred, though not as dramatic as through fear, are just as deadly. And like fear, self-hatred is not natural. We weren't born with self-hatred, it is something we learn. It becomes a habit of the mind. Self-attack takes many different forms and patterns, ranging from guilt and inferiority complexes to self-hatred and suicidal thoughts—all of which bring on the possum response. One of the most common ways we punish ourselves is unforgiving self-criticism that eventually leads to self-hatred. Let's say that you knock over a glass of orange juice at the breakfast table. As you clean up the juice your immediate mental response is, "Oh, that was stupid." You judge yourself harshly, perhaps out of anger or embarrassment, and you feel the consequences. But the only reality is that you spilled the juice. If you quickly forget the incident, the impact of the possum response is negligible. But if you continue to remind yourself about what a stupid act that was, the greater is the impact on your self-respect and on your body. The anger or shame or other feelings are the consequences of your interpretation; they were not part of the event itself. Your interpretation, however, led directly to a possum response and your unhappiness.

Chronic self-criticism leads to chronic feelings of inferiority. Nearly everyone suffers from believing that at some time they are just not good enough. Sometimes this negative self-talk gives us a strong motivation to succeed, but we never seem to achieve enough success to overcome the nagging self-doubt. We try to prove our self-worth over and over. No matter how much we have or how much we achieve, we still feel that we've failed. And to complicate things, we constantly worry that others will find us out. We end up paying a very high (and unnecessary) price for our success.

Another common destructive expression of self-hatred is guilt. Guilt is double-edged misery. Not only do we create strongly negative feelings about ourselves, we reinforce the very behavior that led to the guilt. When we feel guilty, we become preoccupied with the behavior that makes us feel guilty. The more attention we give it, the greater the probability that it will happen again. Guilt leads directly to conflict and resentment, which interfere with our ability to act. The more guilty we feel, the less competent we become, the more we beat up on ourselves, and the more miserable we feel.

Guilt has nothing to do with genuine conscience. When we react with guilt, we simply repeat the condemnations we learn from others. Natural, or real, conscience lies in the more subtle discriminating mind, the next dimension of the personality. The real conscience is not punitive. Nor does it make judgments, so it doesn't activate the possum response. It quietly tells us what is helpful and what isn't, what will benefit us and what will not. Discrimination provides us with the opportunity to recognize mistakes, learn from them, and make more effective choices.

We weren't born guilty. Like other types of self-hatred, we learn to be guilty through our interactions with parents, teachers, preachers, and other members of society. Instead of using our power of discrimination to discern cause/effect relationships and learn from our mistakes, we use our guilt to call names, make value judgments, and, most of all, punish ourselves.

The language of self-hatred is just as destructive as the language of fear, and much more varied. In *The Quiet Mind,* Dr. John Harvey identifies several different categories of destructive inner chatter which feed the dragon of self-hatred.

1. Demands on others, on ourselves, and on life: Frequent use of words such as *should, must,* and *have to,* as in you *should* do this; I *have to* have this position; she *must* have a certain dress.
2. Denial: Using words to avoid facing reality, or the truth of our own actions. There is frequent use of phrases such as *I can't believe* or *I don't understand* or *How could this happen?*
3. Overreaction: We often overreact to disappointments and to things that go wrong, using language that only adds to our troubles. We often refer to this kind of talk as "terriblizing" or "horriblizing." It includes extreme adjectives such as *terrible, horrible, awful,* and *miserable* and such familiar phrases as *I can't stand it, This is awful,* and *It tears me up.*
4. Always/never: This is language that helps us live our negative history. We project our past failures onto the future and refuse to believe that any change is possible. Language becomes prophetic (and pathetic) in such

phrases as *Things will never change; It will always be like this; I'll never get . . .* ; and *She always does this.* These are words of a victim.

5. All/nothing: We generalize faults and mistakes into global realities. By not achieving perfection, we become *a complete failure, good-for-nothing, an utter jerk;* or *we have totally destroyed our careers.*

6. Mind reading: When we think little of ourselves, we project these judgments onto others, and assume we know how they perceive and evaluate us. It includes words and phrases such as *They know I'm a failure* or *She thinks that I'm unattractive* or *They know what a fraud I am.*

The Misleading Mind

IIIIIIIIII We may not have the power to change our situations, but we certainly have the freedom to change how we define them. Often, it only takes changing a word or two to get a different perspective and see new opportunities. But as long as we use the kinds of words and phrases described above, we can't avoid the emotional states these words stimulate in the unconscious. It is our language and the consequent emotional states that reinforce fear and self-hatred and make them stronger. The words we use rob us of our own strength and give it to the two dragons.

The first mistake that we make over and over again is to accept whatever the mind tells us as the "truth" instead of calmly evaluating the usefulness of our mind chatter. The sensory mind was never designed to tell us truth, but to provide us with a perspective, a consistent way to interpret our perceptions. Its function is to collect and present sensory data, all of which are organized by the unconscious habits that control our perceiving and thinking. Our unconscious emotional habits can create many disturbing and unproductive lines of thought that have little to do with reality.

You've seen this happen to your friends many times. They become emotionally upset, and begin to distort the situation. They interpret everything based on their emotional reactions. Remaining outside the fray, you can easily see how their emotions have misled them. But when *your* emotions are involved, it's a different story. You *know* what is happening. You *know* that these people are intentionally giving you a hard time. Have you ever stopped to wonder how your friends' minds can fool them so easily and so often, and yet *your* mind *always* tells you the gospel truth?

Our emotions aren't the only source of misleading information. The mind can offer us completely arbitrary thoughts, images, and sensations. Try this exercise:

THE GREEN FROG EXERCISE

|||||||||| Sit back, close your eyes, and relax. Focus on an even, smooth breath, and clear your mind as best as you can. Let your face muscles relax, and follow that relaxation down to your toes, relaxing the whole body. Now imagine yourself as a great green bullfrog, sitting on a lily pad in the middle of a beautiful, small, clear pool. Over on one side you can see cattails and reeds, and a redwinged blackbird building a nest. Picture a blue sky with puffy white clouds. It's about ten o'clock in the morning of a beautiful August day. The sun is shining, and you feel the heat of the sun on your back. The sunshine feels very warm on your back. Now jump off the pad into the water. *Kerploosh!* Ahh, the water feels cool and nice on your warm skin. Swim down under the lily pad. You see the stem coming up from the bottom, attached to the lily pad. As you look up to the surface of the water, you see the sunshine filtering through the water. Beautiful sight!

Now come to the surface, swim over to the lily pad, and climb back on. Feel the pad moving underneath you as you climb on. Now the sun feels really good on your cool, wet skin. Life is wonderful!

Now open your eyes. Do you really believe that you are a large, green bullfrog? If you do, then you need more help than this book can give you. Most of us distinguish easily between our imagination and what is real . . . or do we? Consider this: what makes the thoughts, images, and sensations of being a bullfrog any less real than the others that your mind chatter presents? They are all nothing more than mind forms. You determine which ones you will believe and accept, and which you won't.

You may not be able to stop your mind from telling you things, but no one says you have to believe them! You don't have to accept as gospel everything your mind chatter says. Take self-criticism, for instance. You probably have some particularly troublesome thought that keeps gnawing at you. You may not feel smart enough, or pretty enough, or you may always feel that what you accomplish is second rate, or worry that someone will find out just how incompetent you really are.

We spend an enormous amount of time and effort proving to ourselves that these thoughts aren't really true, and the very next day we have to prove it all over again. The same thoughts pop into our minds day after day, no matter how much we succeed, how many degrees we earn, or how much money we make. Every time we have to prove ourselves, we reinforce the underlying negative thought by paying attention to it. This is the second mistake: trying to use language to control the consequences of language.

The Limits of Positive Thinking

|||||||||| Recognizing the power of language and changing it to create a more satisfying emotional state allows us to make more effective choices. In neurolinguistics, consciously choosing words and images that are more helpful is called "reframing," a term used by Richard Bandler and John Grinder in their 1982 book called *Reframing*. Long before this, Norman Vincent Peale popularized this same message in his book *The Power of Positive Thinking*. Centuries earlier, Shakespeare wrote, "There is no right or wrong but what thinking makes it so." And in Proverbs we find, "As he thinketh in his heart, so is he." We have long recognized the power of language, and yet we continue to struggle. Even with all our reframing and positive thinking, we still create emotional stress for ourselves. Ultimately, you can't control the sensory mind, the seat of language, as well as perception, emotions, and habits, by using *only* the sensory mind.

The sensory mind collects, organizes, and interprets data; it does not discriminate. At times of stress, confusion, or anger, if we ask the mind to give us an answer, it will find one for us. How helpful and insightful these answers may be is highly questionable. Like any organization, the mind will protect its own structural integrity and tell you whatever it needs to in order to maintain its internal consistency. These defense mechanisms, such as suppression, repression, projection, and denial, are designed to keep unacceptable parts of the personality hidden. Even when you do understand the reasons for what you do, turning to the sensory mind doesn't necessarily give you the skill or power to change anything.

There is a powerful characteristic of the sensory mind that makes changing habits difficult. The sensory mind builds on opposites. In other words, there must be an "up" to have "down," and "good" to have "bad." If things are easy, then somewhere things are hard. If we think positively, then somewhere in the mind we have negative thinking. As long as we deal in opposites, we cannot eliminate just one side of them. When we stand in front of a mirror, smile, and say, "Today is going to be a wonderful day in every way," just guess what the mind is saying on an unconscious level? Probably something very much like "Wanna bet?" or "Yesterday sure was lousy."

When we deal *only* with positive statements, that means we are forcing our negative feelings into the unconscious mind. In fact, the very motivation to think positively comes from a negative condition. Why would you need to think positively unless you had already created a negative state? If you didn't create any negative feelings about yourself, you wouldn't have to think positively. Your mind would be free to focus on problem solving. No matter how many times you repeat positive affirmations, they only subtly reinforce the negative, and you never gain freedom.

When we focus only on positive thinking, we use language to create a false identity, a front that is inconsistent with our real feelings. This inconsistency creates a subtle form of stress that weakens both the body and the will. The insincerity prevents us from dealing with the truth of who we are and from dealing accurately and adequately with our problems. Gradually this mask that we create begins to crack, and we find that we have no idea of who we really are.

An all too common example of this is the person who always has to be "nice." No matter what happens, this person always looks at the bright side of things, or no matter how badly he is mistreated, he will always blame himself and try to be nice. This type of denial leads to superficiality as it isolates us from the power of our emotions. Not only do we seem insincere to others, but we become more and more rigid as we struggle to stay safe.

Positive thinking, rephrasing our language, or reframing our interpretations can be helpful to a degree. They are necessary steps on the path to freedom, particularly if you have been negative about yourself. They can open new possibilities, provide fresh insights, and allow us to create a greater degree of balance and harmony. But they are only a step, not the final goal. If we don't know how to transcend our sensory mind and its power function of language, we remain caught in its subtle traps. As we shall see later on, we can access the deeper levels of the mind and neutralize the power of our emotional and language habits. When we eliminate the *need* to be positive, we will find that we already are.

Mix and Match: The Dragon Twins

|||||||||| Once we understand the power of language, it is easy to see why most of us are quite skilled in finding ways to disturb ourselves. When we aren't worrying about what others think of us, we spend our time thinking badly of ourselves. The two dragons of fear and self-hatred not only come from the same source — uncontrolled mind chatter — but they support and feed off each other. The more fearful we are, the less self-respect we have for ourselves. The less self-respect we have, the weaker we feel, and the more we worry about things.

The difficulty is that we are ignorant of what we are doing in the mind. We aren't sensitive to the organizing faculty of the sensory mind which acts as a filter mechanism, and we seldom, if ever, receive the training necessary to be aware of and to take control of this process.

For example, take a deck of cards on which the spades are red and the hearts are black. If each card was flashed in front of us, we would probably see red hearts and black spades because many of us can't change our conditioned mental categories and don't see what is really there. The same principle can also be observed at just about any sports event. The two groups of fans, one for each team, will generally have two different views of events. In a controversy, each will be absolutely sure of what they saw! Another example of preconditioning is when we believe that a colleague at the office is actively competing with us, when, in fact, he isn't. We tend to ignore those actions which are inconsistent with our beliefs and prejudices and interpret all other actions as proof of them.

What if the colleague really is competing with us? Do we feel threatened, or insecure? Do we give it any importance at all? If we are secure and confident, we may be excited by it—or we may choose not to concern ourselves at all. On the other hand, if we interpret his actions as a possible threat, then we will react with anger, aggression, or fear. It is not what he does that matters; it is how and what we think about it.

What goes through your mind when someone criticizes your work, or gives you a deadline that "must" be met? Are you aware of your own mental preoccupation when that happens, and are you aware of the consequences of that preoccupation? Most of us feel that we are usually pretty cool under pressure and fairly mature in our emotional responses. Sadly, we are often unaware of how the mind is shaping our reactions—unaware of how much time the mind spends in creating problems for us. The fears and punishments from which we suffer are usually not from life-threatening events, but rather from the petty disturbances that we create on a day-to-day basis.

It would be impossible to catalogue all the fears from which we suffer. Fears of failure, of rejection, of being "found out" are only the tip of the iceberg. Fears from financial pressures, time pressures, and deadlines are dangers of a more immediate kind. There are also fears of what others think about us, our work, or our family. The fear of others' opinions is probably the greatest threat that we create for ourselves—with negative self-judgments running a close second. These thoughts are so pervasive and so subtle that we fail to recognize the tremendous pressures they create. Mistakes too often turn into convenient "whipping posts" for self-flagellation, and we lose the benefit of the learning which always takes place when mistakes are made. The fact that we are insensitive to the pressures created by these negative thoughts does not eliminate or negate them; it only allows them to operate unconsciously.

A Habit of Dragons

|||||||||| In order to become free of these two dragons, we must first realize that fear and self-hatred are nothing more than patterns of thought in the mind. They are habits in the form of beliefs and fantasies that we accept as our true self, or identity. The problem is not that we are weak and fearful, but only that we have learned to *see* ourselves as weak and fearful. Once these fantasies become habits, a part of our identity, we lose touch with our powerful inner resources.

Mind chatter follows the pattern of our habits. Most of us pay little attention to our flow of thoughts, and we often aren't aware that our mind chatter is taking us down a track that will create misery for us. *We suffer from fear and self-hatred because we are insensitive to the mental and physical habits which create them.* Only when our discomfort has reached the pain threshold do most of us allow ourselves to become aware of it. By then, however, it is too late to prevent the consequences. If you are sensitive to a particular emotional process before it becomes overwhelming, however, you have the opportunity to redirect the energy into more helpful and satisfying patterns.

Remember when you were a child running down a long hill? Remember how the momentum carried you along and how, at a certain point, it was almost impossible to stop? I remember such a hill in an open field when I was a young lad. About two-thirds of the way down, there was a ditch that you could not see from the top because of the long grass. In fact, you could not see the ditch at all until you were just a few feet from a drop-off into a large muddy area.

We used to take friends from a different neighborhood to the top of the hill and shout, "Let's run down the hill! Last one down is a chicken!" With that, we would take off. By the time we were two feet from the ditch we were going pretty fast, and only then would the poor fellow from the other neighborhood see it right in front of him. What was his reaction? Emotional conflict! He didn't want to run off the cliff into the muck, but he couldn't stop his body's momentum. Of course, since we knew where the ditch was, we could consciously direct the flow of our energy. We would run right alongside of him and then veer off at the last minute—while he sailed off into the ditch.

This is analogous to what happens in our minds. We don't want to be angry, or fearful, but in some situations our emotions are strong, and by the time we recognize them we are out of control. The emotional response is too strong to direct. At best we can stifle it—but then we pay another price.

We know the power of our emotional habits to create suffering, but how many of us have the awareness and the skill to free ourselves from their grasp? Becoming more aware of these habits leads naturally to a greater degree of choice and control. If we can see the ditch from the top of the hill, we can easily direct our energy so that there will be no conflict.

Analyzing our fears and negative mind chatter is useful, but of limited benefit. Our intellect cannot resolve our fear. The tools of intellect—logic, information, reasoning, beliefs—are powerless in the face of fear and self-hatred. The effectiveness of the intellect is hampered by our emotions, attitudes, and experiences. What, and even how, we think is determined by *all* the elements of the mind, not just the intellect. When we ignore these elements, they remain as traps in our unconscious, creating fears and weakness.

Our beliefs are powerful tools as they determine the substance of our reality. But even beliefs become impotent in the face of the powerful, unthinking emotions of fear and self-hatred. Our intelligence, logic, and beliefs have not conquered fear. How often do we know we have nothing to worry about, but still we worry? We have great insights about our personalities, but our emotions prevent us from acting on them.

When we depend only on intellect and on beliefs, and ignore the other dimensions and functions of the personality, we remain unaware of our inner strength. We allow the ego to become unbalanced and fail to develop the other powerful innate resources of the mind such as our emotional power, intuition, and innate self-confidence.

Loneliness: The Final Dragon

||||||||||| While fear and self-hatred arise out of our uncontrolled mind chatter, loneliness has a different source which is far more subtle. We can do much to eliminate fear and self-hatred by taking control of mind chatter. But to overcome our loneliness, we must become aware of the deepest dimension of our being, our spiritual Self, and take back the power that we have given to our ego.

At the center of our loneliness stands the ego, the most powerful function of the mind. The ego's purpose is to establish boundaries, to provide us with a personality center, and to maintain the personality as an integral whole. As manager of the personality system, it must coordinate the different dimensions of the personality, organizing and directing the different power functions of the different dimensions. In so doing, it creates an identity, a sense of ownership and definition that allows us to say that this is mine and that is yours. This is *my* body, these are *my* thoughts, this is *my* spouse, these are *my* children, this is *my* car, *my* house, *my* job, *my* wealth—all relating to me, my, and mine.

We need a healthy, strong ego in order to have a healthy, strong personality. The problem arises when the ego begins to act as if it is actually the owner, the master of the personality, instead of manager and caretaker. Under the influence of our egos, we lose track of our spiritual Self. *We forget that we are really spiritual beings here to have human experiences, and come to believe that we are only human beings trying to have spiritual experiences.* Once we identify ourselves as only the personality consisting of mind and body, we are stuck with all the limitations of this personality.

When we identify with the ego instead of the spiritual Self, we become egocentric, and the ego becomes unbalanced. It is easy to see the destructiveness of an unbalanced ego if we look at the extremes of an overinflated ego and an underinflated or fragile ego. Our society is full of so-called famous people—the Elvis Presleys and Marilyn Monroes—who work desperately hard to get attention but end up so isolated and alone they destroy themselves with drugs or commit suicide. When the ego is overinflated, the world exists to satisfy our ego needs, and even people become objects to be used. The more power the ego gets, the more demanding it becomes, and the less strength we have as a person. Inflated egos look at the world as a feeding trough. Everything and everyone exist only to serve the needs and desires of the individual ego. We may become infatuated with power, with position, with being number one. We continually have to prove how much better we are than others. But even if we get to the top of the heap, we still feel isolated and alone. The more inflated the ego, the more isolated we become, and the more loneliness we feel.

On the other extreme are the fragile egos that are easily intimidated and find threats at every turn. They become the victims, the blamers who find fault with everyone, including themselves. Some suffer quietly, afraid to make changes or confront themselves and the issues around them. Insecure about other people's opinions, they are afraid to express themselves or to rock the boat. Others join groups and find safety in numbers. They see the world in divisive terms, "us" against "them," the "good guys" against the "bad guys," "my religion is better than your religion." Instead of celebrating diversity, they use it as a focus for hate. And no matter how many other people they get to join with them, they still feel insecure, alienated from the rest of humanity, and suffer a great deal of fear and anxiety.

Most of us don't reach these ego extremes. But all of us at one time or another suffer from letting our egos become the center of power. You don't have to drive long in heavy traffic before seeing some ego expressing itself, or perhaps feeling your own ego taking over: "You can't cut in front of ME like that!" In lots of ways, the ego gets in the way. We may "blow up" at some poor clerk, or we gossip and prove that we are better than someone else, or we don't speak up when we should. The need to be right all the time, the fear of admitting mistakes, the inability to form lasting, committed relationships, the unwillingness to share resources, having to have it "my way"—these are common ego-driven attitudes that we all experience from time to time. When the ego takes center stage, the capacity to love, to be open to and share with others, to live in harmony with one another, is diminished.

When the experience of ourselves is limited to the mind and body, then the ego becomes owner and we mistakenly think that all we are is the mind and body. In the tantric tradition, as well as other spiritual traditions, this mistaken identity is called ignorance, and is considered to be the single greatest source of suffering. Ignorance doesn't mean that we don't have enough academic degrees or that we aren't smart enough. Ignorance means to lack awareness. At the most profound level, what we ignore is the spiritual Self, the core of identity. Many of us will even talk about having a soul, and it may be something that we firmly believe. But if we do not feel that soul, if we do not have a conscious awareness of that spiritual reality, we do not have the strength to wrest control from the ego. When experience and identity are locked to the ego, we experience life as an individual leaf instead of a unique expression of the life force within the tree.

The personality is designed to be a unique expression of the spiritual Self. No one can be like another, nor should we even try. Part of the purpose in life is to express the unique talents, views, and beauty of our individual personalities. But that expression must include all of who we are, not just part. When we ignore the spiritual Self, the personality remains limited. We are unable to see the larger picture, and how we are an integral part of something much much greater than ourselves. Isolated, we are unable to draw upon the powerful resources of this larger reality.

We acknowledge that our environment is a complex ecosystem, and that everything great or small within the environment plays a role in maintaining the integrity of the ecosystem. We have discovered that when we ignore the interconnections of the various subsystems, we create problems that are very harmful. The same is true for society. When we ignore the elements that comprise a healthy community—sufficient income and jobs, education, loving and supportive families, a sense of community, an equitable distribution of wealth, respect for self and others—we create ghettos of crime, disease, and violence. When we treat the symptoms by building more prisons, we create even greater problems, even more harsh realities.

The personality is no different from any other complex organization. When we ignore painful parts of the personality, they create distortions within the personality which foster emotional problems and disease. When we ignore the spiritual core, we become trapped by the habits of the mind, locked into fears, self-hatred, and loneliness.

The function of the ego is to maintain a sense of separateness, a boundary between what is "me" and what is "not me." If I identify with my ego instead of the spiritual Self, I also experience separateness, an uncrossable boundary between myself and others. To protect what is "mine," I create barriers, isolating myself from the rest of humanity. The more separate I feel, the more isolated I become and the greater my loneliness. Unfortunately, the more isolated I feel, the greater will be my need to protect myself from others. This can lead to a vicious cycle of even greater weakness, loss of self-respect, and further isolation, all of which only increase my fears and loneliness.

But the most damaging aspect of being ego-centered is that it diminishes our capacity to love. The more self-centered we are, the less capacity we have to give to others, the less able we are to love and to experience love. When we are ego-centered, we love in order to get love. It becomes a trade-off, a position of bargaining. "I will love you if . . . ," then we give our conditions. This isn't love, it's emotional blackmail. And the more we do this, the more we find that what we call love is a bittersweet experience.

The love we experience from the spiritual Self is unconditional. That doesn't mean it accepts any and all behavior. It means that I love you even though I may have to protect myself from your behavior. And I love you no matter where you are or even if you don't love me back. This doesn't make me a sucker, it makes me strong and free of disturbance. Unconditional love isn't foolishness or weakness, it can only come from strength, and this strength comes from the spiritual core.

As we experience the selfless love that characterizes the spiritual core, loneliness comes to an end. We are never lonely when we love. This is what is meant by the word *yoga*, which comes from the root *Yuj* meaning to join together or unite. When we unite our personal awareness with the spiritual Self, we no longer feel isolated or alone. The more skilled we are at achieving awareness of this spiritual Self, the more we overcome any loneliness.

Taking Power Back from the Dragons

||||||||||| The dragons exist only because we do not have the strength to take back the power that we gave them long ago. They have no power or existence on their own. No one else makes us afraid. If someone points a loaded gun at your head, they have the power to take your life, but they have no power to make you afraid. Only you can do that. Fear exists only at our invitation. If we stop using the creative force of the mind to create fear and worry, we no longer suffer from them. If we have the ability to draw upon our inner strength whenever we need it, fear is no longer a part of our lives.

The same is true of self-hatred. Even if we experience the condemnation of others, it has no power unless we join in and condemn ourselves. We will always be judged by external standards. There will always be expectations to meet. But so what? Even if we fail to meet these expectations, that doesn't mean that we must abuse ourselves. Failure, like fear, exists only at our invitation. It doesn't matter how many condemn us or how many praise us, the key is how we respond. If we have control of mind chatter, if we experience the unlimited spiritual core, self-hatred, like fear, becomes a thing of the past.

No one compels us to suffer from loneliness, to live our lives as small, self-centered people. The great sages throughout history have repeatedly told us that we are more than what we see, hear, and feel. But even if we are a spark of the Divine, it has little power in our lives unless we experience it. Loneliness, isolation, self-centeredness—all exist only because of our ignorance. When we quiet the mind, when we go to the very core of our being and experience the power of the spiritual Self, we are free.

But self-knowledge is only the necessary first step. Knowledge has power, but without skill, we have nothing. We know where the power lies within the different dimensions of the personality, but unless we know how to use that power, unless we become skilled human beings, nothing happens.

CHAPTER 4

SKILL: TAKING CHARGE OF THE POWER

Not choice But habit rules the unreflecting herd.
—William Wordsworth

|||||||||| Like Mickey Mouse in Disney's version of Paul Dukas's *The Sorcerer's Apprentice,* we have been bumbling around with our power and creating problems for ourselves instead of helping ourselves. The trick is to be able to make the reality we choose to make, and not allow our inner resources to keep creating dragons for us. To do this, we must come to grips with the other half of self-mastery—skill, the conscious ability to use our inner resources without creating problems for ourselves. We create our skills through our natural capacity for self-discipline.

Self-discipline doesn't mean self-punishment. Self-discipline is about accessing inner strength and developing the ability to do whatever we choose to do. The beauty of this is that we already have everything we need to become skillful human beings. All we need to do is understand a few simple things about the mind and body, and we can use our power in creative and useful ways for ourselves and others.

Our Habits: Channeling the Power

|||||||||| The secret of self-discipline and skill lies hidden in the busy and noisy sensory mind. It is here that we find the power function of habit formation, the conserving force of the mind and one of its most powerful and pervasive tools. This ability to form habits allows the mind to conserve effort and energy. In and of itself, the habit function is neither good nor bad, but like other power functions of the sensory mind—perception, language, and emotions—it can be used in helpful ways (good driving habits, healthy eating habits) or in harmful ways (smoking, poor posture, chronic worrying). The value of the habit

function depends on whether we master this function or allow ourselves to un-consciously and automatically follow whatever habits happen to be developed.

A habit is like a groove that channels the energy of the mind in a certain di-rection. The more often the mind's energy travels down that channel, the deeper the channel, and the stronger the habit becomes. We form these grooves, or habits, through a process called conditioning, repeating behaviors associated with pleasure and avoiding behaviors associated with pain. Some-times these associations are very direct, such as eating a piece of cherry pie that really tastes delicious. The next time we get hungry, we will think about that cherry pie and try to figure out how to get more. Soon we develop the habit of eating cherry pie whenever we have the opportunity. We probably won't think about how we feel four hours later. The immediate taste of sweetness reinforces the desire to have that particular dish. On the other hand, we may eat some-thing that tastes awful, and if so, we probably will never try it again.

We also build habits through association. The cause and effect may not be related to each other but occur close enough in time that we make a connec-tion. A friend of mind had stomach flu just after eating sushi fifteen years ago. Even though she knows intellectually that the sushi was not the cause of her ill-ness, the unpleasantness of the illness is so strongly associated with the sushi that she cannot force herself to eat it again. This process of association is how we become superstitious. If a baseball pitcher wins a couple of games, and no-tices that before each of these wins he ate mashed potatoes and wore a red hat to the game, he may make sure he eats mashed potatoes and wears that same red hat on the day of an important game. After all, it can't hurt!

When habits are practiced and refined, they are called skills. If we do some-thing well or easily, it is because we have the habits that support the behavior. When something is difficult, it means we don't have the habits to support the behavior. We become skilled drivers, skilled tennis players, or skilled accoun-tants because we practice the actions over and over again. We become skilled at brushing our teeth, having good posture, or developing healthy sleeping pat-terns. We also become skilled at worrying, self-criticism, self-doubt, and poor health habits because we practice them. Every time we worry, we are practic-ing worrying. No wonder we become so skilled at worrying.

The most powerful and subtle habits are those learned in the first five or six years of our lives. But we didn't *choose* these habits. They developed uncon-sciously as a result of our interactions with our parents and our society. Once these early habits are established, they become part of our personalities and guide our behaviors for the rest of our lives. If we grow up as Americans, we look at the world with the perspective of an American. If we grow up believing that we aren't important or very smart, it becomes difficult in later life to expe-rience ourselves as important or smart. And we will probably spend a great deal of effort trying to prove that we really are important and smart. As long as we remain unaware of these built-in biases, we don't have any effective way to counteract them.

Bad Habits Bring Bad Outcomes

||||||||||| This is where the power turns bad on us. Many of our habits are certainly not ones that we would choose for ourselves, but they still control us. The most powerful are our mental, emotional, and perceptual habits, which are the hidden source behind our behaviors. These habits allow me to be me, and you to be you. How I understand my world, how I feel about myself, even how I communicate all depend on these subtle mental habits. But they may also create stress, neuroses, and unhappiness. If I develop a habit of self-rejection or of seeing myself as inferior, then I experience myself as inferior and suffer all the emotional trauma that this brings.

We are all too familiar with those habits that create emotional reactions for us. Sooner or later, we all get "our buttons pushed," or we occasionally blow up over a trivial incident. Let's say that you walk into a crowded room and see two people together. One is a stranger, the other is someone you know but don't like or trust. Your eyes meet with this "enemy," and you experience a moment of mutual recognition. Then this person smiles and drops his gaze. You see him whisper into the ear of the person sitting next to him. The next moment the stranger looks in your direction, smiles, and quickly looks away. Now, what does your mind do with this? Are they talking about you? No doubt! Are they saying what a wonderful person you are? Very doubtful! And what is your emotional reaction? Does the term "paranoia" fit?

Did you make a conscious decision to be upset? Highly unlikely. You walked into a situation and unconsciously interpreted actions along the lines of your past experience (habits). The consequence was an emotional reaction, not a choice. Very few of us consciously choose to be disturbed!

You might recall what you felt when you went through this experience. More than likely, your shoulder muscles tensed, perhaps your jaw muscles became tense, and you might have even felt a little nauseated. You might have felt self-conscious, were hesitant to talk to others, and stood off by yourself trying to look occupied. That singular emotional reaction will have an impact on both your body and your behavior.

Over time, our emotional habits, as well as our beliefs and perceptual habits, have physiological consequences. In time, we may develop asthma because of a subtle lack of self-confidence, ulcers because we have a habit of not expressing our anger, migraine headaches because we have a habit of denying negative feelings, or even cancer because we have learned to feel hopeless and helpless about life. Our physiological processes as well as our behaviors reflect the condition of our emotional health. Healthy habits lead to a healthy body and appropriate behavior. But destructive emotional habits will always leave their mark on the body and in our behaviors.

It is the consequences of these physical habits created by our emotional reactions that we often call stress. Eventually, they can lead to disease. From bad habits we gradually develop such problems as migraine or tension headaches, temporomandibular joint (TMJ) dysfunction, or we may develop essential hypertension, a habitual cardiovascular response to stress.

The most troubling habits are emotional. Self-critical beliefs that we developed during our early childhood years, such as feeling that we aren't smart enough, or pretty enough, or lovable enough, are often unexpressed, even unrecognized, but they have a powerful impact on our attitudes and perceptions. We may lack confidence in our work, feel insecure in social gatherings, be hesitant about taking risks and accepting new challenges. Or we may become a raging Type A personality, driven by our inner voices to prove that we aren't second rate. If these early childhood patterns are pathological, we can become very judgmental about ourselves or others, constantly fearful of others' opinions, depressed or neurotic, even psychotic. Definitely not the kind of magic that we really want.

The Unconscious Power

|||||||||| We have this unimaginably powerful instrument we call the mind, but we don't know how to control it. Instead, it takes control of us, and the consequences are often self-destructive. The key to self-control is to take charge of our habits. Habits develop in many ways and for many different reasons. But all habits share one critical aspect—they only operate in, and because of, the unconscious mind. We may consciously build our habits, such as when we practice playing a piano or proper breathing and relaxation techniques. The whole point of the practice is, in fact, to build a habit, to have a certain behavior that we don't have to think about. Not a single habit functions as part of the conscious mind.

Many behavioral scientists believe that while our habits exist in the unconscious, they are really controlled by events in our external environment. These external events provide the reinforcement—the pain or pleasure—that builds and strengthens the habit, and stimulates it to action or inaction. According to the late B. F. Skinner, the "grandfather of behaviorism," we are products of our environment, and are controlled by our environment. If someone knows how to push our buttons, there is little we can do. In other words, we are slaves to our habits, habitual automatons with no real freedom of choice. Whatever stimulates and reinforces those habits in our environment controls our behavior.

For example, let's say you have acquired the deep-seated habit of feeling incompetent. This attitude, learned in childhood, lies in the unconscious, where you are not fully aware of its power. However, whenever anyone questions your judgment, you react with anger or aggression, and overwhelm your questioner with intense, logical argument. The intensity of your response indicates that one of your buttons (your old habit of believing yourself to be incompetent) was pushed, and you react to this threat with the fight-or-flight alarm reaction. When your inquisitor backs down, both the effectiveness of your reaction and the old habit of feeling incompetent are reinforced. More than likely, you rationalize your reaction, never really aware of the real reason behind your actions.

Our eating habits are another example of our environment controlling us. Some people gobble down their dinners in record time, meal after meal. The food is there, and the setting has become a stimulus for the habit of eating fast—even when there is no time pressure. Even though we know that eating fast is unhealthy for us, we still gobble down our food because that is our habit.

The unconscious aspect of habits makes them difficult to change. It is also what makes the unconscious mind so powerful. The experiences embedded in the unconscious mind are like the deep, hidden part of an iceberg. Since the days of Freud, we have become accustomed to the fact that our unconscious mind is a reservoir of great power. Our conscious mind serves mostly as an excuse maker for what is determined by the habits in our unconscious. Just think about the last time you became furious. A few moments before you exploded, I'll bet that you did *not* consciously and rationally think: "Golly gee whiz, this individual's behavior calls for a drastic expression of anger. I better scream and demonstrate some anger here." Instead, you just felt an explosion of anger that came right out of an unconscious emotional reaction. This person pushed one of your buttons, and all your repressed emotional energy got channeled into your reaction. You didn't have a choice, you simply reacted.

Self-Awareness—
Taking the Power Away from the Dragons

||||||||||| What Skinner and other behaviorists never realized is that the laws and principles that define habits only apply as long as the habit remains on the unconscious level. The moment that we become conscious of the habit, it no longer has the power to control the behavior. We can control any habit, and the behavior it evokes, if we are fully aware of all its patterns. Awareness allows us to consciously choose not to act according to the old pattern. We have the capacity to act, think, and feel differently. We do not have to allow the habit to determine our behavior automatically.

Our awareness, however, must be complete and constant. We all know how hard it is to change a habit. Someone looks at us in a "funny way" and we react. We know that our reaction isn't helpful, we may even know why we do it, but we still find ourselves doing what we don't want to do. The problem is that we are only *partially aware* of the entire pattern of the habit, most of which still lies hidden in the unconscious mind. Partial awareness only gives us partial control, and this almost always leads to conflict. We have decided to do one thing in the conscious mind but the unconscious is programming a different behavior. Whichever has the highest emotional charge is the one that usually determines the course of action. As long as we must struggle to control our habit, it means that we still aren't fully aware of the habit.

Intellectual understanding has little power to control unconscious habits. We know how hard it is to quit smoking even though we all know how unhealthy smoking is. We can know about our habits, but that doesn't mean we are aware of the habit pattern itself. Awareness is not "knowing about" a habit; it is direct experience of the habit itself. Intellectual understanding is like thinking about food, where awareness is tasting it.

I remember trying to quit smoking. Of course, I knew that smoking was bad for me, but I was not very conscious of the pain my body felt when I smoked. Like most smokers, I quit several times, but my habit was too strong, so I would start again. One day, after a particularly intense practice of meditation, I lit a cigarette. I was so aware of my inner feelings that I felt the impact of the smoke in my lungs and the depressing effect that the carbon monoxide and other gases had on my body. My enhanced sensitivity to the subtle pain killed all my desire to smoke, and I was able to quit immediately and forever without any difficulty.

When a compulsive eater, for example, becomes overly stressed, he will start snacking. He says that he is hungry, but his "hunger" is not really for food; it is the conditioned response to a high level of tension which eating temporarily reduces. Unfortunately, eating never solves the underlying problem. Eating is an action that will satisfy the stimulus of real hunger or nutrient deprivation. The compulsion to eat stems from another emotional pattern hidden in the unconscious. This emotional pattern may involve repressed sexual urges. The associated guilt, desires, and anything else that is a part of the emotional complex continue to create a disturbance—and, of course, a constant level of stress.

If the compulsive eater gains some awareness of his compulsive behavior and realizes that he is eating mostly as a way to relieve stress, he recognizes intellectually that his behavior is not healthy for him. What then follows is a constant battle between his good intentions and willpower on the one hand and his habits of snacking driven by suppressed sexual feelings on the other.

The compulsive eater has taken an important step—but it is only a beginning. He may have stopped his compulsive eating, but it hasn't reduced the pressures caused by his suppressed sexuality. In fact, he may feel even more stressed since he is no longer acting on his habit and getting whatever relief that provided. He will continue to have conflicts until he takes the next step in dealing with his repressed sexual feelings directly.

We all have personal histories that include enough unconscious conflicts to cause a lot of unhappiness. Sadly, few of us develop the inner sensitivity and self-knowledge necessary to resolve these conflicts. Instead of working with our habits, we try to control the events and conditions in the external world which stimulate and reinforce these habits. We may keep only a few cigarettes with us at any time. But then we find ourselves "bumming" them off another smoker. Or we insist that co-workers behave a certain way so we can be comfortable. As we all know, controlling external circumstances or other people is an impossible and frustrating task. Even partial success can leave us feeling like victims of circumstance. To resolve these hidden conflicts, we must focus our attention inwardly. We must begin to pay attention to our unconscious reactions.

Paying attention makes us aware. Awareness leads to conscious choices. This immediately weakens the habit. The compulsive eater who eats when he is tense has several options. He can continue his habit and then suffer the consequences—or he can substitute an alternative behavior. He may decide to eat only at certain times. Instead of eating between meals when he feels the urge, he practices a relaxation or breathing exercise. The more relaxed he is, the easier it is to deal with the compulsion to eat. In this way he not only controls his compulsive behavior, he also avoids the negative consequences of inappropriate eating. The more sensitive he is to the first stirring of compulsive feelings, the quicker he can act with an alternative response, and the weaker the compulsion becomes. The more skilled he is at relaxing, the more sensitive he is to the thoughts and feelings that drive the compulsion. This gives him even greater insight into the real reasons behind the urge to eat, allowing time to resolve the real reasons for the compulsive behavior. While he must learn and practice new and more effective behaviors, the first step was to bring the habit out from the unconscious mind. The more awareness, the greater the opportunity for choice, and the more control he has.

Becoming aware of your unconscious patterns is not just an exercise in counting symptoms. It means that you become more sensitive to the thoughts and feelings that accompany and even precede your actions. If you watch television while you exercise on your ski machine, you gain very little benefit from the exercise. On the other hand, if you pay attention to your body as you exercise, becoming more aware of your heart's behavior, which muscles are moving, the changes in your breathing, you become more sensitive to what actually is happening in your body. As you become more aware of your internal states, you begin to experience and understand the cause/effect relationships between thoughts and behavior. The more aware you are, the more able you are to choose a different behavior as well as choose different ways of thinking.

Biofeedback:
Using Technology to Enhance Awareness

|||||||||| Biofeedback is a fascinating combination of modern technology and awareness. A biofeedback instrument monitors a physiological process, such as skin temperature (which indicates whether blood vessels are constricted or dilated) or electrical activity in the muscles (which determines muscle tension). For example, an electromyograph (EMG) biofeedback instrument tells you when the neurons in your muscle are firing and when they are not. This tells you exactly what is happening in the muscle at the moment. The more electrical activity, the more tension in the muscle.

The biofeedback instrument doesn't do anything to you, it only indicates what is happening inside your body. With its help, you become aware of very subtle physiological events, like nerves firing or blood flow, of which you had no previous awareness. By paying attention to the different thoughts and feelings associated with the changes going on inside your body, you soon learn how to direct these thoughts and feelings to change the nerve activity or the blood flow. Instead of letting your body continue with old patterns, you can consciously alter the response, and create a new, more helpful and healthy habit pattern. With a little training, you can control blood flow, increase or decrease your pulse rate, change your brain waves, or lower your muscle tension.

Proper training with biofeedback produces astonishing results: people who have suffered from tension headaches for ten or even more years quickly learn to relax their muscles and eliminate their tension headaches; patients with migraine headaches change blood-flow patterns by consciously learning to increase blood flow to their hands; people suffering from paralysis caused by spinal injury or stroke have regained use of their limbs. To suggest even twenty years ago that this kind of control was possible would have brought derisive laughter from the medical and scientific community. Yet the Tantra Yoga Masters have demonstrated this kind of control for thousands of years. And they do it without any help from biofeedback machines.

As the biofeedback experience shows, you don't have to be a Yoga Master to control your body. The people who accomplish this day in and day out in biofeedback clinics are ordinary people, with no special training. Nor is the awareness limited to just physical problems. In fact, becoming aware of the underlying emotional habits is the key to resolving the physical symptoms.

One client, a middle-aged woman suffering from migraine headaches, came to the biofeedback program seeking relief. After several weeks of training and several biofeedback sessions, it was obvious that she was becoming quite skilled at relaxing, at least during the biofeedback sessions. But something was missing because there was no change in her headaches. We talked at some length about possible conflicts, but she kept insisting that everything in her life was just wonderful. Her only problem was these awful headaches.

I decided to use the next biofeedback session to explore her emotional reactions. After hooking her up to an EMG instrument, I asked her to focus on relaxation and breathing. After only a few moments, the signal from the biofeedback instrument became very slow and steady, indicating a state of relaxation. I asked her if she had any problems or difficulty at work. She answered "No." There was no change in her level of relaxation. I asked her if she had difficulties with her children. Again, the answer was no, and the instrument maintained a slow, steady signal. Then I asked if she had any conflicts with her husband. She quickly answered "No," but the biofeedback instrument took off like a rocket.

She was stunned. She couldn't believe that this question could create so much tension. Although she was skilled at relaxing, she was even more skilled at denying conflict between herself and her husband. She was so skilled, in fact, that she didn't even recognize it consciously. Using the biofeedback instrument allowed her to become aware of a conflict that she had unconsciously suppressed. Once she became aware of the problem and was willing to face it, within weeks her headaches had mostly disappeared, and she and her husband were dealing more openly and honestly with their conflicts.

The biofeedback instrument didn't change her headaches. It was her increased awareness that allowed her to change the biofeedback signal and take control of her headaches and hidden conflicts. Once she used the biofeedback signal as a mirror to reflect her own internal processes and to develop awareness, she very quickly began to deal with the problem. As she became skilled in introspection, she found that the biofeedback equipment wasn't even necessary. In fact, in many cases, the machine interferes with inner concentration and awareness.

Biofeedback doesn't teach us how to control the body. It allows us to become conscious of the control we already have. Once we are aware of these controls, we use them to create a healthier process. By becoming skilled in the use of sophisticated internal tools, such as hatha yoga and breathing and meditation practices, we become sensitive to our own internal biofeedback systems and we change our unconscious misery-producing habits to more useful ones.

The belief that we cannot, and do not, control the body, our thoughts, or our emotions is false. The truth is that we have absolute control over everything in the personality. The crucial factor is whether we are conscious or unconscious. When we are unconscious, our habits are in control; when we are conscious, we have the power to choose!

We have a far greater ability for self-control and self-discipline than most of us realize or have experienced. Our bodies and minds have both extremely sophisticated internal sensory mechanisms and control systems. We use these mechanisms when we learn how to control blood flow or to fire a single muscle neuron through biofeedback. The body/mind complex is the most sophisticated biofeedback instrument you can find. The greater our self-awareness, the more choices we have, and the less we disturb ourselves.

Focused Attention:
The Secret Power of the Conscious Mind

||||||||||| In a recent seminar I led, one of the participants was a jogger. He told the group that while jogging with a colleague, he had developed the habit of discussing work problems. Over a period of time he noticed that he did not enjoy the jogging as much. He was running more slowly and could not maintain his speed. During the seminar, he realized that his habit of thinking about work problems while jogging had unconsciously created stress and reduced his efficiency. The very next day, he refocused his attention on running, and did not allow his mind to follow the habit of going over work problems. Immediately, he began running as fast as his best time. His joy of running returned, and he felt better than he had for months.

The jogger took charge of his thoughts. He chose different thoughts, altered the pattern, and improved his efficiency in running. He tapped the secret power of his conscious mind. This power is our ability to focus our attention, to focus the energy of the mind. It is secret because we seldom acknowledge the power of attention. We are told to pay attention in school, but no one shows us how. We learn all sorts of facts and methods, but we seldom learn how to use the mind. As a consequence, we don't know how to systematically expand our awareness into the subconscious and unconscious areas of the mind.

Many scientists, psychiatrists, and psychologists speak appropriately of the hidden power of the unconscious mind and the power of habit. Most believe that we can only have indirect communication with the unconscious mind through symbolic representation such as dreams and ink-blot tests. Psychoanalysts believe that we can become aware of the unconscious only after years of analysis, and only with the help and guidance of an analyst. The myth that we cannot directly confront our own unconscious has been the basis for much of Western psychology and psychiatry, particularly behaviorism. As a result, we don't have a systematic approach to introspection and self-awareness. Nor do we have a science of self-mastery.

My scientific, academic education taught me that conscious control over my body and my emotions was not possible. My tantric Master showed me not only that it was possible, but that I could do it myself, and do it well. The key was not my unconscious, but my ability to focus my conscious mind. The conscious mind has one powerful ability—the ability to direct attention. With the right approach and the right tools, we can refine the ability to pay attention and direct the entire mind and body and all of their resources—knowledge, creativity, will, emotional energy, even habits. By refining our attention and expanding our awareness, we expand the capacity for choice, and take the power back from the dragons.

AN EXERCISE IN MIND/BODY AWARENESS

||||||||||| Try it for yourself. If you pay attention, you don't need a biofeedback machine to tell you when your muscles are tense and when they are relaxed. Sit quietly for a moment, and pay attention to the muscles in your face—the jaws, around the eyes, and the forehead. What do you feel? Be aware of the muscles in the back of your neck and your shoulders. What do you feel here?

Think about the last conflict you got involved with at work. Go over the situation clearly in your mind as if you were reliving it. What is happening to your muscles? Now picture these muscles as being very relaxed and loose. Imagine yourself sitting in your favorite vacation place, relaxing in the sun. Pay attention to what happens to the muscles in your face, neck, and shoulders. Notice how your thoughts about your favorite spot seem to relax these muscles.

Which thoughts and feelings would you rather have? Which condition would you choose for your muscles? Your awareness gives you the opportunity to make a choice.

Bringing the unconscious mind and its contents to awareness is not impossible. We only need to train our power of attention. By learning to concentrate and focus attention inwardly with detachment, we create a state of neutral observation. As we become more skilled in the ability to be an observer, we become more aware of the patterns and movements of the mind and we have a greater opportunity to choose the patterns and behaviors we want.

The Secret of Self-Discipline

||||||||||| No one consciously chooses to be afraid, hate themselves, or feel isolated and alone. But unconsciously, our habits create and feed these dragons and make our lives miserable. As long as we remain insensitive, ignoring our unconscious habits, B. F. Skinner is right. We don't really have any freedom. Instead of experiencing our power as human beings, we are enslaved by the habits and patterns of the mind. We learn to see ourselves as weak, ineffectual, unlovable, stupid—all the negative judgments we learned growing up. The consequence of ignorance is constant fear, self-hatred, and loneliness, a denial of the true strength and joy of the Self.

But we don't have to suffer because we don't have to remain ignorant. These habits are not who we are, they are only habits, grooves in the mind that we unconsciously developed at some point in our lives. Once we understand the power of habits, we see that self-discipline is nothing more than consciously choosing and practicing habits which help us grow and be joyful. We can take charge of this powerful function in the sensory mind and create the habits that we want.

On the most profound level, ignorance means to be unconscious or unaware of the spiritual Self. This truth of attention and awareness is known in all great spiritual traditions. John's declaration in the Gospels (8:32), "The truth shall make you free," doesn't refer to some secret "truth" hidden in a musty book on some forgotten shelf. It is about awareness—at a spiritual level as well as a mundane level. When you become conscious, when you become aware of the truth inside yourself, you are free—to choose your responses, to live without fear, self-hatred, and loneliness, and to experience joy, tranquillity, and love.

CHOICE, NOT STRUGGLE

||||||||||| The emphasis must be on choosing the habits we want to build, not struggling to eliminate the old habits. Most of us think of self-discipline as making ourselves do something we don't want to do. If this is the case, very few of us will ever succeed. We can successfully learn to be self-disciplined if we remember three key points:

1. *Inspiration is 90 percent of the success for self-discipline.* Work on building habits that you really want to have. Don't waste energy and effort struggling against already established habits, which only leads to conflict and strengthens these habits. Instead, focus your efforts on the habits you want to build, the patterns you are interested in having.
2. *Practice makes perfect.* Once you decide on the habit or pattern of behavior or the thinking that you want, practice that behavior or thinking pattern every day. You won't create change by wishing something will happen, or by imagery alone. You must act on your choices in order for the choices to become deeply grooved in the mind.
3. *Determination and persistence will always lead to success.* There is no failure, only premature stopping. A habit takes time to establish itself in the mind. Once you decide on a particular behavior that you want to build, allow at least three months to begin to groove the habit into your mind.

ABOVE ALL, BALANCE

||||||||||| To be successful, self-discipline must be tempered with balance. We don't grow much as human beings if we become overdeveloped in one area and remain retarded in everything else. We may become highly skilled in our careers or professions, but this should not be at the sacrifice of the other elements of our humanity.

Genuine balance is not a static condition, but a dynamic process, constantly evolving as we grow and evolve. When we are balanced, we are spontaneous instead of programmed, relaxed instead of tense, responsive instead of reactive, and in tune with the world around us. Balance involves the integration of all dimensions of the personality. On a physical level, balance is regulated primarily through the autonomic nervous system which controls our organ systems. When our physical systems are out of balance, we suffer from the symptoms of stress. Knowing how to control this powerful control mechanism is a key factor in our ability to live in this pressure-cooker society of ours and remain relaxed, calm, and effective.

But physical balance must involve emotional balance. Even the best food becomes toxic and our exercise becomes just another pressure if we don't know how to balance our emotions. Emotional balance requires practice, just as physical balance requires practice. If we become fanatical in our practice, we lose perspective, reinforce our fears, and create greater problems for ourselves. Balance is characterized by both persistence and patience. Emotional balance requires that we build our relationships with others with the same care that we build the relationship with ourselves.

Both emotional balance and social balance emerge naturally from our increasing spiritual awareness. If we become zealots in our religious or philosophical beliefs, if we think that our way is the only way to live life or to express religious or philosophical beliefs, we only increase our fear and loneliness, and become small and egocentric. As we grow in our capacity to experience ourselves as the life force within the tree, as a part of the universal Spirit, our respect, compassion, and regard for others evolve naturally and completely. We must always remember that there are as many ways to understand the reality as there are individuals. I recall the phrase used by my great and enlightened friend Rabbi Gelberman, "In addition to . . ." — in addition to my way, there is your way, and his way, and her way, and all the ways of seeing and living life.

The same tools and techniques that give us control of ourselves also help us to become balanced human beings. But along the way, there will be times when we must allow ourselves and others the freedom to think in different and unusual ways and to make mistakes. We need only be patient with ourselves and with others. The practice of patience is just as much a part of self-mastery as anything else we may do. Like other skills, patience takes sincere practice and effort.

Laziness: The Path to Nowhere

||||||||||| Like any organization, the personality resists change. This resistance comes mostly from our habits. Once we build a habit of worry in the mind, the body builds the habit of the fight-or-flight alarm reaction. When we build the habit of self-hatred, the body also builds the habit of the possum reaction. All these habits have some resistance to change. If we allow resistance to limit our choices and actions, we have little chance to take control of our power. Laziness is one of the most pervasive ways in which we experience this resistance. The mind says, "Why bother?" It's easier to take an aspirin for a headache, a drink to relax, or to watch television to dull the mind than to spend fifteen minutes a day doing an exercise.

It's all too easy and more familiar to feel a little miserable than to create a change. Our fast-food mentality constantly hunts for the easiest, quickest way out, whether a lottery, a shorter workweek for more pay, or drugs and alcohol. We don't realize that we are shortchanging ourselves. The less effort we invest, the less we gain, and the more damage we do to our personalities and sense of self-esteem.

It's easy to rationalize laziness. It often takes the form of not having enough time. In our society, everyone is busy. We are "action oriented" but with a heavy dose of couch potatoism. The most common complaint is, "I don't have the time to do the relaxation exercise [or anything else]." Yet we find the time to watch an average of three hours of television a day, the time to waste in idle chatter, the time to "hoist a few cold ones." We find time to clean our bodies, our cars, our homes, but we don't take the time to clean our minds.

The great danger of laziness is that it turns us into victims. Once we become victims we are guaranteed lives of misery. If we are unwilling to make the effort necessary to take control of our own inner resources, or our own inner chatter, there is no way we can take the power away from our dragons or solve the problems of stress.

Developing the Whole Person

|||||||||| But we won't be successful if we only work with one part of the mind. Remember, we function on a number of different dimensions at the same time, and we must work with all of our resources if we want to become skilled human beings. The power of habit formation is a tool that we must learn to use, but we must also use the other tools that we have—our physical tools and controls, insight, strength and courage, sensitivity and creativity—in order to be successful.

The tantric Masters are very practical. They have researched and studied all the dimensions of human life because they realize that we live in all dimensions. They use the resources of the mind and body in a systematic way. Like professional athletes, they know that in order to become skillful, you must approach the building of skills in a very systematic way. My Master taught me about food and exercise as well as about spiritual truths. He taught me about breathing as well as concentration exercises. At first, all I wanted was to learn about the mind, but I finally realized that I couldn't think clearly if my body was troubled or my emotions were clouded. Systematically, he led me through all the dimensions, providing me with a strong foundation to build upon.

We will do the same here. In the second part of the book, we will explore each of the dimensions of the personality and discover the most practical techniques to use in order to build useful habits and develop conscious skills. You see, our goal isn't only to get rid of the dragons or to become healthy. Certainly we will do that. But the real purpose is to become a Master ourselves, to free ourselves from our self-imposed limitations and unlock the power and beauty of the body, mind, and spirit.

Self-Mastery—Reaching for Our Birthright

||||||||||| How would you like to live your life without worrying about every little thing or even big things? How would you like to have unlimited self-confidence, and be able to face failure without being upset or disturbed, to use failure as an opportunity to increase your skill and wisdom? How would you like to experience love without limitations? Or be able to freely use your creativity to solve problems? How would you like to dance with life instead of being dragged through it? This is what self-mastery is really about. It isn't about self-therapy, it is about self-transformation. We become so focused on what is wrong with us that our troubles and our weaknesses become all-consuming issues that devour our energy and our lives.

It is time to put an end to this self-defeating behavior. We are far more than our failures, we are much greater than our pettiness, and we are more powerful than our technology. Self-mastery is knowing ourselves for what we really are, a unique spark of the Divine, the life force within the tree. But unless we come to know and master that force, unless we become skilled human beings, we limit ourselves to the ego, and become the pawns and slaves of our own habits.

The power does not lie anywhere outside of yourself. You can wear a crystal but that piece of mineral rock, no matter how polished and refined, is nothing compared to the power of your mind. You can use technology to alter your brain waves, and you can have highs with drugs. But what will you do when the batteries are dead and the drugs have created side effects?

Self-Training: Taking the Steps to Freedom

||||||||||| It is up to each of us to make the choices necessary to be free. No one can be aware for another, and no one else can slay our dragons. When we blame others or ourselves for our behavior, we end up with even greater weakness and fear. Our habits are ultimately our own responsibility. If we choose to ignore

them, no therapist, doctor, friend, spouse, teacher, or even God can help us. We alone choose to be unaware, we alone allow our habits to remain in power, and we alone suffer the consequences.

The path to self-mastery and freedom lies in our conscious decision to use our own power to create and sustain balance, to develop and use our inner resources. Everything we need is sitting right there within us, hidden only by our ignorance. Take the next step. No one asks that you believe, only that you experiment, practice, and become strong. We can take back the power. We can become Masters.

PART II

THE
SKILLS
OF
SELF-MASTERY

Just as we begin our journey with self-knowledge, we can only complete it with self-discipline. It doesn't matter how many resources we have if we don't know how to access and use them. Nor do we realize the power of our human spirit simply by believing in it. Inspiration is very helpful, but without perspiration, it only ends in disappointment. Faith and belief are powerful tools, but without direct experience and skill, they lead to impotence and ineffectiveness. How many times have you heard someone give an inspiring talk only to have a feeling of futility and sadness a few days later when you realize that nothing really has changed?

There are no "easy" answers—a magic crystal, the right book, a powerful teacher—that will solve all our problems and make life beautiful. Only we have the power to do that for ourselves. This is our freedom—to know and to do for ourselves. It is only when we become skilled, when we can "walk our talk," that we gain freedom from the dragons of the mind and open the power and strength of the personality and spirit.

In Part II, we explore specific techniques used by the great Masters. We will learn a number of different exercises and techniques that will help us take command of our inner resources. Of course, you won't use every exercise or technique. And you will very probably find other techniques that might work as well for you. But you will find a complete approach to working with all dimensions of yourself, and this is essential.

As you read through the next five chapters, try the different exercises to get a sense of what they do and how they feel when you do them. Don't try to become an expert at any of them at this point, and don't worry about which ones to focus on. In the addendum following Chapter 9, we will explore how to design a self-training program that will meet your own unique needs.

The great traditions of self-mastery are very systematic, taking care to build the foundation so strong that it can support any height that we can achieve. They also acknowledge that we must begin to master all dimensions—physical, mental/emotional, and spiritual—if we want to become skilled human beings.

We will do the same here. We begin with the physical foundation, the knowledge and skills we need to make the body healthy, strong, and flexible. In Chapter 5 we explore basic knowledge, skills, and techniques about relaxation, diet, and flexibility training. We will learn about the different levels of relaxation we can achieve through different exercises. By making a few simple changes in how we approach diet, we can put an end to many of the problems that poor eating habits create for us. We will also learn an integrated stretching exercise that has been used by yogis for thousands of years to keep the body flexible, to build strength, and to increase energy.

Then we turn to the more subtle dimension of energy. In Chapter 6 we learn how to use the breath to bring balance and harmony to body and mind, and to create a healthy cardiovascular system. We will see how what we have come to regard as "normal" breathing leads to heart disease and discover how to return to our natural breathing motion.

Once we know how to minimize the effects of stress and create a relaxed, balanced foundation, it is time to confront the dragons of fear and self-hatred found in the sensory mind. In Chapter 7 we explore the techniques that give us the ability to take command of the creative force we call the sensory mind. With these techniques we can regain our power from these two dragons and create a calm, clear mind.

Once we gain the upper hand over the dragons, we learn how to increase the power of the mind and use it to gain access to inner strength and wisdom. In Chapter 8 we explore how to enhance the power of concentration and then refine that power through meditation techniques.

Finally, in Chapter 9, we learn how to use the power of the mind to access the spiritual Self and put an end to the dragon of loneliness. Once we have the foundation, we can access the spiritual Self and begin to use its unlimited strength in our day-to-day lives. In this chapter we will discover how to resolve emotional disturbances through the power of selfless love and other positive emotions.

Learning and doing these exercises is not meant to be work, but an engagement of intention, effort, and joy. Learn to play, to experiment, to see what you discover as you systematically explore your capacities with the exercises. It is time to dance, so let's turn the page and begin.

CHAPTER 5

BODY SKILLS: RELAXATION, DIET, AND EXERCISE

If anything is sacred, the human body is sacred.

—Walt Whitman

|||||||||| The great Masters know that the body is a powerful and useful instrument. The body is a sophisticated biocomputer which not only serves as our mobile home, taking us here and there, but at the same time provides us with an enormous amount of information both about the world around us and about our own inner states of knowledge. It lets us know when we are in danger, what kind of food is healthy for us, and it even signals when we are making a wrong choice. Depending on how we train the body, we can use it as a weapon to defend ourselves or as a tool to enhance the lives of ourselves and others. Because of its power and usefulness, the body is seen as a sacred temple by all spiritual traditions. Many of the most powerful traditions, such as Tantra Yoga, have gained a profound knowledge on how to keep the body healthy and use its power.

Yet most of us hardly know how to treat the body or even how to begin to use the power that we have. We seldom think of the body as an instrument, a tool to develop and use. Instead, we let our bodies suffer from stress and disease, and they become obstacles instead of tools. Not only do we suffer from pain and discomfort, but we also do not think clearly or creatively, our relationships suffer, and we waste incredible amounts of money on drugs to relieve symptoms but do nothing to change the cause.

My tantric Master was raised from the age of three in a cave monastery at 10,000 feet in the Himalayan Mountains. Needless to say, there were no doctors, drugstores, health spas, or personal trainers. Yogis had to rely on themselves to maintain a healthy body. Of course, they have extensive knowledge about healing, using herbs, plants, and other natural products. But the emphasis has always been on prevention, on making the body so healthy and strong that it is naturally resistant to disease.

The exercises and techniques they developed to maintain wellness are highly refined and very sophisticated. Hatha yoga, for instance, is designed to bring balance to body and mind through stimulation of critical neural and glandular centers as well as creating flexibility throughout the body. Martial arts, such as tai chi and kung fu, are recognized as powerful and sophisticated systems of self-defense and combat, but what is not commonly known is that they began as a way to keep the monks of the Shao Lin Temple healthy. A Yoga Master from the Himalayas visited the temple and taught the monks self-defense in order to help them protect themselves and to restore their health.

Naturally, the different approaches to physical health emphasize different aspects. But there are three key elements that are found in every system, whether it is hatha yoga, tai chi, or karate. These are the heart of physical health and are essential to the achievement of self-mastery: relaxation, diet, and flexibility.

Relaxation: A Critical Foundation Skill

|||||||||| We *must* master two skills if we want to free ourselves of suffering and develop our inner resources: relaxation and diaphragmatic breathing. These two crucial skills provide the foundation for self-mastery and personal development. Unless we know how to maintain a relaxed mind and body, and breathe properly, there is no way we can eliminate stress or develop the power of our inner resources effectively. (In fact, breathing is so critical to self-mastery that we will spend the entire next chapter on it.)

Deep relaxation is much more than a stress-management technique. It opens the gateway to your inner resources. When you are relaxed, you work more efficiently, think more clearly, solve problems more creatively, and feel better physically and emotionally.

When we think of being relaxed, however, most of us think about *deep* relaxation. We see ourselves as completely unable or unwilling to move. While this may characterize the first level of deep relaxation, being relaxed does not mean being limp and lethargic. The term "relaxation" simply implies *no excess tension*, a condition of physical and mental balance and efficiency. To be relaxed at work (or anywhere else) doesn't mean you walk around like a wet noodle, but rather that you work without tense shoulder muscles, a clenched jaw, or a hectic mind.

Unnecessary tension interferes with physical actions. The martial arts, for instance, demand a relaxed mind and body for effective, balanced, and quick movement. When students first begin karate training, they are always too tense in their movements. This slows their reflexes, interferes with perception, and creates awkwardness. Karate, like all martial arts, is a combination of relaxation and tension, of softness and hardness. The skilled martial artist is completely relaxed, moves in a balanced way, and uses tension only at a point of contact, and then moves quickly back into a relaxed stance. The ability to be relaxed and use tension is a key element in almost everything we do.

You become skilled at deep relaxation by practicing a series of systematic exercises, which eliminates all tension from the body. Practicing deep relaxation quiets your organ systems, eliminates chronic tension, strengthens your immune system, and helps you stay calm and focused during daily activities.

As with any skill, relaxation requires a consistent practice of systematic techniques. The more skilled you become, the less time it takes. When you become skilled at deep relaxation, what once took fifteen minutes can be done in a few breaths.

THE THREE LEVELS OF DEEP RELAXATION

||||||||||| The depth of your relaxation depends on two things: your degree of skill and the particular technique. Each level has its own purpose, and each provides us with certain benefits.

Level 1: Structural or Muscular Relaxation

The most common techniques achieve deep relaxation through the release of muscle tension. Two major forms are used: tense-release exercises and imagery (auto-hypnosis) exercises. In tense-release exercises, individual muscles or groups of muscles are tensed and then relaxed. For those who don't know what it means to relax, this is an excellent way to experience the difference between a relaxed muscle and a tense one. Auto-hypnosis techniques use imagery (such as picturing your muscles as very warm and loose or picturing yourself lying in the warm sunshine on a secluded beach) or auto-suggestion (repeating such phrases as "My arms are very warm, my arms are very heavy") in order to create a state of muscular relaxation.

These exercises require no previous experience or skill at relaxing. They are excellent beginning exercises and result in a light to moderate level of deep relaxation. When done effectively, they leave the body feeling very heavy and warm, as if it were encased in lead. Your mind is lethargic, and you feel reluctant to work or make any effort. These exercises effectively reduce chronic stress and muscle tension and reduce or even eliminate a variety of symptomatic problems related to muscle tension, such as tension headaches, back problems, and neck and shoulder pain. Detailed instructions for a systematic muscle-relaxation exercise are given in Appendix B.

Level 2: Autonomic Relaxation

A deeper, more complete level of relaxation is achieved by directly influencing the autonomic nervous system. This powerful nervous system controls the fight-or-flight alarm reaction and the possum response in the body. By consciously and systematically altering the motion of the lungs, you can change the dominance pattern within the autonomic nervous system. By changing the motion and rhythm of the breath, you increase parasympathetic activity and achieve a deeper state of rest in the body. Instead of feeling heavy and lethargic, your body feels light, and your mind becomes clear and alert. As we shall see in the next chapter, breathing is an excellent way to maintain balance and create the conditions for effective problem solving. There are a number of different breathing techniques, each one leading to progressively deeper states of relaxation.

Level 3: Concentration

We create the most profound states of relaxation through concentration. The more focused, or concentrated, the mind, the deeper the relaxation and rest in the body. Any concentration exercise calms the body, but the 61 Points Exercise given in Chapter 8 is extremely effective because it reaches the deepest systems of the body. While muscle-relaxation exercises are helpful for muscle-related problems, they are not so effective for more complex problems such as essential hypertension. Because of the depth of the relaxation it creates, "61 Points" is particularly helpful in treating and preventing high blood pressure.

BECOMING SKILLED AT RELAXATION

|||||||||| The most effective way to practice deep relaxation is to use the Relaxation Posture (Figure 5.1), which is called the Corpse Posture in hatha yoga. This posture allows every muscle in the body to achieve a deep state of relaxation. Any other position creates muscle tension to sustain the position, or at least will allow some muscles to remain tense. We use this posture to practice the breathing techniques given in Chapter 6, and to develop skills in deep relaxation.

The best time to practice relaxation is when no one will disturb you for at least fifteen minutes. At the end of a workday, go to a quiet room and take fifteen minutes to clear your mind and body of stress, tension, and all the pressures from work. At first, it may be difficult to take this time when your family wants your attention. But if you persist, you will find that you feel more refreshed and calm, and your interactions with your family and friends will be

||||||||| **RELAXATION POSTURE** |||||||||

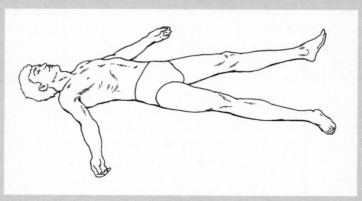

FIGURE 5.1

This basic posture should be used for all relaxation exercises.

Lie on your back on a pad or carpeted floor, and gently close your eyes. Place your feet a comfortable distance apart, about 12 to 18 inches, and your arms and hands slightly away from the body, palms facing up, and fingers gently curled. Use a small pillow or a folded blanket under your head to support the curve of your neck. Do not lie haphazardly or place the limbs too far apart. Lie in a symmetrical position. In this posture the body lies still and relaxed. It is important to avoid drowsiness; keep the mind alert and focused on the flow of the breath.

much better. In fact, after a few weeks your family will probably insist that you take this time.

Obviously, the more you practice, the more skillful you become. Start with fifteen minutes a day. As you gain skill, the time required shortens dramatically. *After* you have built your skill, never spend more than five minutes doing relaxation. The rest of your time is better spent making your mind stronger with concentration and meditation exercises, developing your creativity, or working with your intuition.

You will soon realize that the harder you try to relax, the more tense you become. Relaxation is like floating. Simply lie back and allow it to happen. This is called passive volition, or effortless effort. The best way to learn relaxation exercises is to use an audiocassette until you have memorized the exercise. The tape allows you to listen and follow directions without getting actively involved.

You can purchase tapes commercially or make your own. Detailed instructions for the three major relaxation exercises are given in Appendices B, C, and D. First, read through the exercises and make sure you understand the systematic approach. Then slowly read the instructions while recording them on a cassette tape. The periods between the sentences indicate a pause of a few seconds. After you have taped the exercise, lie down in the Relaxation Posture and listen to it.

People often tell me that their favorite relaxation technique is to listen to music. Others listen to whale sounds, the sound of waves on a beach, or "white noise." Obviously, certain kinds of music and sounds will help you relax. But listening to music or whales communicating with each other does not teach you the skill of deep relaxation, nor will the relaxation be as complete or as deep. Also, you won't always have the opportunity to turn on your stereo or plug in your earphones. If you have the skill, you can relax at any time, in any situation.

Diet: Fuel for Self-Mastery

|||||||||| The diets of the great Masters of self-mastery vary as widely as the cultures and climates in which they live. Many are vegetarian, but not all. Regardless of the differences, the diets of these great Masters share important similarities. First of all, the attitudes that Masters have toward food are remarkably similar. They consider food an offering, and eating as an act of worship. Great respect and attention are given to the freshness and quality of the food, its preparation, and the eating of it. Second, these Masters all eat simple meals and avoid rich, complex foods. They know the negative impact that rich food has on the mind as well as the body. Third, attention is always given to individual needs. The great Masters avoid fanaticism in their diets as in all aspects of life. They approach food as they approach life, with attention, experimentation, and flexibility. And while diets vary from tradition to tradition, we find that the key elements in all traditions are a respectful attitude, simplicity, and balance.

Unfortunately, in our culture many of our eating habits can only be called abusive. Although we have become much more sophisticated about nutrition, our knowledge and practices are primitive and our attitudes are disrespectful. We forget that diet is the basis for physical health and has a profound impact on our emotional health.

There is no question that a low-fat diet helps prevent arterial disease. Dr. Dean Ornish's programs prove that a combination of a low-fat diet, exercise, and yoga even reverses arterial disease and improves the efficiency of the heart. As we reduce our intake of fat, we reduce the incidence of cardiovascular disease. Almost every day, we hear about new discoveries concerning the relationship of diet and disease. In a recent fourteen-day period, *Science News*, a weekly magazine that reports on scientific research, had two articles on diet and disease. One (May 22, 1993) summarized studies that show that vitamin E appears to "dramatically cut heart disease risk in middle-aged men and women" and possibly even protects against degenerative diseases. Another (June 5, 1993) discussed two studies showing that two nutrients in fresh fruits and vegetables help prevent colon cancer, a disease that kills about 57,000 Americans a year.

As a source of misery, a poor diet is second only to emotional disturbances. We eat several times a day. Given the disastrous dietary habits of the average person, we have ample opportunity to create problems. We don't pay attention to the quality of the food we eat, and we allow junk food to dominate. We don't prepare or cook our food properly. We eat too fast. We eat when we are tense and under pressure. The stress that all this creates is evident in the high and increasing incidence of "digestive diseases" such as Crohn's disease, ulcers, and diverticulitis.

Our dietary problems are serious, but we can do a great deal to minimize them with a little understanding and a few simple practices. The digestive system involves two complementary processes—nourishing and cleansing. If we don't build the proper habits, the body gradually builds up toxins which lead to mental and physical diseases. To prevent dietary misery, we have basically three areas to manage: what we eat, how we eat, and when we eat.

THE QUALITY OF THE FOOD WE EAT

|||||||||| The foods most conducive to health are fresh, simple, and nutritious. But amazingly enough, fully 60 to 70 percent of the average American diet is of suboptimal nutritional value. This is not because there isn't enough to eat, but because much of what we eat is of little or no value. Refined sugar, for instance, which contains absolutely no nutrients, makes up about 25 percent of our diets. Fats, which also contain no nutrients, make up about 45 percent. For many, this combination of fats and refined sugar constitutes as much as 70 percent of their food intake. However, to process refined sugar and fats, the body must utilize nutrients.

Besides increasing our nutrient debt, refined sugar leads to a number of other serious problems, such as obesity, a serious and prevalent problem in our society. In addition, when sugar is refined, the body doesn't need to process or digest it in order to absorb it into the bloodstream. The sugar is immediately absorbed, leading to a quick increase in blood sugar levels. If, for instance, you eat a candy bar on an empty stomach, this precipitous rise in blood sugar keys a high insulin release to break down the sucrose so the body can use the sugar. This large insulin output reaches the bloodstream just as the blood sugar is dropping; it causes the blood sugar level to plummet below normal levels; and we feel depressed and enervated. Since we don't like to feel that way, we take another sugar hit, creating the same blood sugar spiking and overproduction of insulin as before. Figure 5.2 shows what happens to blood sugar levels when you eat a lot of refined sugar on an empty stomach.

The precipitous rise and decline in blood sugar often leads to a strain on the liver, which has to clear the insulin from the bloodstream, as well as imbalances in insulin production. This in turn can lead to both hypoglycemia and diabetes. A more serious consequence is the danger posed to the nervous system—such as a diabetic coma. Low blood sugar can also intensify emotional problems, anxiety, and restlessness as well as tiredness and depression. Physical problems related to high sugar intake include kidney irregularity, fluctuations in blood pressure, and adrenal imbalances.

If, instead, we eat an apple, which has to be digested before the sugar is available, a very different process occurs (Figure 5.3). First, the sugar in an apple consists of both sucrose and fructose. You don't need insulin to process fructose inside the body as you do with sucrose. Second, you must take the apple through a digestive process to get to the sucrose. Not only is the level of sucrose lower, but the sucrose is released over a period of time as you digest the apple. This keys a much smaller production of insulin, creating less work for the liver. Unlike the candy bar with its refined sugar, an apple satisfies your nutritional needs without stressing your systems.

Blood sugar is the major fuel for our cells, but we can usually get enough naturally occurring sugar in fresh fruits, vegetables, and grains. Sugar in any form is a stimulant and leads to heightened arousal; refined sugar is too much of a stimulant for the body to be able to handle comfortably. When we add caffeine to the refined sugar, we double the stimulants. There is a rush of sympathetic activity which we feel as a new burst of energy. Unfortunately, the end result is autonomic imbalance (stress), which leads to even more fatigue—particularly in those who suffer from low blood sugar. The "relaxing" coffee break is actually a stress producer!

When we need a break, a relaxation and/or breathing exercise would be far more helpful. These reduce stress, clear our minds, and leave us feeling wonderfully refreshed. Instead of being overstimulated from refined sugar or caf-

FIGURE 5.2

BLOOD SUGAR REACTION LEVELS WITH REFINED SUGAR

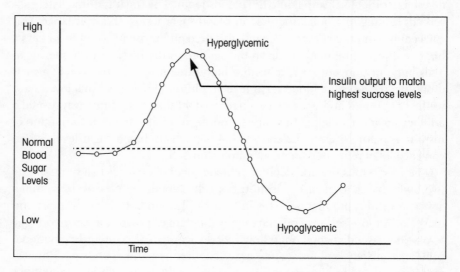

FIGURE 5.3

BLOOD SUGAR REACTION LEVELS WITH NATURALLY OCCURRING SUGAR

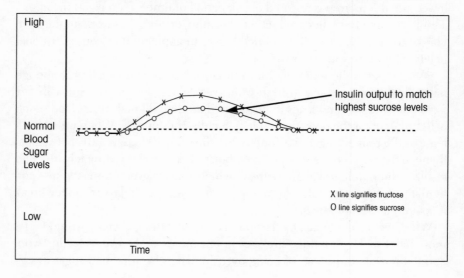

feine, our energy would be appropriate to the task, and the mind would be focused. Releasing tension would leave us more flexible both mentally and physically. We also avoid the withdrawal problems associated with stimulants.

Unless you have a clinical problem, there's no reason to eliminate all refined sugar from your diet. But you should know how to use it intelligently. An average yearly consumption of about 125 pounds per person, or 25 percent of the diet, is certainly not intelligent. Epidemiological studies clearly show that in countries where people consume large amounts of refined sugar the population has a high incidence of blood sugar diseases. In countries where the inhabitants consume more naturally occurring sugars, there is a low incidence of blood sugar diseases.

By being sensitive to the impact of refined sugar on our bodies, we make better choices. Eating a piece of pie on an empty stomach has quite a different effect than eating it after a full meal. When treats become the rule instead of the exception, we aren't using sugar intelligently.

While we have become more sensitive to the fat in our food, fats still make up as much as 45 percent of our diet. These are also "empty" calories with no nutritional value. While a certain amount of fat is necessary, the American Heart Association recommends not more than 30 percent, and Dr. Dean Ornish recommends 10 percent or less. Medical authorities agree that a high-fat diet is associated with heart disease as well as certain forms of cancer, such as colon and prostate.

THE "ARTIFICIAL" PROBLEM

|||||||||| Other things that we ingest can also lead to serious stress problems. For instance, Americans yearly consume an estimated 5 pounds of chemicals which do not occur naturally in the food chain. Did you know that over 2,000 additives are commonly used by the food industry? The basic research on how these additives affect us *has not been done*. No one can tell us what happens when we combine additives (which we do when we eat different foods together) and subject them to the refining process of digestion. Add to this combination the herbicides and pesticides which enter the food chain, and we are looking at chemical mixtures that are potentially dangerous.

Recently, scientists have discovered that chemical pollutants in water and food have had an impact on the sexual development of both men and women as well as animals. Since 1938, sperm counts of men in the United States and in twenty other countries have dropped by an average of 50 percent. One researcher told a congressional panel, "Every man in this room is half the man his grandfather was." The problem of decreased sperm count seems to be caused by estrogen and pollutants that mimic estrogen's structure. More research is needed, but it is clear that both animals and humans have undergone dramatic changes in sexual development that indicate increasing fertility problems.

Long-term effects over generations on such delicate mechanisms as genetic structures and reproductive capacities are largely unknown. Of course, there is a great deal of research showing that the minute quantities of any one chemical that we ingest are not going to create a problem for us. But no one investigates the whole picture. We ingest minute quantities of a broad range of chemicals, not just one, and over a long period of time. What is the cumulative effect over several years of this broad intake? To assume that it is safe to take all these chemicals into our bodies is more than naive; it is foolhardy. Chemicals which do not occur naturally in the food chain upset neurological functioning. It is absurd to think that they have no impact on the body or mind.

THE UNHEALTHY CONVENIENCE

|||||||||| Since World War II the consumption of soft drinks has gone up by 80 percent, pastries by 70 percent, and potato chips by 85 percent. On the other hand, the consumption of dairy products has decreased by 21 percent, vegetables by 23 percent, and fruits by 25 percent. Recent statistics show an alarming pattern:

1. We consume an average of 221 cans of soft drinks per person. This translates roughly into 22 gallons of carbonated sugar.
2. Soft-drink consumption exceeds milk consumption.
3. Americans spent 46 percent of their food expenditures on restaurant meals.
4. One-third of all adults are overweight to the extent that it impairs their health. (Only 2 percent of this can be attributed to glandular problems.)
5. The top ten TV shows are supported by 91 commercials for fast-food restaurants.

The main ingredients found in snack foods are sugar, refined flour, salt, and chemical additives that enhance flavor and color—and extend shelf life. How can anyone doubt that this negatively affects our health! The nature of even the "nutritious" food that we consume has been adversely altered in the past twenty years. "Convenience," or processed, foods are notoriously lacking in both nutritional value and fiber.

The irrepressible drive for convenience has led to a far more subtle and even more serious problem. Microwave cooking is a social experiment on a grand scale. We know little about the effects of this approach on the subtle energy levels of food. Recent research has shown that in microwave cooking, about half the L (levo) isomers switch to D (dextro) isomers, and D to L. Our enzymes are designed to fit as mirror images to these isomers in order to break down and access the nutrients in the food. When the isomers are switched, these enzymes cannot fit, and so the nutrition is unavailable. The longer the food is microwaved, the more switching that occurs. It appears that up to half the nutritional value of the food can be lost in microwave cooking. If this research is accurate, then we are creating even bigger problems with our diets.

TO CHEW OR NOT TO CHEW

|||||||||| How we eat is just as important as what we eat. Unfortunately, most of us are in too much of a hurry to take the time to really chew and taste our food. After two, three, or four quick chews, we swallow it, expecting the rest of our overworked system to break it down further. But contrary to popular belief, neither the stomach nor the liver has teeth. Neither can adequately break down pieces of food that have been reduced in size just enough to be swallowed.

There are several important consequences of gulping down food. First, the digestive process is incomplete. Gulping food prevents the proper mixture of digestive enzymes with the food and interferes with the absorption of nutrients that is supposed to occur in the mouth. This creates stress within the entire digestive system. And when gulping food becomes a habit, the stress becomes chronic.

Furthermore, when we gulp our food, we don't really get an opportunity to taste it. We only experience a few strong flavors—sweetness, saltiness, and sourness. The more subtle flavors (which require a more complete breakdown of the food as it mixes with the digestive juices) are not tasted. Thus, we don't allow our taste buds to tell us what is good for us and what is not.

Most processed food, and, in particular, snack or junk food, is intentionally designed to appeal to the obvious tastes—sweet, salty, and sour. These products contain either sugar or salt as a major ingredient, and eating quickly will leave this taste in the mouth. Their real appearance, odor, and flavor are disguised by a variety of chemicals. The word *enhanced* or *imitation* on the label usually indicates the addition of chemicals.

While artificial colorings can fool the eyes, it is much more difficult to fool the nose—and even more difficult to fool the taste buds. Our taste habits are primarily conditioned by a few strong flavors, and gulping food reinforces our dependence on them. But if our olfactory and taste capacities are given a chance to do their work, it is very difficult to hide or "enhance" the real flavor or smell of what we are putting into our mouths.

Here is an experiment which will give you an opportunity to discover your potential for tasting food. You will need two pieces of bread. One should be the fluffy white kind made from highly refined, enriched white flour, complete with all sorts of artificial additives. The other should be a piece of fresh whole-grain bread made without any additives or preservatives. Rinse your mouth with water. Then take the white fluffy bread, hold it to your nose, and sniff several times to get a good smell. Put it into your mouth and chew until it becomes liquid. Spit it out, rinse your mouth, and repeat the same process with the whole-grain bread. Do your senses of taste and smell tell you anything about which bread you should be eating?

This same experiment should be tried with a piece of snack food (such as a packaged chocolate cupcake) and a piece of fresh fruit. Make sure you chew each until there is nothing but liquid in the mouth. Give your taste buds a chance to work, then decide what you want to put into your system.

Another reason not to gulp food is that when we chew completely, we generally eat about a third less than if we "wolf" it down. Approximately one-third of digestion is supposed to take place in the mouth. When we bypass it by chewing only two or three times, we also bypass about a third of the nutritional value in our food. Consequently, we will eat about a third more than what we really need. When we thoroughly chew each bite, digestion takes place more efficiently, hunger is satisfied more quickly and thoroughly, and we require less intake. Compulsive eaters, or overeaters, rarely if ever really chew their food. If this is a problem for you, taking the time to chew your food will be very helpful. If you are on a weight-loss diet, take particular care to chew thoroughly. A participant in one of my seminars reported that he lost 10 pounds in two weeks simply by chewing his food thoroughly.

Eating when you are calm and quiet is also helpful. The emotional disturbances of anger, sadness, and fear create an "impossible" internal environment for the digestive process. Even the most perfect food creates serious digestive difficulties when eaten under these conditions. When you pause for a moment of silence before meals, it gives you time to clear your mind of disturbing emotions—and thus calm your body—before you eat. Silent prayer cultivates an attitude of thankfulness and prepares the mind and body to receive grace in the form of food. It allows you to focus on positive, joyful emotions. This, of course, leads to a restful condition and the proper neurological balance required for efficient digestion.

In the growing pressure and hurry of our lives, we have lost track of this simple wisdom. Instead of being the center of peace, the dinner table is all too often a battleground, or we eat when we are under pressure. The price we pay for this is reflected in the epidemic of digestive tract diseases we suffer from today.

THE HURRY TO INDIGESTION

|||||||||| While this is somewhat oversimplified, it is essentially correct to say that the more hurried we are, the less able we are to digest food properly and the greater the stress we cause the system. The pervasive habit of "grabbing a bite to eat" or "eating on the run" almost guarantees digestive misery. The more frequently we do this, the more likely it will lead to ill health. Yet how many times do we approach our meals with any degree of calm?

Eating at the wrong times leads to more problems. Constantly snacking (which forces our digestive process to work continually), eating before bedtime, and eating right before or immediately after engaging in strenuous mental or physical activity all tax the digestive system. Asking the body to perform two neurologically opposing tasks invites misery. For example, wining, dining, and then lovemaking is the romantic ideal, but its real consequence is decreased digestive efficiency, decreased sexual capacity, and increased stress. More practical and far less stressful for your body's systems is to make love first and then wine and dine. This way you are not asking your body to perform two conflicting activities at the same time. If thus performed in proper order, all activities—the functioning of the nervous system, digestion, lovemaking—are enhanced.

It isn't difficult to slow down. Before you eat, simply take two minutes to focus on the breathing exercises you will learn in the next chapter. You may reflect on a silent prayer or focus on your breathing. When you feel calm and relaxed, you will notice that you have more saliva in your mouth, indicating that your body is prepared to digest food. Once you have the habit of doing this at every meal, you'll notice that you feel better after you have eaten, and you will also find greater enjoyment in the activity.

PAYING ATTENTION: GAINING RESPECT AND CONTROL

|||||||||| We can solve the problems created by poor diet if we pay attention to what we eat, how we eat, and when we eat. There is no one diet for everyone. Within general guidelines—fresh, nutritious food natural to the food chain, eating in an atmosphere of serenity, and proper chewing—each of us is unique in our nutritional needs. We can discover what we need by paying attention to how food makes us feel not just immediately, but four hours after we eat it.

Again, the key is relaxed awareness. The more sensitive we become, the better choices we make, and the fewer problems we create for ourselves.

Exercise: Creating Flexibility and Awareness

|||||||||| Research leaves no room for doubt: those who exercise consistently will be healthier, have less cardiovascular disease, experience fewer frustrations, and generally have greater satisfaction with life than those who do not. They also have fewer medical expenses and ingest smaller quantities of drugs. This is true regardless of age or sex. In his book *Ageless Body, Timeless Mind*, Deepak Chopra reports on a program conducted by gerontologists from Tufts University in which a group of the frailest residents from a nursing home were selected for a weight-training program. "Within eight weeks, wasted muscles had come back by 300 percent, coordination and balance improved, and overall a sense of active life returned. Some of the subjects who had not been able to walk unaided could now get up and go to the bathroom in the middle of the night by themselves, an act of reclaimed dignity that is by no means trivial. What makes this accomplishment truly wondrous, however, is that the youngest subject in the group was 87 and the oldest 96."

No one seriously disputes the fact that exercise is necessary to maintain a healthy body. But little is said about the impact of exercise on the mind. Most people exercise to build muscular strength, cardiovascular endurance, flexibility, and physical balance. These are important and necessary for health. There is a great deal of good information available about aerobic exercise and weight lifting, so we don't need to focus on these here. Instead, our focus will be to use exercise to increase inner awareness as well as to enhance flexibility. The simple exercises that follow will strengthen both body and mind, build balance and coordination as well as strength, and enhance concentration and confidence.

If you exercise regularly, you will recognize that there are times when your exercise program doesn't seem very helpful. Jogging wasn't enjoyable, you didn't feel invigorated after your handball game or martial arts session, or you felt low after your walk in the park. It isn't the fault of the exercise program— your mind was not properly engaged. Whenever the body is exercising but the mind is not involved, the exercise yields fewer benefits. In fact, if you merely exercise your body without paying attention, it can be harmful.

A classic example of this is the "screaming" Type A personality who has been told by his doctor to start jogging every day. In true Type A form, he compulsively sets up a jogging schedule in which he attempts to achieve certain goals as quickly as possible. After all, if he is going to run, then, by God, he will be "the best damn runner on the block." He runs against the clock just as he works against the clock. The result is that he adds another strain to his day rather than a beneficial interlude for his body. Working or jogging, his mental attitude creates his stress. What happens to his body is determined by what happens in his mind.

If we want to use exercise as a tool to increase our self-mastery, we must pay attention to how the exercise affects the body and mind. We must coordinate mind, body, and action, and this takes attention, which is the key to successful exercise.

Like the Type A jogger, we create stress and other problems when we allow the mind to think about future threats or past mistakes and hurts, instead of focusing on what we are doing. This is why competitive sports can be very stressful, particularly when there are heavy emotional attachments (such as financial or self-esteem considerations) involved with winning or losing.

Both professional and amateur athletes now recognize that the mind plays a key role in performance. Early books on the subject, such as Timothy Galway's *The Inner Game of Tennis*, point out how concentration and mental imagery (performing the actions perfectly in the mind before performing with the body) enhance performance. Now sports psychologists work in all fields of professional and amateur sports, using imagery to develop performance skills. However, the focus is still on performance at the physical level.

Western physical-fitness programs are just beginning to use exercise as a way to sharpen the mind and increase inner awareness. In Eastern systems, on the other hand, the focus has always been to perfect control of the mind over the body. We don't have to become yogis or martial artists to use exercise to increase our conscious control over the body/mind interaction. We can easily bring balance to our physical-fitness regimens and enhance control over both mind and body.

EXERCISE FOR MIND/BODY COORDINATION

||||||||||| The interdependent relationship between mind and body is very complex. The mind has ultimate control, but events in the body deeply affect the mind. If you don't believe this, simply spend a few hours hunched over and see how you feel. When the body becomes rigid and inflexible, it means that the same conditions exist somewhere in the mind. If we make the body more flexible, we also make the mind more flexible.

The most common symptoms of rigidity are stiff muscles, backaches, and painful joints. We retain inflexibility through muscle tension. This problem is exacerbated when the tendons become short and rigid, allowing for little flexibility and leading to sprains, torn ligaments and muscles, and dislocated joints. More serious, and also stress related, is arthritis, the crippling joint disease.

We know that we must loosen up before playing handball or tennis, and that exercises which systematically stretch muscles and tendons are very important. So what do we do to warm up? A few jumping jacks, a shrug of the shoulders, a few quick deep knee bends, running in place, or other quick, short, and choppy movements. Unfortunately, this is the wrong way to stretch muscles!

To relieve tension, to stretch and loosen tight muscles and tendons, requires slow, sustained movement together with holding the stretched posture. Pumping muscles with quick movements does not stretch them out; it builds more tension within them. These movements energize muscles, but don't necessarily release tension.

A wide variety of simple stretching exercises are available (at the end of this chapter you will find several which are excellent for increasing flexibility). But there is one important secret to doing stretches—coordinate your breathing with the movement. This dramatically improves your capacity to stretch. If you pay close attention to both the movement and your breath, you can determine whether that movement should be done on an exhalation or an inhalation. A general rule is to exhale whenever you stretch down or bend over, and inhale whenever returning to the original position. This coordinates the mind with the movement. Breath coordination also ensures that the movements will not be done too quickly.

Breathing is also an important variable in holding the stretch. For example, when you stretch down to touch your toes, don't bounce up and down as if you were bobbing for apples. Rather, bend down to touch your toes, and then stay bent as far as you comfortably can. Do not bend until you feel pain. You are exercising, not taking a course in pain control!

Do not hold your breath. That only increases tension. After a few moments, concentrate on relaxing the point in the body at which you feel the stretch most. Then, on an exhalation, bend a little bit more, and hold the stretch. Concentrating on the flow of the breath, relax into this posture as much as possible. Then, after a few moments, rise slowly and relax standing up. The longer you comfortably hold the stretch, the more benefit you gain from it. Slowly increase your capacity to hold or remain in the stretch posture. Work within your limits and your limits will certainly increase. Go beyond them and you will certainly suffer.

With concentration and comfortable breathing, you will be able to stretch much farther than you thought. However, use the exhalation and bending technique only once or twice after the initial bend. Otherwise you may extend yourself too far, and you will feel the consequences for the next few days.

By moving gently and relaxing into the posture (holding the limit of the stretch) you begin to develop the most important skill that comes from exercising. *By paying close attention to the internal feelings and movements, you become conscious of the subtle feedback cues of the muscles and systems involved. This increased sensitivity leads to a greater conscious control over these muscles and systems.*

You are learning how to use your own innate biofeedback machine. You must develop this sensitivity if you ever want to have control over your body and to be able to use your mind to keep your body healthy and free of stress and disease. The more skilled you become, the greater your power.

Most people are not sensitive to the tension in the shoulders and neck until they feel soreness or pain or even a headache. The muscles use pain as a final signal in order to grab your attention. The problem isn't your shoulders. These poor muscles are only following instructions, and all along they have been sending signals back to the brain with every change or increase in tension. The problem is that no one was paying attention to the feedback signals! The muscle was forced to remain tense. Finally, the muscle sends a pain message, and you begin to pay attention.

Why wait until the tension becomes so chronic and extreme as to cause pain? By becoming aware of your internal messages and controls, you can listen more carefully to the messages of the body and do something much earlier to prevent a problem from developing. While exercising, if you think about how wonderful you look while stretching, or how far you bend in comparison to others, or about your job, or anything else, you have wasted your time. You have missed the most important element of the exercise—developing awareness of your changing physical and mental states.

Even just five minutes of stretching done consistently with intense concentration develops your internal awareness. You actually need very little time to become aware of and develop control over your muscles. You can do it with all the muscles, as well as your heartbeat, blood pressure, and just about any system in the body. The deeper the system, of course, the more time and attention it takes.

BODY, MIND, AND CONSCIOUSNESS

|||||||||| Hatha yoga is a sophisticated and practical exercise system that consists of a series of postures designed to bring balance and flexibility to both mind and body by stimulating neural and glandular systems. Hatha yoga is very pre-

cise and effective in correcting physical problems. Research in England has shown that hatha yoga is more effective for healing back problems than any other exercise system, and far more effective than surgery.

Several of my clients and associates have used hatha yoga as a therapeutic system for problems stemming from accidents as well as from congenital defects. One example is an elderly gentleman, Bua Swami, from a small farming village in India. I met Bua Swami about eighteen years ago and attended several of his classes. At the time we met, he was seventy-three years old and was capable of bending his body like a pretzel, accomplishing the most difficult of yoga exercises. What was most fascinating was that he was born crippled. Early in his life, he was sent to study hatha yoga with an accomplished Master. Through his training, he was able to overcome his disability completely, and went on to teach hatha yoga all over the world. At the present he is still teaching and doing postures at age ninety-one.

On the physical level, hatha yoga strengthens organ, glandular, and neurological systems. In addition, it reduces physical tension by slowly stretching the muscles and tendons and eliminating the physical habits which sustain stress. It consists of stretches and held postures alternated with relaxation, all of which work synergistically to coordinate mind and body. Hatha yoga also includes practices which cleanse the body of accumulated toxins and waste products. But its ultimate goal is to bring perfect balance and harmony into the body/mind/spirit relationship and eliminate conditions of "dis-ease."

In the West, hatha yoga is taught primarily as a beauty regimen to keep oneself young and healthy. The real purpose of hatha yoga, however, is not only to strengthen and balance the body, but to calm the mind, increase concentration skills, and expand inner awareness. It isn't by accident that the postures are centered around the spine and central nervous system. Through proper manipulation, exercise, and concentration, the postures benefit particular glandular, structural, and organic systems. In this way our physiological systems achieve harmony and balance, which allows us to sustain deep concentration and a one-pointed mind, the key tools for self-mastery. This, in turn, leads to emotional equilibrium and a powerful mind, building blocks for a healthy life.

Beginning exercises, such as those for joints and glands and some of the stretches, can and should be practiced on your own, and several of the more immediately helpful ones are described at the end of this chapter. The ideal, however, is to find a competent instructor and learn the postures. Then develop a routine that fits your nature and needs.

When selecting a teacher, remember that the ultimate purpose of the system is to work with the mind and internal concentration skills. The competent teacher knows her subject well and practices what she teaches. One critical point is breathing, a necessary part of hatha yoga. If the teacher is not knowledgeable about the breath, including the neurophysiology of breathing, she is not competent.

You can usually find a variety of classes in hatha yoga and martial arts in your community. Sample the classes, study the teacher and the methods used, and choose wisely. There are many fine traditions and excellent teachers. It is simply a matter of taking the time to check out your resources, finding what best fits your temperament and needs, and then committing yourself to a consistent practice.

Hatha yoga does not replace sports or aerobic exercises. You need balance in your exercise program just as you need balance in the other areas of your life. A short daily period of hatha yoga postures, which will prevent many physical and mental problems, can (and should) supplement your regular exercise routine.

STRETCHING EXERCISES FOR FLEXIBILITY AND BALANCE

‖‖‖‖‖‖‖‖ The following are a series of exercises which anyone can do easily and quickly. The first set consists of desk exercises, simple stretching exercises for the face, neck, and shoulders, designed to increase circulation and decrease tension in the various muscle, joint, and glandular areas of the body. You can do these easily while sitting at a desk (and at any time during the day). If used often, they provide immediate and effective stress reduction.

The second group details simple cross-pattern movements that coordinate left-brain and right-brain hemispheres. They are part of Brain Gym, a system of educational kinesiology developed by Dr. Paul Dennison that uses simple movements to enhance learning abilities. These are useful morning exercises to help balance and coordinate mind and body.

The third set is more involved; the stretches require some time and space to perform. Integrated with relaxation, they offer a practical series of beginning stretching exercises.

When you exercise, it helps to keep several points in mind:

- Be consistent. Set a specific time each day for your practice, and practice at least a little each day. Don't rush—take the time you need to do them properly. Consistency builds very helpful habits.
- Morning and evening are the two best times to practice. Morning exercise helps you remain calm and alert during the day. In the evening, the exercises help relieve the day's tensions so that you can enjoy a peaceful night's sleep.

- Do the exercises in a clean, quiet, and well-ventilated room. Wear loose, comfortable clothing.
- Always practice on an empty stomach.
- Women should not practice strenuous exercises during menstruation. However, all the exercises given below can be done. Just remember to relax and work gently with the body.
- Do not become discouraged if your body does not respond the same way each day. Just practice regularly, and don't compete with others or yourself.
- Study your body and its movements. Be aware of your capacity and learn not to go beyond it. Your capacity will increase with practice.
- Let the body movements flow evenly and gently with the breath. Do not hold your breath at any time unless specifically instructed to do so.
- Follow any exertion with relaxation. However, do not allow the mind to drift toward sleep while you relax.

Remember, the purpose of the stretches is to relieve tension, increase flexibility, and increase internal awareness and control of bodily processes. Concentrate on what you are doing. Keep the breath even, steady, and coordinated with the movement. Most important, enjoy the exercises.

Desk Exercises

||||||||||| *Shoulders* Do these simple exercises several times during the day. Be sure to coordinate the breathing with the movement, and pay attention to what you feel. This will not only stretch the muscles but also increase your awareness of each one, which in turn will increase your control and reduce chronic muscular tension.

Stand or sit with the arms hanging loosely at the sides. Begin to rotate the left shoulder in a complete circle, first moving it forward and in toward the center of the chest, exhaling as you do so. Then move it up toward the ear and back while inhaling, trying to touch the shoulder blade to the spine, and then down, back into the starting position. Rotate three times in this direction and then reverse and rotate three times in the opposite direction. Do the same for the right shoulder, and then do both shoulders together. Relax.

||||||||||| *Neck* These exercises are very good for relieving accumulated tension in the back neck muscles. If you have tension headaches or are bothered by a stiff neck and shoulders, these will be very helpful, and can be practiced several times daily without any difficulty.

Forward and Backward Bend: Exhale slowly, bringing the head forward and taking the chin toward the chest. Feel the stretch of the muscles in the back of the neck. Inhale slowly, lifting the head up and back, stretching the muscles at the front of the neck. With an exhalation, slowly return to the forward position.

Chin over Shoulder: With an exhalation, turn the head as far to the left as possible and try to bring the chin in line with the shoulder. Inhale and bring the head back to the forward position. Repeat in the same manner on the right side.

Ear over Shoulder: With an exhalation, bring the left ear toward the left shoulder. Inhale and come back to the center. Exhale and bring the right ear toward the right shoulder. Again inhale, come back to the center, and relax. Only the head and neck should move. The shoulder should not be raised to meet the ear.

Neck Rolls (Figure 5.4): Lower the chin to the chest and *slowly* begin to tilt the head in a clockwise direction. Inhale as you tilt the head to one side and then to the back. Exhale as you tilt the head to the other side and then forward. Remember to tilt the head, bringing your ear to your shoulder, and not to turn the head. Your chin should always face the front. Reverse and rotate the same number of times in the opposite, counterclockwise direction. The head, neck, and body should be relaxed, allowing the head to tilt and rotate freely and loosely. Do three or four rolls in each direction several times a day.

Neck rolls can be done safely if you move slowly and methodically. If you feel any slight dizziness, or if there is any pain when tilting the head back, simply do not allow the head to tilt as far back, avoiding any pain or discomfort.

|||||||||||| *Forehead and Sinus Massage*
- Sit in a comfortable posture with the head, neck, and trunk straight. Using your fingers or the heels of your palms, begin to massage the forehead by working up and out with a stroking motion. Follow the bony structure around the eyes and continue out across the temples.
- Next, massage just below the eyes and next to the nose. Make the same motions, moving outward across the face and temples.
- Using the thumbs and forefingers, gently slide across the upper rim of the eye sockets toward the temples. Put pressure on the bony ridge, but don't put any pressure on the eye itself.
- On the lower ridge of the eye sockets close to the nose, use your fingers to press down gently, then release. Don't rub, just press. Then move your fin-

FIGURE 5.4

NECK ROLL EXERCISE

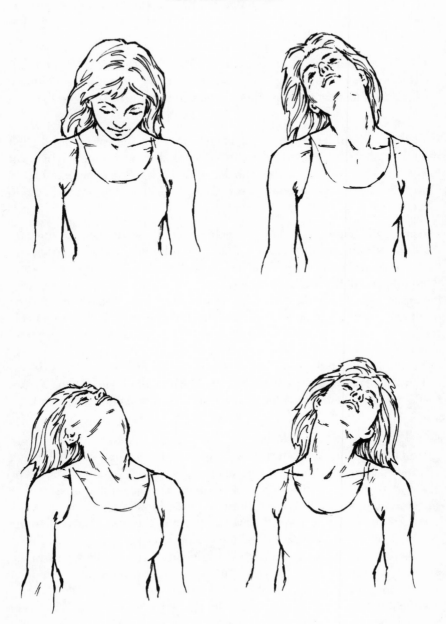

gers over, and press again. Continue to move and press until the entire bony ridge has been massaged. Don't put any pressure on the eye.

- Massage around your mouth and up the jaw line to the temples. Ease up on the pressure whenever you come to the temple area. All of these movements begin at the center of the face and move outward. This pushes all the tension off the face, forehead, and temples, and smoothes away any wrinkles on the forehead or crow's-feet at the eye edges.
- Rub the palms of your hands quickly together until the hands become very warm. Then gently lay the palms of the hands on your closed eyelids, without pressing, allowing the heat from the skin to permeate the eyelids. Visualize the warmth moving from your hands and penetrating all the way to the back of your eyes. Feel your eyes relaxing in the warmth. This is called palming, and is very useful, particularly if you work with a computer.

Balancing Exercises

These simple movements help balance brain hemispheres. They are adapted from Paul Dennison's book *Switching On*. Cross-motor patterning or cross-crawling "is any rhythmic, balanced movement which requires the individual to dynamically relate the right side of his body to the left side, while at the same time being aware of the top half of his body and the lower half.

Cross-crawling requires precise switching on and off of the muscles by the brain at exactly the right time, and requires feedback and feed forward from and to the muscles to maintain the exercise. This highly intricate bilateral integration is learned by the infant during the creeping and crawling stages before walking. It is the same type of cooperation of the cerebral hemispheres that is required for reading and writing."

These exercises begin with a simple cross-pattern, touching the knee with the opposite-side hand, and move to more complex patterns of touching the knee with the opposite-side elbow. These movements coordinate left/right, top/bottom, and back/front areas of the brain and body simultaneously, leading to better coordination and balance. Start these exercises slowly and rhythmically. Slowly increase your speed as you feel more coordinated. Most people (myself included) who do these simple exercises in the morning feel more coordinated throughout the day.

|||||||||| *Hand-to-Knee Cross-Pattern (Figure 5.5)*: Lift your right knee upward and bring your left hand down to touch the knee. Then lift your left knee, bringing your right hand down to touch your knee. Alternate between the two until you have done at least ten repetitions on each side.

FIGURE 5.5
HAND-TO-KNEE
CROSS-PATTERN

FIGURES 5.6
ELBOW-TO-KNEE
CROSS-PATTERN

FIGURE 5.7
ELBOW-TO-KNEE
CROSS-PATTERN
FRONT TO BACK

|||||||||| *Elbow-to-Knee Cross-Pattern (Figure 5.6):* This is similar to the above exercise except that you extend the arm and opposite leg in opposite directions and form an X to complete the movement. Lift your right knee, touching your left elbow, and then stretch the right leg out to the right and the left arm out to the left. Then lift your left knee, touching the knee with your right elbow, and then stretch the left leg out to the left and the right arm out to the right. This creates an X pattern with the arms and legs. Do at least ten repetitions on each side.

|||||||||| *Elbow-to-Knee Cross-Pattern Front to Back (Figure 5.7):* This exercise is the same as the above except that instead of stretching the arms and legs to the side, the arms are stretched to the front and the legs to the back. Lift your left knee and touch your right elbow to the knee. Then stretch your right arm forward as if reaching in front of you, and simultaneously stretch your left leg out behind you. Then lift your right knee and touch your left elbow to the right knee. Then stretch your left arm forward as if reaching in front of you, and simultaneously stretch your right leg out behind you. Do a minimum of ten repetitions on each side.

Stretches

Before doing the following stretches, lie in the Relaxation Posture (see Figure 5.1). This centers the mind and prepares it for focusing on the body. It helps you to relax the skeletal muscles, enabling you to go further into the stretches while reducing the likelihood of injuries. Relaxing between stretches helps prepare the mind for the next exercise in the sequence. Lie in the Relaxation Posture until respiration and heartbeat return to normal. However, beginners should not remain in this position for more than ten minutes. After finishing your stretches, complete your exercise period by lying on your back, breathing from the diaphragm and concentrating on the breath for five minutes. This is an excellent time to practice 2:1 Breathing as described in Chapter 6.

|||||||||| *Side Stretch (Figure 5.8):* Assume a simple standing posture with feet about shoulder width apart and legs and knees relaxed. Movements should be made slowly as if you are standing in water and moving your arms or legs through the water. Begin inhaling, and slowly raise the right arm out to the side with the palm facing downward. When the arm reaches shoulder level, turn the palm upward. Continue inhaling and raise the arm until it is next to the ear. Still continuing to inhale and keeping the feet firmly on the floor, stretch the entire right side of the body upward. Then, without allowing the body to

bend forward or backward or the right arm to bend, begin exhaling and slowly bend at the waist, sliding the left hand down the left leg. Breathe evenly for three complete breaths. Inhaling, slowly bring the body back to an upright position. Exhaling, slowly lower the arm to shoulder level, turn the palm downward, and return to the simple standing posture. Concentrate on the breath until the body relaxes completely. Repeat the side stretch in the opposite direction. When you first begin to stretch, hold the stretch for at least three breaths on each side. As you become more flexible, you can hold the posture for as long as you are comfortable, but make sure that you hold each side for the same length of time.

Note: For a more intense stretch repeat this posture standing with the legs together.

||||||||||| *Simple Back Stretch (Figure 5.9)*

Assume the standing posture. With the fingers facing downward, place the heels of the hands on either side of the spine just above the buttocks. Exhaling, gently push the hips forward, slowly letting the head, neck, and trunk bend backward as far as comfortable without straining. Inhaling, return to the standing pose, keeping the hands in the same position. Keeping the entire body relaxed, exhale as you slowly bend the body forward from the hips as far as possible. Hold this position until all the muscles of the back relax completely.

Note: The forward bend balances the effects of the backward bend.

||||||||||| *Angle Posture*

First Position (Figure 5.10): Assume the simple standing posture with the feet two to three feet apart. Placing the arms behind the back, grasp the right wrist with the left hand. Keep the heels in line and place the right foot at a 90-degree angle outward from the left. (Beginning students may turn the left foot slightly inward—to the right—if it is more comfortable.) Inhaling, turn the body toward the right foot. Exhaling, bend forward from the hips and bring the head as close to the knee as comfortable. Breathe evenly; hold this position for five counts. Inhaling, slowly raise the body, and exhaling, turn to the front. Turn the right foot so that it faces forward. Repeat the exercise on the left.

Second Position (Figure 5.11): Keeping the arms straight, interlace the fingers behind the back. With the right foot at a 90-degree outward angle from the left, turn the body and exhaling, bend forward from the hips, bringing the head toward the right knee. Raise the hands overhead as far as comfortable. Breathe evenly; hold this position for five counts. Inhaling, slowly raise the body and exhaling, turn to the front. Repeat the exercise on the left side.

FIGURE 5.8

SIDE STRETCH

FIGURE 5.9

SIMPLE BACK STRETCH

FIGURE 5.10

ANGLE POSTURE 1

FIGURE 5.11

ANGLE POSTURE 2

FIGURE 5.12

ANGLE POSTURE 3

FIGURE 5.13

TORSO TWIST

1

2

3

Third Position (Figure 5.12): With the arms straight, interlace the fingers behind the back and press the palms together. Exhaling, raise the arms and bend forward as far as comfortable. Breathe evenly and hold for five counts. Inhaling, push the hands toward the floor and bend the head, neck, and trunk back as far as comfortable without straining. Breathe evenly; hold for five counts. Slowly return to a standing position and relax.

|||||||||| *Torso Twist (Figure 5.13)*

First Position: Assume the simple standing posture with the feet two to three feet apart. Raise the arms overhead; interlace the fingers. Keeping the arms next to the ears and stretching the body from the rib cage upward, rotate the upper torso, arms, and hands in a clockwise direction. The waist, hips, and legs remain stationary. Inhale as the body leans to the right and to the back; exhale as the body leans to the left and to the front. Repeat three times clockwise and then three times counterclockwise. Continue by moving into the second position.

Second Position: Keeping the hips stationary and bending from the waist, repeat the above exercise three times clockwise and three times counterclockwise. Continue by moving into the third position. (Remember to breathe as described in the first position.)

Third Position: Keeping the legs stationary and bending from the hips as far as comfortable, rotate and twist the entire upper part of the body in a large circle. Repeat three times clockwise and three times counterclockwise. (Remember to breathe as described in the first position.)

Relax. Concentrate on the breath.

THE SUN SALUTATION:
AN INTEGRATED STRETCHING EXERCISE (FIGURE 5.14)

|||||||||| This is an integrated exercise that stretches and limbers the spine as well as all of the limbs and joints. The Sun Salutation is a series of twelve positions, each one flowing into the next in one graceful, continuous movement. First become familiar with the movements, and then coordinate your breathing with them. You will find, as you progress from doing two or three every morning to doing seven or eight or more, that you will feel the difference on the days you do not do them. If you feel like you only have the time to do one exercise in the morning, this is the one to do. (It is my favorite wake-up exercise.) The benefits are innumerable.

FIGURE 5.14

The Twelve Positions of the Sun Salutation

1   2   3   4

5   6

7   8

9   10   11   12

During sleep our body is very inactive. Our metabolic rate decreases, the circulation of body fluids slows, and all of the body's functions are reduced. When we wake up, we must make a transition from an inactive condition to an active one. By not stretching properly, the body isn't prepared to function adequately, and this can lead to problems, including strained and pulled muscles.

The Sun Salutation is excellent for the transition between sleep and activity. The exercise massages and stimulates the glands, organs, muscles, and nerves of the body. The breath rate increases, bringing more oxygen into the lungs, and the heart rate speeds up. This in turn causes more blood to pass through the lungs, which picks up more oxygen, providing a greater supply of oxygenated blood throughout the body.

It's a wonderful exercise. Try it for a month, gradually increasing the number of salutations you do each morning until you are doing at least eight to twelve. The first one you do will be difficult as the body is not used to stretching. The second one will not be as difficult, and by the third or fourth salutation, you will feel as if your body has been oiled at the joints and your internal energy is beginning to flow. You will notice the difference in how you feel for the rest of the day.

Position 1 (exhale during movement): Stand firmly with the head, neck, and trunk in a straight line. Beginners can stand with the feet slightly apart. With palms together in a prayer position, place the hands at the heart level and gently close the eyes. Standing silently, concentrate on the breath.

Position 2 (inhale during movement): Inhaling, slightly lower and stretch the hands and arms forward with the palms facing downward. Raise the arms overhead until they are next to the ears. Keeping the knees slightly bent and the head between the arms, arch the spine and bend backward as far as possible without straining.

Position 3 (exhale during movement): Exhaling, bend forward from the hips, keeping the back straight and the arms next to the ears. Continue bending; place the palms next to the feet, aligning the fingers with the toes. Bring the head to the knees, keeping the legs straight. Note: If you cannot place the hands on the floor without bending the legs, then lower the upper body only as far as comfortable without straining.

Position 4 (inhale during movement): In this position bend the knees if necessary in order to place the hands on the floor. Inhaling, stretch the right leg back, rest the right knee and the top of the right foot on the floor, and extend the toes. The left foot remains between the hands; the hands remain firmly on the floor. Arch the back, look up, and stretch the head back as far as comfortable. The line from the head to the tip of the right foot should form a smooth and graceful curve.

Position 5 (retain the breath; this is the only position in which the breath is held): While retaining the breath, curl the toes of the right foot and extend the left leg, placing it next to the right. The arms remain straight but not locked and the body forms an inclined plane from the head to the feet. This position resembles a starting push-up position.

Position 6 (exhale during movement): Exhaling, drop first the knees and then the chest to the floor, keeping the tips of the fingers in line with the breasts. Tuck in the chin and place the forehead on the floor. In this position only the toes, knees, hands, chest, and forehead touch the floor. The nose does not touch the floor and the elbows remain close to the body.

Position 7 (inhale during movement): Without moving the hands and forehead, relax the legs and extend the feet so that the body rests flat on the floor. Inhaling, slowly raise the head. First, touch the nose and then chin to the floor; then stretch the head forward and upward. Without using the strength of the arms or hands, slowly raise the shoulders and chest; look up and bend back as far as comfortable. In this posture the navel remains on the floor. To lift the thorax, use the muscles of the back only. Do not use the arms and hands to push the body off the floor, but to balance the body. Keep the feet and legs together and relaxed.

Position 8 (exhale during movement): Without repositioning the feet and hands, exhale, straighten the arms, and push the buttocks high in the air. Bring the head between the arms and try to gently press the heels to the floor.

Position 9 (inhale during movement): Inhaling, bend the right knee and place the right foot between the hands. Align the toes with the fingers. Rest the left knee and the top of the foot on the floor and extend the toes. Arch the back, look up, and bend back as far as comfortable.

Position 10 (exhale during movement): Exhaling, place the left foot beside the right, keeping the palms on the floor. Straighten the legs and bring the head to the knees.

Position 11 (inhale during movement): Inhaling, slowly raise the body, stretching the arms out, up, and back. Remember to keep the arms next to the ears and to bend the knees slightly as you arch the spine and bend backward as far as possible.

Position 12 (exhale): Exhaling, return to an erect standing position. Slowly lower the arms and bring the hands to the chest in prayer position.

Repeat the Sun Salutation, but alternate the leg movements by extending the opposite leg in Positions 4 and 9. Then relax in the Corpse Posture and practice a few minutes of even diaphragmatic breathing.

CHAPTER 6

THE BREATH OF LIFE

If you know the breath, you will know everything.
—Tantra Yoga Master Swami Rama

Once there was a great gathering of all the active and passive senses of man for the purpose of deciding which of them was to be king. They each dressed in their finest, most impressive clothing, and each was busily trying to impress the others with his importance and power. The sense of sight was dressed in shimmering, brilliant colors and spoke movingly of the utility and beauty of his power. The sense of sound, garbed in subtle clothing that moved and sounded like a gentle wind in the trees, and wearing jewelry that tinkled like tiny, clear silver bells, argued just as movingly for his power. All the others, beautifully robed, were equally as insistent, each attempting to outshine the others.

Finally, breath, unnoticed in his common and ordinary clothing, grew tired of the useless noise and senseless argument, and announced in a strong voice that the decision was already made. He, the breath, was the most vital, and thus king of all. There was a stunned silence, and then a clamoring of denial and argument as each sense pointed out its own beauty and power. Having heard enough, and somewhat irritated by all the hubbub and foolishness, breath decided to leave, and quietly slipped out the door. Within a few moments, all the other senses began to dim, and their power and beauty began to fade. Finally realizing the power of breath, all the other senses called after him and begged his return, paying full respect to his sovereignty.

This ancient tantric parable is as relevant today as it was 2,000 years ago. In our fast-paced, exciting, technologically driven society, we are charmed and hypnotized by the sensory experiences of life. We become addicted to the changes, stimulation, and distractions that are so characteristic of modern culture. The more dependent we become on our technology, the more we lose touch with the fundamental realities within ourselves and the more insensitive we are to our inner harmony and strength. As a consequence, we become victims to the whims of our senses and the unconscious play of our habits. Even our relaxation is often done with music and soft lights, or to the accompaniment of the various tones, beeps, and lights of sophisticated biofeedback equipment.

Like the senses in the parable, we don't pay much attention to breath until it isn't there. Yet breath is the most powerful tool we have for achieving self-mastery. Because of its unique relationship to the autonomic nervous system, the powerful nervous system that controls our organ systems, breathing plays *the* critical role in determining whether or not we suffer from stress. Breath is part of both the voluntary or sensorimotor nervous system and the involuntary or autonomic nervous system. We can either consciously control the way we breathe or let it run on automatic. This dual connection allows us to use the breath as a doorway to the autonomic nervous system, giving us the control we need to regulate autonomic balance and eliminate stress.

Western sciences study breathing from the perspective of ventilation perfusion and blood gases. The great traditions of self-mastery, from yoga to Taoism to the martial arts, have gone far beyond this limited view, and have also studied the impact of breathing on the nervous system. For thousands of years, the science of yoga has researched, experimented, and verified methods of breathing that lead to direct control over the autonomic nervous system. Through yoga science, we know that changes in neurological functioning are related to changes in our breathing patterns. This is critical information if we are to achieve self-mastery.

Let's explore the relationship between breathing and the autonomic system. Take your fingers and find a place where you can feel your own pulse, either on the inside of your wrists or in your neck. Pay attention to your pulse for a few moments. Notice that your pulse doesn't tick like a clock. Instead, it fluctuates slightly. There is a slight slowing and speeding up of your pulse. This gentle rhythm is related to another process going on in your body.

As you keep track of your pulse, pay attention to your breath. As you inhale, notice how your pulse begins to speed up, and as you exhale, your pulse begins to slow down. This is called sinus arrhythmia, and is a healthy and natural rhythm or fluctuation in your pulse. Western medical science has known about it for hundreds of years, yet no one has paid attention to its implications. Your pulse is controlled by the autonomic nervous system, the control system that controls your organ systems. The sympathetic arm of the autonomic system, which creates arousal in the body, speeds up the heart rate. The parasympathetic arm, which creates rest for the body, slows the heart rate. Recall from Chapter 2 that the sympathetic system controls the fight-or-flight alarm reaction, the physical reaction created by the dragon of fear, while the parasympathetic system controls the possum response, the physical reaction created by the dragon of self-hatred.

The fluctuation in the pulse reflects the influence of your breath on the autonomic nervous system. Your inhalation reflects and stimulates sympathetic activity, in turn speeding up the heartbeat, while your exhalation reflects and stimulates parasympathetic activity which, in turn, slows the heartbeat. This influence is so strong that you can use your breath to regulate autonomic balance. *Taking charge of your breath is the crucial "first step" to self-mastery. If you know the secrets of breathing, you learn the secret to controlling the physical reactions to fear and self-hatred. Not only do you now have control of your stress reactions, but you also have a powerful tool to begin to take control of your emotional reactions and the two dragons of fear and self-hatred.*

Breath and Energy: The Vital Link

|||||||||| All traditions of self-mastery see the breath as the major vehicle for the second dimension of the personality, the subtle life force that connects mind and body. They use a variety of breathing techniques to develop inner balance, strength, and self-control. These traditions are extremely sophisticated, such as the yogic science of *Swar Swarodayam,* a vast and intricate science which details the relationship between breathing rhythms and states of consciousness. The great masters of the martial arts use breathing to develop their ability to use their energy to throw their opponent several yards without any effort. However, the practical aspects of these subtle sciences are very accessible, and provide powerful tools for self-mastery.

For instance, when you are angry, you can calm yourself by simply slowing down the flow of the breath and making sure that you don't hold it at any time. Panic disorders are intimately linked with bad breathing habits. By taking control of your breath, you can often resolve this difficult and common anxiety reaction. Even insomnia can be resolved by a particular breathing exercise, the Sleep Exercise, given later in this chapter. All of this is possible because of the connection between the breath and the autonomic nervous system.

We generally ignore the breath except when we have a severe problem such as asthma or emphysema. As a consequence, we develop unconscious breathing habits which often create stress and reinforce the dragons in the mind. These habits can also prevent us from taking control of the mind and body no matter how many stretching and relaxation exercises we may do.

If we understand the basic and simple principles about how and why we breathe, we can take control of our inner resources. We can use our knowledge and skill to create a healthy body free of the problems of stress and develop the power of the mind. There are three key points about breathing:

1. *Efficiency:* The primary purpose of breathing is to provide oxygen to the bloodstream. The diaphragm is the breathing mechanism designed by nature to utilize the natural efficiency of our respiratory system. Proper *diaphragmatic breathing* will minimize pressure on the cardiovascular system and prevent essential hypertension.
2. *Neural Connections:* The direct relationship between breathing, the autonomic nervous system, and our emotions gives us a mechanism to control both stress in the body and emotional reactions in the mind. By taking control of the way we breathe, the physical motion of our lungs, we take control of the autonomic nervous system. This gives us the power to control the fight-or-flight and possum alarm reactions.
3. *Nose Breathing:* The nose serves as a switchboard for the entire nervous system. Breathing through the mouth alters neural patterning and can lead to greater physical weakness and even dangerous health conditions.

The Physical Process of Breathing

|||||||||| Obviously, we must breathe to stay alive. The primary function of the lungs is to enrich our blood with oxygen and remove the waste product of carbon dioxide from the blood. This entire process is called ventilation perfusion. When we breathe, we take air into the lungs. This consists, roughly, of 21 percent oxygen, 78 percent nitrogen, and 0.9 percent argon and other gases including carbon dioxide. As we bring air in, it is dispersed to the smallest functional part of the lung—a small air pocket, an alveolus, which is surrounded by microscopic blood vessels, as shown in Figure 6.1. The lung is literally shaped like a tree. The windpipe (trachea) is the main trunk which divides many times into smaller and smaller branches; the alveolus corresponds to a leaf. Just as a tree breathes from its leaves, so do we breathe at the alveoli. In the alveolus there is a constant exchange going on. When oxygen enters the alveolus, it diffuses into the bloodstream. At the same time, carbon dioxide diffuses from the blood back into the alveolus.

As the oxygen enters the bloodstream, it turns the blood a bright red color. This energized blood is pumped by the heart to every cell in the body. Body nutrients, which provide energy fuel to the body, need to burn oxygen. This burning produces carbon dioxide and water as waste products, which are elimi-

FIGURE 6.1
THE PHYSICAL PROCESS OF BREATHING

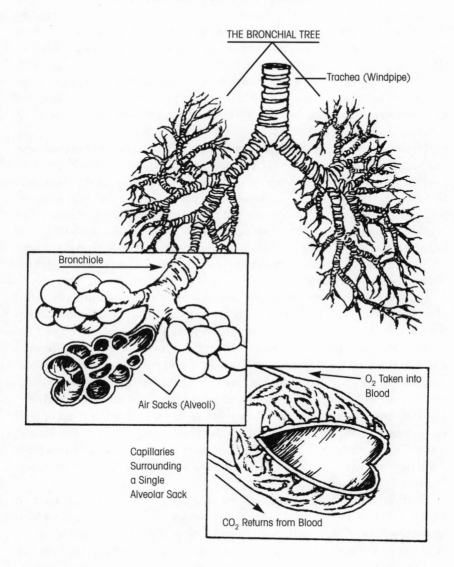

THE BRONCHIAL TREE

Trachea (Windpipe)

Bronchiole

Air Sacks (Alveoli)

Capillaries
Surrounding
a Single
Alveolar Sack

O_2 Taken into
Blood

CO_2 Returns from Blood

nated from the body through the lungs and kidneys, respectively. If a cell doesn't get oxygen, it dies. This is what happens when a stroke occurs. The brain cells are deprived of blood and oxygen, and they die. The consequence is loss of speech, paralysis, or death, depending on which brain cells are affected.

The upper part of the torso is designed to ensure that enough air gets into the lungs. Imagine the torso as a somewhat flattened cylinder divided into an upper chamber (the chest cavity) and a lower chamber (the abdominal cavity). The chest cavity is defined structurally by the rib cage, which provides rigidity. The widest part of the chest cylinder is the lower area where the ribs have their greatest length of curvature, and most of the space in this cylinder is filled by the lungs.

When the cylinder expands, it creates a suction which pulls air into the lungs and we inhale. We exhale when counterpressures (primarily from the elasticity of the lung, but also from the external, rigid structure of the chest cavity) force the entire structure back to its original position.

Respiration is so crucial that we have three different ways to bring air into our lungs. The first is very minor, and used only for emergency breathing. This happens when we lift our shoulder blades, create a vacuum, and pull air into the upper part of our lungs. This is the kind of breathing we do when someone sneaks up behind us and startles us. Try lifting your shoulders quickly. Notice how there is a small natural intake of breath. What if you had to walk around breathing like this all day? You would use more energy than what you get from your breathing. We use this mechanism only in emergencies, or when we want to completely fill our lungs with air.

The second breathing mechanism is thoracic breathing, commonly called chest breathing. We use the intercostal muscles (the specialized muscles which surround and are sandwiched between the ribs) to expand and contract the chest. When we inhale, the external intercostal muscles pivot the ribs upward and forward, increase the diameter of the chest, and pull air into the upper two-thirds of the lungs. The internal intercostals then perform the opposite function for the exhalation—pulling the ribs downward, reducing lung volume, and forcing air out of the lungs. Place your hands on your upper chest and fill your lungs with air. You will feel your upper chest expand. Now as you exhale, you will feel your upper chest contract. Notice that you can get a lot of air into the lungs this way, certainly much more than when you lift your shoulders to breathe.

The third mechanism we use for breathing is the diaphragm. As you see in Figure 6.2, the diaphragm is a large, dome-shaped sheet of muscle which forms the floor of the chest cavity, separating it from the abdominal cavity. When you inhale, the diaphragm contracts and flattens, pulling the chest cavity down and expanding the lungs. This creates a vacuum which pulls air into the lower two-thirds of the lungs. When the diaphragm flattens, it pushes against the abdominal organs, and they, in turn, push out against the abdominal wall. Instead of the upper chest going up and down as happens when you chest-breathe, the lower chest cavity expands slightly outward.

When you exhale, the diaphragm relaxes. When you sit or stand, the ab-

FIGURE 6.2

THE PROCESS OF DIAPHRAGMATIC BREATHING

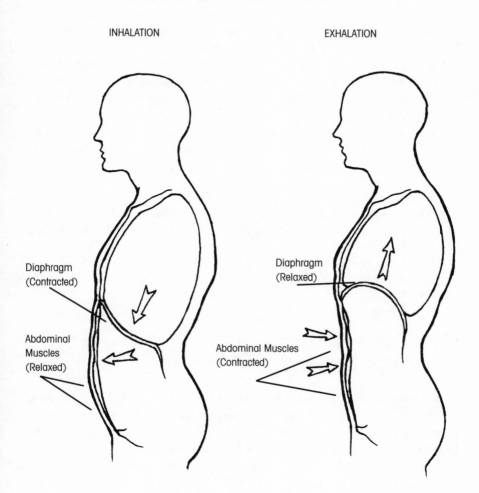

INHALATION   EXHALATION

Diaphragm
(Contracted)

Diaphragm
(Relaxed)

Abdominal
Muscles
(Relaxed)

Abdominal Muscles
(Contracted)

dominal muscles, acting as an "antagonist," contract slightly, and push the organs back and up. This forces the relaxed diaphragm into its original dome-shaped position and reduces chest cavity volume, pushing the air out. This action is a significant part of exhalation. When you lie down, gravity serves as the "antagonist" to the diaphragm, pulling the raised belly down and forcing the flexible abdominal organs up. This also pushes the diaphragm back into its dome-shaped original position, creating an exhalation.

Sit back, place your hands on your upper stomach, right below the chest, and breathe as if you are filling a small balloon in your stomach. When you inhale, your stomach will rise gently; when you exhale, your stomach will fall gently. Your upper chest shouldn't move at all. You might find this a bit difficult to do at first, particularly if you have a very strong habit of chest breathing. But after a few moments, you will notice that it seems to take less effort to breathe with the diaphragm than with the chest.

Diaphragmatic breathing gently massages the internal organs, pushing them back and forth. This contributes to proper blood perfusion in these organs and is one of the driving forces behind the normal digestive movement of the intestines. This massaging action doesn't happen during chest breathing.

But more important, diaphragmatic breathing plays a crucial role in creating inner balance. It makes three necessary contributions to healthy and relaxed functioning. These are:

- Increased efficiency of the cardiopulmonary system;
- Maintaining autonomic balance, creating a balanced relaxed state, and countering the fight-or-flight alarm reaction which occurs during chest breathing;
- Regulating the motion of the lungs, the actual flow of breath in and out of the body.

Cardiopulmonary Efficiency— Taking the Work Out of Breathing

|||||||||| Obviously, the heart and lungs are intimately connected to each other. Blood is pumped from the heart directly to the alveoli where fresh oxygen molecules are exchanged in the bloodstream for carbon dioxide molecules. The first of the freshly oxygenated blood goes directly to the heart itself, keeping that muscle supplied with lifesaving oxygen. Most heart attacks happen because clogged arteries prevent enough oxygen-rich blood from getting to the heart. When this happens, our heart-muscle cells die. We may have warning signs such as severe chest pain (angina pectoris), a signal that our heart is being starved of oxygen and that the cells are beginning to die. But many times we won't feel any symptoms. When enough cells die, it interferes with the electrical activity of the heart, which stops pumping. Then we have a heart attack.

How does diaphragmatic breathing relate to this? Doesn't chest breathing supply oxygen to the blood? Yes, it does, but not efficiently. Figure 6.3a shows the distribution of blood in the lungs. Because of gravity, most of the blood distribution for gas exchange takes place primarily in the lower half of the lungs. When we breathe with the chest, the expansion pulls air into the top

two-thirds of the lungs, as shown in Figure 6.3b. The gas exchange is inefficient, making the heart and lungs work harder to accomplish the proper
amount of oxygenation.

When we breathe with the diaphragm, it pulls air all the way down into the
blood-rich lower lobes, as illustrated in Figure 6.3c. This increases the efficiency of the gas exchange, requiring less effort. There is no difference between chest and diaphragmatic breathing in the amount of air entering the
body, or in the oxygen consumed by the body. But there is a vast difference in
how efficiently oxygen is taken up in the bloodstream. By breathing with the
diaphragm instead of the chest, we reduce the workload of our heart and lungs
by as much as 50 percent.

We can easily see the difference simply by counting the number of times we
breathe per minute. Chest breathers will average 16 to 20 breaths per minute.
It may go as low as 12 breaths per minute when sitting quietly, or be as high as
24 breaths per minute. On the other hand, diaphragmatic breathers average
only 6 to 10 breaths per minute. In one twenty-four-hour period, a chest
breather will take 22,000 to 25,000 breaths, while a person who breathes with
her diaphragm will take only 9,000 to 12,000. Chest breathing demands double the effort to accomplish the same task of ventilation perfusion.

When Normal Means Stressed

|||||||||| Let's take a quick test to determine your breathing habit. All you have to
do is count the number of times you breathe in one minute. An inhalation and
an exhalation together count as one breath. If you have a normal pattern, you
will breathe somewhere between 16 and 20 times a minute. If you are sitting
quietly, it may go as low as 12. You may also notice that your breathing slows
down slightly when you pay attention to it. Your actual moment-to-moment
breathing rate will probably be a little higher than your count in this test. It can
be as high as 24 times a minute and still be considered normal.

Chances are you breathe normally. So-called normal breathing is done with
the chest. However, the term "normal" does not mean "healthy." It is a statisti-
cal term meaning "most cases." And most people breathe with the chest. If you
are a "normal" breather, then it's absolutely certain that you suffer from
chronic stress!

We believe that chest breathing is natural for us when it's really a habit we
developed over the years. The best example of natural breathing is the breathing done by a healthy infant. If you observe the infant closely, you will see little
or no movement of the chest when he breathes—only the stomach goes up

FIGURE 6.3
DISTRIBUTION OF BLOOD IN THE LUNGS
CHEST VS. DIAPHRAGMATIC BREATHING

BLOOD DISTRIBUTION

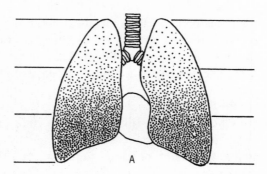

A

CHEST BREATHING   DIAPHRAGMATIC BREATHING

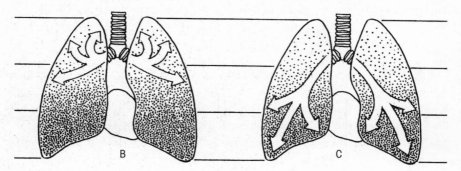

B   C

and down, indicating diaphragmatic breathing. Even under stress, a newborn infant still breathes with the diaphragm. It's only later that we develop the capacity to breathe with our chest.

As we grow, we develop unhealthy habits which interfere with our natural innate breathing patterns. Eventually the habit of chest breathing becomes so strong that we no longer use the diaphragm in our normal, day-to-day resting breathing pattern. In fact, in many people the diaphragm becomes "frozen," showing little to absolutely no movement at all. They hold it rigidly in place and breathe totally with the chest muscles.

There are any number of reasons why we develop poor breathing habits. Social and cultural conventions play a significant role. We are told that flat stomachs are attractive, and we learn to hold in the stomach. By tensing the abdominal muscles, the internal organs are prevented from moving out of the way in order for the diaphragm to flatten. This freezes the diaphragm, forcing us to rely on chest breathing. Any kind of tight clothing around the waist also hinders the natural expansion of the abdominal cavity and interferes with diaphragmatic breathing.

Men, particularly, often puff their chests out, in the classic macho pose. Watch what happens to a young man walking casually down the street when he suddenly meets a couple of young women. What does he do with his chest? The exaggerated expansion of his chest interferes with diaphragmatic breathing and forces reliance upon chest breathing. This lifting of the chest is actually part of military training. Military organizations want their soldiers to stay very alert, in a constant fight-or-flight reaction. They think that this makes better soldiers. It certainly makes for more tense soldiers. For normal day-to-day, moment-to-moment breathing, a "macho" chest is dysfunctional—it creates stress as well as extra pressure on the cardiovascular system.

Psychological trauma is the most important reason we become chest breathers. If you watch children when they are being scolded by their parents or other authority figures, you will see their stomach muscles tighten, forcing them into chest breathing. You will see how fear literally tightens the stomach muscles, preventing diaphragmatic movement. We all experience traumas as we grow up—and they have a powerful effect on our breathing patterns.

Our posture also affects the way we breathe. Most people do not sit properly, with their head, neck, and trunk straight. Instead, they slouch or slump, with the spine curved out and a slight bend in the abdominal cavity. This prevents the diaphragm from moving, forcing us to rely on chest breathing. In addition, poor posture doesn't allow the sympathetic and parasympathetic nerves to function properly, which affects the entire system.

As you can see, a number of powerful influences lead to chest breathing and the inefficient use of our lungs and heart. We learn to be "normal" breathers. On the other hand, natural diaphragmatic breathing reduces pressure on the heart and vascular system, and the entire system operates in a more balanced, relaxed way. When we feel the symptoms of heart disease such as angina, diaphragmatic breathing is the one immediate step we can take to ease the strain on the overworked heart. But why wait until you have heart trouble?

Relearning Diaphragmatic Breathing*

||||||||||| If you do no other exercise, be sure to practice this one. Everything else you do to develop self-mastery depends on your ability to breathe with the diaphragm. Fortunately, it takes very little effort to reestablish diaphragmatic breathing as your moment-to-moment breathing habit. To replace your old habit of chest breathing, you should lie down and practice diaphragmatic breathing at least twice a day for ten to fifteen minutes each time. Since you are already lying down twice a day, when you go to bed and when you wake up, this exercise is easy to practice. Gradually, the easy rhythmic motion of diaphragmatic breathing will replace the strained, unnatural chest breathing of your old habit. You can speed the process by being aware of your breathing pattern as much as possible during the day. The more aware of it you become, the more often you correct it, the faster you will replace your old habit of chest breathing with diaphragmatic breathing.

Even Diaphragmatic Breathing

||||||||||| While you are practicing diaphragmatic breathing, concentrate on making the breath very smooth and even. The inhalation and exhalation should be of the same length and have the same pressure. Do not exhale all the breath at the beginning of the exhalation. Concentrate on keeping the flow pressure even throughout the entire cycle. Eliminate all pauses, stops, and shakiness in the breath, including the pause between inhalation and exhalation. Imagine that the breath is like a large wheel moving through the body without any pauses or stops. It is often helpful to picture the breath flow as a completely smooth, even sine wave (see Figure 6.5).

Don't worry if it feels as if you aren't getting enough air and you feel that you have to take a deep breath after a few minutes of diaphragmatic breathing. This sometimes happens when you first change from chest breathing to diaphragmatic breathing. You are getting plenty of oxygen into your system, but your mind isn't comfortable with the change. Your mind is used to your old habit of

---

*The breathing exercises presented in this book can be safely and easily practiced on your own. However, since breathing is so intimately connected with neurological functioning, it is highly advisable that you do not engage in advanced or rigorous breathing practices except under the guidance of a competent teacher. *Do not practice breath retention under any circumstances unless you are being given expert instruction.*

To Practice: Lie in the Relaxation Posture and practice diaphragmatic breathing for a minimum of ten to fifteen minutes twice a day. (Again, the easiest time to practice is when you go to bed and when you first wake up in the morning. Doing it before you go to sleep will help you have a restful sleep.) In the Relaxation Posture, place your right hand on your stomach, your little finger over the navel, and the other fingers stretching up toward your chest. Place your left hand on the upper part of your chest, with the little finger between the two breasts. When the diaphragm contracts, it flattens out and pushes against the internal organs in the abdominal cavity. Instead of the chest going up and down, the stomach moves out and in as if there were a small balloon inside. Now breathe as if you are filling this small balloon in your stomach. Your stomach and right hand will rise with the inhalation and fall with the exhalation. This should be very gentle, no effort or work required. Don't try to completely fill or empty your lungs. Let your body decide how much air it needs. There should be no movement at all in the left hand. You should feel a slight motion in the lower portion of the chest cavity, but the upper portion should remain still.

Within a few moments you will become more rested and quiet. Do not try to force the breath. Allow the motion to be gentle and effortless. Notice how easy it is to breathe deeply and easily, without any effort. Practice being an observer, or witness, allowing the body to do the breathing for you. The evenness and balance of the breath will balance the nervous system.

To build a quicker and stronger diaphragmatic response, place an 8- to 10-pound pliable weight, such as wrist or ankle weights, a sandbag, or a sack of beans or rice, across the upper abdomen when you practice. This weight lifting strengthens the diaphragm, and establishes diaphragmatic breathing more quickly as your moment-to-moment breathing response.

chest breathing, and when you change your breathing pattern, it isn't sure you are breathing properly. Go ahead and take a deep breath. After a few weeks of practice, this feeling will disappear as your mind registers the beginning of a new habit.

Benefits: Practicing even diaphragmatic breathing leads to autonomic balance and a relaxed state. After some weeks, depending on your particular habits, you will begin to notice subtle and gradual changes in your daily breathing pattern. Its movement will be more relaxed and rhythmic.

When you change from the habit of chest breathing to diaphragmatic breathing, you will notice that you aren't so tired at the end of the day. By using the natural efficiency of your lungs, you reduce your body's workload, and use less energy. Moreover, when you feel under stress, you will be able to regulate your breathing. After a few moments of even, rhythmic diaphragmatic breathing, the feelings of pressure will disappear and you will feel balanced and calm. Diaphragmatic breathing will allow you to breathe more efficiently and to achieve balance in your autonomic nervous system.

Breath and Autonomic Balance

|||||||||| There is a very close connection between the way you breathe and your emotions. Whenever you become emotional, your breathing pattern becomes disturbed. When you are tense, frightened, angry, or intently focused, you often unconsciously hold your breath, or have pauses of different lengths between your breaths. Similarly, if you are depressed, your breathing will be very shallow with frequent sighs. Shallow, jerky breathing in itself disturbs the mind. And when the mind is disturbed, it affects the biochemistry of the body. If you want a calm, steady mind, your breath must be calm and steady, without any noise, jerkiness, shallowness, or prolonged pauses.

The key to this relationship between mind and breath is the autonomic nervous system and its control center in the brain, the limbic center. The way we breathe directly influences two key neural systems. The first, the tenth cranial nerve, called the vagus nerve, separates into two paths and passes through the left and right chest cavity. The vagus nerves account for nearly 80 percent of the parasympathetic system. The way that we breathe creates a certain pressure on the left and right vagus nerves, causing them to either increase or decrease their activity. The second key neural system, the Herring-Breuer reflex, consists of nerve receptors scattered throughout the lungs. These receptors send signals directly back to the limbic system in the brain indicating the exact motion of the lungs.

When we breathe with the chest, we send a signal to both the limbic system and the autonomic system that says, "Get ready! There is danger. Take protective action!" *Chest breathing is our body's emergency breathing system.* Chest breathing activates the fight-or-flight alarm reaction. It doesn't matter whether or not there is actually any danger, once we use the chest mechanism the body responds as if we really are in danger. When we are in danger, we need to be fully alert and aroused. When this happens, it's appropriate to use the full capacity of our lungs, bringing into action all the mechanisms at our disposal. However, when we are skilled in self-mastery, we take command of these resources and respond with self-preservation, instead of reacting out of a habit of fear.

Rarely do we face life-threatening emergencies, and we seldom need to put ourselves on emergency status. If you chest-breathe while reading this book, you may think you are calm and relaxed, but your breathing is sending an alarm message to the brain and into the autonomic system. The message may be very subtle, but it is still an alarm, and it is constant. Like water dripping on a rock, any one drop is insignificant, but over time, it has an enormous effect. Any one "emergency" breath is insignificant in its impact, but over a period of time it wears and tears at the system. Your "normal" habit of chest breathing maintains a chronic stress in both the body and the mind, and you can never completely relax. The longer you continue to utilize your emergency capacity without any need for it, the more ingrained becomes your imbalance.

On the other hand, the motion created by diaphragmatic breathing sends a message that says, "Everything is calm . . . stay relaxed . . . all is well . . . you are in control." Smooth, even diaphragmatic breathing is the key to regulating the autonomic nervous system, and taking control of inner resources.

Figure 6.4 illustrates the relationship between breath and the autonomic nervous system. Inhalation directly but subtly reflects and stimulates sympathetic discharge, while exhalation directly but subtly reflects and stimulates parasympathetic discharge. What is fascinating about this relationship is that we already know it. We simply never paid attention. Earlier we saw that if we pay attention to the pulse, we find that it increases slightly as we inhale, and slows slightly as we exhale. Medical scientists, laboring under the illusion that we could not control the autonomic nervous system, attributed this phenomenon to mechanical pressure, ignoring the role of the vagus nerves and the Herring-Breuer reflex.

Even the language we use indicates that we unconsciously understand this relationship between breathing and the autonomic nervous system. We have all heard someone say, "Let's take a breather." Why use that term? Why not "Let's take a liver," or even "Let's take a bladder." At least we could justify the latter expression. Even more dramatic is what happens when we experience a

FIGURE 6.4

BREATH AND THE AUTONOMIC NERVOUS SYSTEM

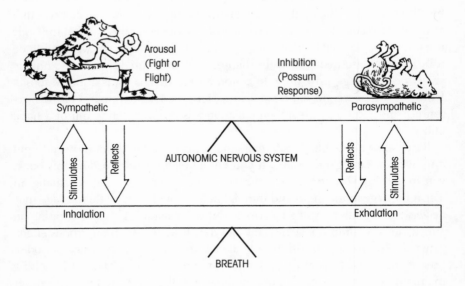

sharp invasive attack to the body. Let's say that you were right in the middle of an exhalation and, at that moment, you received a sharp slap on the face. Internally, this slap results in an immediate and strong sympathetic discharge, an instant arousal reaction as your body prepares to defend itself. But what happens to your breathing? Your exhalation stops as you quickly gasp (quick inhalation) for breath. We've all heard of a "gasp of pain," reflecting the relationship of inhalation to sympathetic discharge.

We find different expressions when we speak of periods of relief or strong parasympathetic states such as depression. Have you ever heard anyone use the expression "a gasp of depression" or "a gasp of relief"? Instead, we hear about "sighs of relief" or "sighs of depression," reflecting the strong relationship of our exhalation to parasympathetic dominance.

Any emotional state, such as anxiety or anger, also disrupts our breathing patterns. When we are angry, we inhale and hold the breath, and the moment we do, we become a little more angry. When we are depressed, we sigh, and then there is a long pause before we breathe in, and we become a little more depressed. Whenever we pause or hold the breath, it intensifies the emotional state. Because of the direct relationship between inhalation and sympathetic activity, and exhalation and parasympathetic activity, uneven, arrhythmic breathing leads to uneven stimulation of sympathetic and parasympathetic discharge—in other words, autonomic imbalance, or stress.

Yoga science sees the breath as the flywheel mechanism in the autonomic system. If a flywheel becomes unbalanced, it unbalances the entire system. So it is with breathing and the autonomic system. The evidence for this relationship between the autonomic system and the breath is extensive. An increasing number of scientific studies show that changes in respiratory patterns accompany changes in a wide variety of emotional states and mental and physical activities. Breathing techniques are used to solve a variety of problems, ranging from stress and anxiety management to postsurgical care and treatment of stuttering.

The best evidence, however, is your own experience. The next time you feel pressure, or you are beginning to get tense, sit back and take two minutes to practice diaphragmatic breathing. Focus on your breath becoming very even and steady. Watch what happens to the pressure you feel. The situation will not have changed—deadlines are still there, people are still making demands, problems still need your attention—but the pressure you felt will have dissipated. Whenever you feel stressed or under pressure, you can use your breath to restore your inner balance. The more you do this, the more skilled you become, and the greater benefit you gain.

When you understand this relationship between breathing and the autonomic nervous system, you can use it skillfully to relax or create more energy. One of the easiest ways to stay relaxed is 2:1 Breathing, in which you exhale twice as long as you inhale. The extended exhalation provides a greater stimulus to parasympathetic discharge, leading to a deep and balanced relaxation. This is the reason for the common practice of focusing on exhalation as a technique for inducing relaxation. But this should be done skillfully, and you should not exceed your personal limits. You should always be comfortable when doing breathing exercises.

Benefits: The exhalation stimulates the parasympathetic system twice as long as the inhalation stimulates the sympathetic system. This rhythm greatly reduces tension and creates a deeper state of rest for your heart and vascular system. Once you become skilled with 2:1 Breathing, you can use it anytime during the day or night. Several of my clients who are joggers use the 2:1 pattern while they jog, coordinating their stride with their breathing. This allows them to go farther with less effort, and provides a more stable and complete conditioning for the heart.

Do not reverse the rhythm, however, and inhale twice as long as you exhale. This reversed pattern can make you tense and nervous. Also do not practice 2:1 Breathing if you suffer from chronic depression. In chronic depression, the

> ||||||||| 2:1 BREATHING: A RESTFUL PATTERN |||||||||
>
> During your practice of diaphragmatic breathing, when your breathing is balanced and even, and has become very smooth with no jerkiness, stops, or pauses, gently slow the rate of exhalation until you are breathing out about twice as long as you are inhaling. (It might be necessary to shorten the length of inhalation very slightly.) You are simply changing the rhythm of the breath, not trying to fill the lungs completely or empty them completely. The purpose is to alter the motion of the lungs in a very systematic way. You may count to six on the exhalation and three on the inhalation, or eight on the exhalation and four on the inhalation—*or whatever is most comfortable for you*. Then, after you have established this gentle rhythm, stop the mental counting and focus on the smoothness and evenness of the breath flow. Eliminate all jerks and pauses. Maintain 2:1 diaphragmatic breathing for as long as you wish. Pay attention to what happens to your heartbeat and any other changes in your body.

parasympathetic system is already too dominant, and you don't want to emphasize its dominance with long exhalations. For depression and low energy states, the Alternate-Nostril Breathing Exercise given below is much more appropriate.

The Importance of Motion

||||||||||| As you might gather from the above discussion of 2:1 Breathing, it is important to control the motion of the lungs skillfully. While the intercostal muscles can control the movement of the chest cavity, they cannot adequately control the smoothness and evenness of the breath itself. Only the diaphragm is large enough to really control breathing motion and depth.

The flow of the breath (the smoothness and evenness of lung motion) can be measured on an instrument called the Cottle rhinomanometer. As you breathe into the nosepiece of the instrument, it records a wave motion on a strip chart. The exhalation is measured above the baseline, the inhalation below it. Each of us has a unique pattern of breathing, just as we each have unique fingerprints. The ideal breathing motion looks like a perfect sine wave—an even, smooth wave that indicates an even, uninterrupted flow of breath (Figure 6.5).

Researchers find very few people who can even begin to approach this type of breath-flow pattern without proper training. Most people have patterns which differ dramatically from this ideal.

Chronic emotional states also seem to have characteristic wave patterns. For instance, a person who is constantly angry often has a distinctive type of mid-cycle pause just after the inhalation and before the exhalation (Figure 6.6).

The effects of irregular breath-flow patterns are very subtle and often go unnoticed. However, if you pay close attention to your own breath and the thoughts, feelings, and sensations that go along with it, you will begin to notice these patterns. If you observe carefully, you will see that when your breath is uneven and unstable it is impossible to concentrate. Take a few moments to observe your breathing patterns closely. Do you breathe with your chest muscles? Are there any pauses or stops in your breath? Is your breath uneven? Do you sigh a lot? Do you hold your breath and not breathe for periods of time? Through simple observation you will quickly determine the kinds of breathing habits you have.

As an experiment, simply concentrate on diaphragmatic breathing, making the inhalation and exhalation as smooth and even as possible. Picture in your mind your breath flowing exactly like the ideal wave form shown in Figure 6.5—no bumps, no pauses, no shakiness. Do this for five minutes, paying close attention to the flow of breath in and out of the nostrils. Then see how you feel both physically and mentally.

Also experiment during the day. The next time you face a situation in which you are becoming angry or upset, concentrate a few moments on your breathing. Breathe with the diaphragm, keeping your breath very even and steady. Then observe what happens to your feelings. You will notice that your ability to remain calm in the face of adversity is vastly improved. And the one who remains calm is able to think and act more creatively in any situation. Similarly, when you are feeling depressed or sad, observe how shallow your breathing has become. Then concentrate on diaphragmatic breathing and observe what happens to your mood.

Alternate-Nostril Breathing: An Exercise for Control

||||||||| One of the most important breathing exercises you can do is Alternate-Nostril Breathing. It increases the capacity of the lungs as well as your control

FIGURE 6.5

IDEAL BREATHING PATTERN

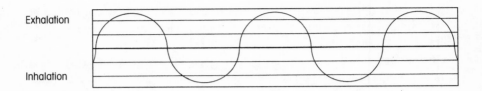

Exhalation

Inhalation

FIGURE 6.6

BREATHING PATTERN ASSOCIATED

WITH CHRONIC ANGER

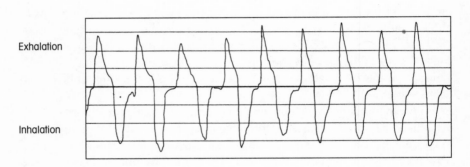

Exhalation

Inhalation

over the breathing process and the autonomic system. It is also very useful in developing your power of concentration. It should be practiced three times daily, and it only takes a few minutes to do. There are several ways to do this exercise. The following is the most simple.

You should begin the exercise with whichever nostril is active, or most open. The entire exercise consists simply of exhaling and inhaling through the active nostril and then through the passive nostril and repeating this procedure two more times. There are only six complete breaths in the exercise, three on each side. Notice that you begin the exercise with an exhalation, not an inhalation.

Begin with a count that is comfortable and concentrate on making the breath smooth and even at this length. It is the smoothness of the flow which is important here, not how long you can make your breath. Maintain the same count until you can breathe comfortably and effortlessly without any bumps, jerks, or pauses. Make sure the flow of air is evenly distributed throughout the entire cycle. When you are very sure of your control, increase the length of the breath (for example, go from a count of six to a count of eight). The length of your breath will gradually increase as your control increases.

After completing the exercise, resume your normal breathing. Focus as much attention as possible on the flow of the breath during the exercise. As you develop your ability to concentrate, gradually learn to direct the flow of breath by using only your mind and not your fingers. This enhances the power of your concentration.

Benefits: With this exercise, you learn to control the motion of the lungs,

---

|||||||| ALTERNATE-NOSTRIL BREATHING ||||||||

Close your eyes and sit comfortably, with your head, neck, and trunk in alignment (the back should be straight but allow for the natural S curve of the spine). Rest the index and middle fingers of the right hand on the space between the two eyebrows. Determine which nostril is active. (The active nostril is the one in which the air is flowing freely. The passive nostril is the nostril in which there is some natural blockage due to the natural cyclic swelling of the mucosa.)

1. If the right nostril is active, press your ring finger against the left nostril, closing it, and gently exhale through the right nostril, counting to six (or about six seconds) mentally as you exhale. Then inhale immediately through the same nostril for a count of six.

2. Now press the thumb gently against the right nostril, closing it off, and at the same time release the pressure on the left nostril. Exhale for a count of six, and then inhale for a count of six through the left nostril.

3. Now press the ring finger gently against the left nostril, closing off the flow, and at the same time release the pressure from the thumb on the right nostril. Exhale for a count of six, and inhale for a count of six through the right nostril.

4. Close the right nostril and open the left. Exhale and inhale for a count of six in the left nostril.

5. Close the left nostril and open the right. Exhale and inhale to counts of six in the right nostril.

6. Close the right nostril and open the left. Exhale and inhale for counts of six through the left nostril. You have just done three rounds. This completes the exercise.

and gradually take control over the autonomic nervous system. It strengthens the autonomic nervous system and leads to increased lung capacity. This allows you to maintain balance, develop control over your emotional reactions, and enhance your power of concentration. Alternate-Nostril Breathing also corrects unhealthy breathing patterns and is a subtle but helpful exercise for resolving depression. The benefits of doing this exercise are usually not dramatic, but over a period of time, it calms the mind and stabilizes the emotions. The tantric Masters become so skilled using this exercise that they gain complete conscious control over the autonomic nervous system.

The Pause That Kills

‖‖‖‖‖‖‖‖ It's not only our emotional states that are affected by irregular breathing. Preliminary research indicates that the wave patterns can reflect severe pathological states. For example, research by the late Dr. Maurice Cottle, an ear, nose, and throat specialist who practiced in Chicago, shows a distinctive wave pattern associated with heart attacks. This pattern, too, is characterized by a mid-cycle rest, or pause, but in a way different from that associated with chronic anger.

As you can see in the simulated pattern in Figure 6.7, the mid-cycle rest is a constant pause in the breathing pattern after the exhalation and before the inhalation. This is a form of apnea, and may reflect a very dangerous condition. The longer the pause, the greater the danger. When this pause occurs during sleep, it is called sleep apnea, and is characterized by loud, open-mouthed snoring with periodic silences between the snores. Sleep apnea is considered a central nervous system disease, and is a major reason why people suffer heart attacks at night.

FIGURE 6.7

CHARACTERISTIC APNEA BREATHING PATTERN

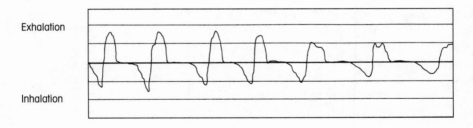

Exhalation

Inhalation

It's the focus of much joking, but if you have heart disease, snoring is no longer very humorous. There are two kinds of snoring. If you snore with your mouth closed, the sound is created by the vibration of the uvula and is harmless. If, on the other hand, your mouth is open, the snoring sound is created by the collapsing of the larynx—by a total relaxation of the muscles, which temporarily closes the air passageway. The breath flow is blocked, and breathing may pause for relatively long periods of time. The snoring sound is made when enough pressure is created to force air through the collapsed larynx.

Dr. Alan Hymes, a thoracic surgeon who researched sleep apnea and its relationship to heart attacks and mouth breathing, points out that when we stop breathing we create oxygen imbalances in the blood gases. This creates a strain on the heart. While a variety of treatment modalities have been tried, particularly drugs, there has been little success in treating this potentially life-threatening condition. Dr. Hymes reports, however, that simply closing the mouth of the person who is snoring (thus forcing nasal breathing) corrects the sleep apnea — the snoring stops, the breath becomes even and steady, and chest breathing appears to change into diaphragmatic breathing. The patient's respiratory efficiency is increased, and the strain is off the heart. The stimulation of the nerve endings in the nasal mucosa appears to restore respiratory balance and lead to diaphragmatic breathing.

Preliminary studies by Dr. Hymes have shown that over 75 percent of those who have heart attacks breathe through the mouth instead of through the nose. What is more, nearly all of those who habitually breathe through the mouth also snore; and of those who snore, 84 percent showed patterns of sleep and waking apnea lasting for periods of six to thirty seconds or longer. *On the other hand, the patients who breathe through the nose exhibit little or no apnea.*

Dr. Hymes suggests that it may be possible to minimize or even eliminate the apnea by retraining ourselves to breathe diaphragmatically and through the nose. This not only relieves a very serious breathing problem, it also ensures restful sleep. We revitalize the body, relieve stress, and create balance in the most natural way there is. By practicing the proper breathing exercises, we can bring about deep, restful sleep without sleeping pills.

Breathing and the Heart

‖‖‖‖‖‖‖‖ Several years ago I had a meeting with a lieutenant general (three stars) to talk about a stress-management program for his staff. The appointment was actually engineered by the general's sister, who was concerned about his health. A hard-driving individual, the general was taking medication for high blood pressure. Typical of any busy executive, the general started the interview by saying how overscheduled he was, and that he could spare only thirty minutes. In the process of the interview, the general mentioned his high blood pressure and asked if I thought stress had anything to do with it. We discussed this for a few moments, and then I pointed out that he was breathing with his chest, which could affect his blood pressure. I could see that the general wasn't exactly convinced. Like most people, he simply accepted the fact that he had the problem. He was fairly sure that, other than taking medication, there was little he, or anyone else, could do. Fortunately, I had a blood pressure monitor with me, and I asked if we could try a little experiment. Out of politeness, he agreed. We took his blood pressure. It was 147/95. I then had him lie on the carpet in the Relaxation Posture, and instructed him in Even Diaphragmatic Breathing and 2:1 Breathing. After four minutes of focused, diaphragmatic breathing, I had him sit up and we measured his blood pressure again. To the general's great surprise, his blood pressure had dropped 27 points systolic and 12 points diastolic. Our interview went on to last for over an hour and a half. Since then, I have been a trainer for several agencies within the Defense Department.

It's not coincidence that we call chest breathing "normal" and we suffer a high rate of cardiovascular disease. According to University of Chicago cardiologist Dr. D. S. Gupta, when we breathe with our chest, we can create problems for our heart in at least four ways:

- *Heart Rhythm:* The heart creates its own electrical impulses through a sodium chloride/potassium chloride ion exchange in the pacemaker cells of the heart. This ion exchange is regulated by the autonomic nervous system. If autonomic balance is disturbed by sleep apnea, it can lead to severe rhythmic dysfunctions in the heartbeat, such as atrial fibrillation, and then ventricular fibrillation. Once ventricular fibrillation begins, survival becomes problematic. For those already suffering heart damage, sleep apnea is a grave danger.
- *Chronic Arousal:* Chest breathing, our emergency breathing pattern, stimulates sympathetic arousal. As part of the arousal response, the peripheral blood vessels constrict, sending more blood to the center of the body. This constriction can contribute to higher blood pressure levels.
- *Coronary Effort:* Chest breathing exerts pressure on the heart cavity, which increases the amount of blood that enters the heart; this is called *preload.* The more blood that enters the heart, the harder the heart muscle must work to pump the blood out; this effort is called *afterload.* Higher levels of preload and afterload lead to higher levels of blood pressure.

- *Carbon Dioxide Cleansing:* Carbon dioxide is a waste product eliminated through exhalation. During chest breathing, the lower lobes of the lungs are not properly cleansed, resulting in a buildup of carbon dioxide. This carbon dioxide reenters the bloodstream and elevates the level of carbonic acid in the blood. This can change the acid/base balance of the body and may eventually disturb the inner linings of the blood vessels, which can lead to hardening of the arteries. It may also influence the reactivity of the blood vessels, which in turn can affect blood pressure.

Both Dr. Hymes and Dr. Gupta point out that only chest breathers develop essential hypertension. It's clear that chest breathing increases your risk of high blood pressure in several important ways. On the other hand, if you breathe with your diaphragm, your chances of getting essential hypertension are very, very small. By breathing with the diaphragm, you maintain internal balance and reduce pressure on the vascular system, which helps prevent high blood pressure. The lesson here is very clear and simple: *If you don't want to suffer from essential hypertension, then don't become a chest breather.* I offer the six-point list Behavioral Training for Essential Hypertension as a self-training program to help resolve and prevent this disease.

There is a great deal that we can do to help ourselves. Our breathing is a tool that we always have with us. If you become skilled in its use, you become skilled at living without stress. It only requires that you practice. Diaphragmatic breathing is just the beginning. At the end of this chapter are several more simple exercises. One you will use to energize yourself, another will take you to the second level of relaxation, and the third you can use to eliminate insomnia and train yourself to have a very restful sleep. But first, there is one more facet of our breathing that we must understand.

The Nose—A Sophisticated Neurological Organ

llllllllll The nose, surprisingly enough, is an extremely important organ. It is not simply twin exhaust pipes for the lungs. While we may worry about its size and how it looks, we seldom think about what happens inside the nose until we get congested or have a sinus headache. In fact, many of us breathe through the mouth and don't properly use the nostrils at all. This is a serious mistake. The nose is a switchboard for the entire nervous system. When we don't breathe through the nose properly, it can affect every system in the body, as well as the mind.

||||||| BEHAVIORAL TRAINING FOR ESSENTIAL HYPERTENSION |||||||

1. 10–15 minutes of Diaphragmatic Breathing on the bed or floor before going to sleep and before getting up in the morning (Chapter 6, pages 147).

    A. Place an 8- to 10-pound pliable weight (such as a sandbag, a bag of rice or beans, or wrist or ankle weights) on the upper part of the abdominal cavity right below the rib cage. This added weight will strengthen the diaphragm.

    B. Begin with Even Breathing (page 146), then after breath is even and steady, shift to 2:1 Breathing (page 152), exhaling twice as long as you inhale.

2. "61 Points" Exercise once daily (Chapter 8, page 200).

    A. Lie on a firm surface (not a bed) in the Relaxation Posture (Chapter 5, page 106).

    B. Begin by concentrating on Even or 2:1 Breathing for 5 minutes.

    C. Do "61 Points" using a blue star or a blue flame at each of the 61 points.

3. Emotional control: Anger, worry, and other emotions can underlie and aggravate essential hypertension. The following techniques help regulate emotional energy.

    A. A 2-minute period of Breath Awareness (Chapter 7, pages 172–74) every hour will help clear the mind and calm the body.

    B. Use a 10-minute relaxation break in the morning and in the afternoon.

    C. Try not to identify with any of the problems you must solve on a day-to-day basis. Use Breath Awareness and focus on the problem at hand, not one that might happen in the future.

4. Diet: Adapt a prudent approach to diet; don't overeat, and reduce the amount of red meat, caffeine, and sugar in your daily diet. Follow a sensible low-cholesterol, low-fat, and low-salt diet.

5. Aerobic exercise: A minimum of 20 minutes three times weekly with an appropriate level of aerobic exercise such as jogging, walking, bicycling, swimming, active sports.

6. Stretching Exercises (Chapter 5, page127): 5 minutes of stretching in the morning, 5–15 minutes of stretching in the evening. Morning stretches free energy, stimulate vital neural and glandular functioning, and make you feel alert and alive. Evening stretches will increase flexibility, remove structural tension, and allow for a more peaceful sleep.

FIGURE 6.8

DIAGRAM OF THE NOSE

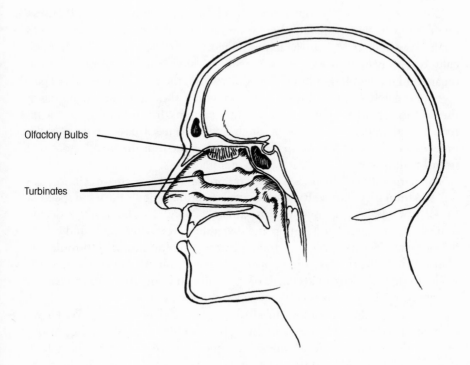

Olfactory Bulbs

Turbinates

As you can see in Figure 6.8, the nasal passages occupy a unique position. The roof of the mouth forms the floor of the nasal cavity, and the roof of the nasal cavity forms part of the floor of the brain. Thus the nose is in a strategic position, for it is very near the nervous system and the pituitary gland. The mucosa (the inside lining of the nose) is saturated with nerve endings that connect with all major neural systems. The most important are the olfactory bulbs, which are part of the limbic system, the brain's emotional center. The olfactory bulbs, which provide our sense of smell, are the only part of the limbic system that has direct contact with the outside world. All other input to the limbic center is mediated through other parts of the brain. There are also nerve endings from both the sensorimotor and the autonomic nervous systems.

The passageways in the nose are not straight channels where air flows directly into the lungs. A series of structures within the nasal cavity guide and direct the air as it flows in and out of the nostrils. The most important are three seashell-like bulges called turbinates. They serve to baffle the air, to stir it up. They force the air moving through the nostrils to go through a series of winding, bending, looping, convoluting passageways. This creates a great deal of turbulence.

Check the air flow of your nostrils by closing off one nostril and then the other. You will very likely find that the air flow is not even. The nasal passages are lined with erectile tissue which can engorge with blood and swell dramatically. The only other place you find erectile tissue in the body is in the sexual organs and the nipples. As blood flow shifts within the nose, different nasal passages alternately swell or shrink. This continuous shrinking and engorging of the nostrils creates an infinite variety of flow patterns. It constantly alters the direction and reshapes the flow of air through the nasal passages in a cyclic process. In a healthy person this change of air flow shifts the breath from one nostril to the other over regular periods of time.

The narrowness of the passageways compresses the air, increasing its force as it passes through the nose. Even when you are sitting quietly, the wind speed in the narrow nasal passageways is approximately 20 miles an hour. If you decide to really exert yourself and run up and down steps, you will create wind velocities of up to 200 miles an hour inside the nose. And this flow is all turbulence. Can you imagine what would happen to the community you live in if it was subjected to turbulent wind speeds of 200 miles an hour? And yet, you can do this easily inside your nose with some good aerobic exercise.

There is a definite purpose to all this speed and turbulence. When we breathe, the turbulent air flowing through the nostrils stimulates the various nerve endings. This creates a switchboard effect for the entire nervous system. If you alter this neural stimulation, you create changes elsewhere in the body. You can verify this for yourself. The next time you have indigestion, check which nostril is open and is allowing the air to move freely. Almost every time, you will find that the left nostril will be the dominant, or open, nostril, and the right will be mostly closed. Instead of taking an Alka-Seltzer, lie down on your left side. Gravity will force the flow of blood from the swollen right nostril over to the left. In a matter of a few minutes, the mucosa in your left nostril will begin to swell. The mucosa in the right nostril will shrink, and air will begin to flow freely through the right nostril. When you can breathe freely through the right nostril, you will find that your indigestion has disappeared. By changing the flow of air through the nose, you change the neural patterns in the body and consequently change the digestive process. Why spend money on an antacid which only relieves the symptom when you can alter the underlying condition yourself for free?

This isn't the only effect of nose breathing you can notice. You will also find that when you breathe through your mouth, you tend to lose approximately 10 to 15 percent of your physical strength. If your muscles can be so weakened, what about the more sensitive systems of your body, such as your immune system and your endocrine system? Only mouth breathers develop sleep apnea. Those who breathe through the nose, even when they have heart disease, seldom, if ever, develop sleep apnea.

Even Sigmund Freud found a connection between what happens in the nose and certain systems in the body. He and Wilhelm Fliess, an ear, nose, and throat specialist, found that menstrual cramps were often related to an inflammation and discoloration of specific areas in the lining of the nose. When these were anesthetized, the menstrual pains disappeared until the effects of the anesthetic wore off. They then decided to do a surgical removal of this part of the nose. This radical move led to so many problems that they quickly stopped doing it. There are instances where cosmetic nasal surgery becomes so involved that it impinges on the neural centers in the nose. This can lead to personality changes that are totally unpredictable, and not always beneficial.

Breathing through the nose is a critical process, yet Western science still does not recognize the neurological role of nose breathing. In fact, almost all respiratory research is done on mouth breathing. There is very little attention being paid to the nose and its role.

According to yoga science the physiological effects associated with the air flow through the two nostrils are quite different. Interestingly enough, when research was conducted on discharge from the two nostrils, it was found that the electrical potential of the discharge was different for each nostril. While this puzzled the researchers, who clearly did not understand its implications, it confirms the experience of yoga science. Modern research is also finding that emotional states appear to be related to an overdominance of either right or left nostril activity. For example, preliminary research indicates that some forms of depression are related to overactivity in the left nostril, while excessive air flow in the right nostril has been found to be associated with hyperactivity. This doesn't necessarily mean that a constantly overactive left nostril causes depression, or that an overactive right nostril leads to hyperactivity. What it does show is the connection between the way we breathe, certain neural conditions, and physical and emotional states.

Yoga science states that when you are doing active work, the right nostril should be open and dominant. When you are quiet and reserved, the left nostril should be dominant. Consciously working with your breath in this way gradually allows you to establish control over your breathing with your mind. The goal is to be able to establish *sushumna*, the ability to willfully direct both nostrils to be open equally at the same time. According to yoga science, this creates a calm mind, and balance in the autonomic nervous system and between the two hemispheres of the brain. The purpose of *sushumna* is to allow the mind to be deeply concentrated without effort. To practice meditation, you must apply it in order to reach the deepest states of meditation. One of the most important techniques for developing this control is the Alternate-Nostril Breathing Exercise given on page 155 of this chapter.

The Nasal Wash

|||||||||| For healthy nasal passages, a daily nasal wash with saline solution is extremely helpful. The most difficult part of this technique is our attitude. Whenever I present the nasal wash in a seminar, many of the participants roll their eyes. You can tell by the look on their faces that they think that washing out the inside of the nose is disgusting. What is disgusting is that we walk around with

|||||||||| **THE NASAL WASH** ||||||||||

As a part of your morning wash, fill a regular kitchen glass (8 ounces) with lukewarm tap water. Add approximately one-eighth teaspoon of either kosher salt or sea salt. (Commercial salt has chemicals added to it that create a slight burning sensation in the nose.) The water should be about as salty as tears. The salt acts as a drawing agent, helping to cleanse the nose. You will be able to tell if the solution is too salty—it will sting slightly. If it isn't salty enough, it may create an unpleasant pressure inside the nose. Bring the glass up to the nostrils, slightly tilting the head back. Relax your throat, mouth, and jaw, and pour just enough to fill the nasal passage. As you tilt the glass, inhale just enough to help pull water into your nasal passages. Then drop your head, exhale with a gentle force through both nostrils, and let the water drain back out. A little water may trickle down into your throat as you first begin, causing you to cough or slightly choke. Don't worry, you will quickly learn how to close off your throat.

After a little practice you will be able to tilt your head back and to one side. Then bring the water in through the upper nostril and let it drain out the lower. This cleans and rejuvenates the mucus membrane lining the inside of the nostrils. After a little more practice, you will be able to take the water through both nostrils, down into the throat, and out the mouth. This cleans the entire passageway.

all that excess mucus inside the nose and sinus cavities. We carry it around like a national treasure.

This simple, easy wash is one of the most beneficial techniques we can do, particularly if we have sinus problems, such as allergies or sinus headaches. A daily nasal wash keeps the lining of the nose healthy and free from excess mucus. It helps drain the sinuses, reduce allergies, and prevent colds. You can pay $45 to have the same procedure, called a nasal irrigation, done at a doctor's office or follow the simple procedure outlined above for less than the cost of an eighth of a teaspoon of sea salt.

One of the most consistent messages I hear from past participants in my seminars is how helpful the nasal wash has been for them. Sometimes the relief is immediate, and for others it happens over a period of time. But everyone who really uses the wash reports some benefit from doing it.

Benefits: This nasal wash cleans and rejuvenates the mucus membrane, alleviating congestion and helping to prevent infections in the sinus area. It helps eliminate the problem and pain of sinus headaches, reduce the symptoms of allergies, and prevent colds and other minor infections of the mucus membrane. This can also be a very important exercise in helping to eliminate open-mouth snoring. Open-mouth breathing often occurs because a slight sinus infection partially blocks nostril passages. Doing the nasal wash before going to sleep helps clear the nasal passages, allowing you to breathe more easily through the nose.

Taking Control:
Using Breath as the Key to Health and Freedom

|||||||||| Our breathing is a very powerful tool for controlling stress. The basic exercises are not at all difficult, and they take very little time. All that you need is a little consistent practice. The easiest way to eliminate an unhealthy breathing (or any) habit to replace it with a healthy one. We can use the breath to create and maintain balance, to minimize the pressure on the heart and vascular system, and to stay relaxed throughout the day. We can also become skilled at deeper states of relaxation, control our energy, and learn how to sleep peacefully.

You can use the same breathing technique that I have found useful. It's called the Complete Breath, and utilizes all three breathing mechanisms—collar bones, ribs, and diaphragm—to completely fill the lungs with air. Read through the exercise before trying it.

||||||||| THE COMPLETE BREATH |||||||||

In this exercise all three mechanisms for breathing—diaphragm, chest, and collarbones—are brought into use. When you first practice this exercise, place your right hand on your upper stomach area and your left hand on your upper chest. When you breathe with the diaphragm, the right hand will rise on the inhalation and fall on the exhalation. The left hand will rise when you inhale with the chest mechanism. Once you are sure of the proper movement of the diaphragm, chest, and clavicles, you can do the breathing without using your hands.

Inhale first, using the diaphragm and expanding the belly; then continue the inhalation by expanding the chest; then let the inhalation continue to the very top of the lungs, at which point a slight upward movement of the clavicles may be experienced. The exhalation is done in reverse motion, letting the clavicles drop slightly, then letting the chest wall collapse slightly, then letting the belly collapse as the diaphragm moves upward, pushing the air out of the lungs. The breath should be slow and smooth, without any pauses or jerks.

The Complete Breath is a very useful technique to use when you are sitting at your desk and feel a lot of tension in your shoulders. A few minutes of practice will be very helpful in reducing not only muscle tension but also mental fatigue. The Complete Breath is an energizer and can be used any time you feel mentally dull, or need to be more alert. For instance, when you have been driving for some time and are beginning to feel a little tired, you can energize yourself by taking six or seven complete breaths.

Deep-State Breath Relaxation: The Second Level of Relaxation

||||||||| We achieve the second level of relaxation, autonomic relaxation, by using the breath to shift the balance in the autonomic nervous system. By systematically changing the motion and rhythm of the breath, we increase parasympathetic activity and create a deeper state of rest in the body. Autonomic relaxation provides a different kind of experience than muscle relax-

||||||||||| **SWEEPING BREATH EXERCISE** |||||||||||

Begin by lying in the Relaxation Posture. Breathe with the diaphragm, allowing your breath to become very even and smooth.

Now visualize the body as a hollow reed. Then breathe in as if inhaling through the toes and filling the body with breath to the crown of the head. Exhale as if you are breathing back down the body and out the toes. Breathe easily and gently, without any effort. Do not try to force your breathing; let your body decide how much air you need.

Focus your concentration on feeling the entire body breathe, and imagine every cell and pore in your body breathing in and out. It's as if you are feeling your entire body expanding on the inhalation and contracting on the exhalation.

After a few moments, visualize the breath as a wave washing upon the shore on the inhalation and receding back into the sea on the exhalation. Maintain this imagery as long as you wish.

ation. Instead of feeling heavy and lethargic, our body feels light, and our mind becomes clear and alert.

We can breathe in a number of different ways to create progressively deeper states of relaxation. The simplest is the 2:1 Breathing discussed on page 152 of this chapter. Another simple but extremely effective relaxation exercise is called the Sweeping Breath. This exercise is very direct and easy to use. A few minutes of concentration on the Sweeping Breath brings on a deep, restful state. Use this exercise as a preliminary exercise for the "61 Points" concentration exercise given on page 200 in Chapter 8, or as a finishing exercise to other relaxation techniques.

More complex is the Deep-State Breath Relaxation. Detailed instructions are provided in Appendix C. In this exercise, you systematically alter the motion of the lungs, moving from very deep and slow breathing to very shallow, rapid breathing, and then returning to very deep, slow breathing. The effectiveness of this exercise lies in the systematic and gradual change in the motion of the lungs. The impact on the autonomic system creates a profound state of rest for the body. As your breathing becomes more shallow, it naturally becomes more rapid. Breathe as quickly as you need to feel comfortable. But you shouldn't have to pant. All breathing should be done effortlessly and without any sense of struggle or panic.

This exercise is very sophisticated, and takes practice. Any disruption of the systematic rhythm, such as a yawn, makes it somewhat less effective. But don't let this discourage you. Even if you do it imperfectly, you will be more relaxed than if you do the muscle relaxation exercise in Chapter 5 (Muscular Relaxation, page 104). Like the muscle relaxation exercise, this exercise is easier to do if you first read through the exercise, and record it on a cassette tape. Then lie in the Relaxation Posture and listen to the cassette.

The Two-Minute Breath Break

||||||||| During the day, every hour on the hour, or as often as you can remember, take a two-minute breath break. Close your eyes and concentrate on either Even Diaphragmatic Breathing or 2:1 Breathing for two minutes. This important practice clears your mind and breaks the daily tension habits that can lead to headaches and high blood pressure. Make sure to breathe through your nose and not your mouth.

You can easily check to see if you are breathing properly with your diaphragm while sitting or standing by using a wide belt or piece of cloth. Put the belt around your lower rib cage. When you inhale, the lower rib cage and upper abdominal area should expand, using more of the belt to encircle you. When you exhale, the lower rib cage and upper abdominal area contract, and the belt can be tightened. Remember, don't try to fill the lungs completely, or exhale completely. Your breath should be effortless, rhythmic, and diaphragmatic, with no movement in the upper chest.

Sleep Exercise

||||||||| Many of us struggle with chronic fatigue due to sleep deprivation. We usually have enough time, we just don't know how to get restful sleep. We don't usually think about sleeping as a skill. However, it isn't any different from any other kind of behavior. It all depends on our habits. With a little practice, we can train ourselves to sleep peacefully. This is also an excellent exercise to teach children who suffer from night terrors or sleepwalking.

We can also use the 2:1 pattern of breathing as an effective sleep exercise to minimize and eliminate insomnia, a common and difficult stress symptom.

|||||||| **SLEEP EXERCISE** ||||||||

- All breathing is 2:1. Exhale for twice as long as you inhale.
- Use a comfortable count such as 6:3 or 8:4. You are not trying to completely empty or fill the lungs. The 2:1 ratio should be effortless.
- Pay close attention to your breath. There should be no stops, pauses, or shakiness during either the inhalation or the exhalation. Minimize the pause between inhalation and exhalation.

The exercise goes as follows:
8 breaths lying on your back
16 breaths lying on your right side
32 breaths lying on your left side

Whether the problem is not falling asleep or waking up in the middle of the night and not falling back asleep, insomnia is most often caused by an agitated mind. You can easily remedy this problem with a little training. The nice thing about this and the other breathing exercises is that they don't depend on anything but your own willingness to practice.

This ancient yogic sleeping exercise takes advantage of the relationship between breathing and the autonomic nervous system, the impact of posture, and our ability to focus the attention. Follow these steps closely. If you don't fall asleep the first time, repeat the exercise. Practice every night until you can fall asleep easily and stay asleep all night.

From Body to Breath to Mind

|||||||||| You must take control of your breath if you want to achieve self-mastery. Once you start practicing the exercises and consciously working with your breath, you will have a powerful tool that you can use at any moment to relieve pressure and tension, and prevent stress. With breathing and relaxation skills, you now have a strong foundation for freedom. We are ready to take the next step. We must now turn to the creative mind and learn how to take power back from the dragons, and use it to create a life of joy and fulfillment.

CHAPTER 7

MIND AND MASTERY: TAKING ON THE DRAGONS

Untwisting all the chains that tie
The hidden soul of harmony.
—Milton

|||||||||| Breathing and relaxation skills provide the foundation for self-mastery. If these skills were all we needed, solving our problems would indeed be easy. As powerful as it is, breathing only reflects what goes on inside the mind. Watch someone become angry, and you will see her inhale and hold her breath. Watch someone who is depressed, and you will see him exhale and then hold his breath for a few moments. Someone who is anxious will be breathing very quickly and very high in the chest.

It's apparent that the real power and control lie within the mind, not the body. It's time to face the real source of our miseries, the dragons of the mind. If we don't take control of the creative force we call the sensory mind, all the breathing and relaxation in the world won't keep the dragons from breathing fire and creating unhappiness. In Chapter 3 we saw how the dragons of fear and self-hatred disturb the coordination between mind and body, which leads to stress. The greatest cause of stress is fear. It sets off the fight-or-flight alarm response, and we worry ourselves to death. When we identify with all the hurts, mistakes, and disasters of the past, we react with the possum response and suffer from depression and guilt. This is the second greatest cause of stress. Many of us are quite capable of doing both at the same time. Because we aren't skilled in using our inner resources, our habits dominate the mind and we become victims of our own misdirected creative force.

When we use the sensory mind skillfully, we solve problems, create new possibilities, tap our instinctual knowledge, and bring balance and harmony into our lives. But left unmanaged, this creative force is disrupted by emotions, made rigid by habits, and limited through beliefs. Instead of visualizing solutions, we fantasize harm and failure. We all know someone like Sharon, a middle-aged, very attractive and intelligent woman, whom I met at one of my seminars. She spends a great deal of emotional effort just trying to cope—not with the world, but with her own fears of rejection and thoughts about how stupid and unlovable she is. Sadly, like many others, Sharon had a difficult childhood. Her father was rejecting and cold, and her mother was incapable of providing the love and security every child needs. It's easy to see how these early patterns of rejection created such strong feelings of fear and self-hatred. Sharon understands this, but this analysis doesn't change the habits of her mind. She still accepts these early judgments that continue to play in her mind as her identity. Even though she practices relaxation and breathing exercises, she still feels fearful and unloved. Sharon must and can learn to distance herself from these habits locked into her sensory mind. If she learns how to quiet her mind and take control of her inner chatter, she can free herself from these old patterns.

To take command of the sensory mind, we must master four steps:

1. Stabilize our emotional reactions by taking charge of mind chatter. In this way, we cut the circuits to our past emotional reactions and redirect our emotional energies.
2. Carefully choose our language to create the realities we want and not waste time and energy on nonproductive thinking and emotional reactions.
3. Develop effective strategies to eliminate fear and self-hatred. With the right techniques and practice, we can overcome our fears, minimize negative self-criticism, and maintain a calm, clear mind even in the face of conflict and attack.
4. Refine our perceptual sensitivity and develop our instincts to provide us with a better sense of timing and the ability to make more effective decisions.

Stabilizing: Focusing the Power

|||||||||| It should be fairly obvious by now that even on our best days mind chatter can be difficult to deal with. And when fear and self-hatred raise their ugly heads, it seems impossible. The harder we try to control the chatter, the more it fills the mind. Try not to think for fifteen seconds. Don't think about not thinking, as this is still thinking. You will quickly find how difficult this is. The mind is a field of intelligent energy in constant motion. Like a crazed monkey jumping around in a tree, the mind hops from one thing to another, often making unexpected and undesirable leaps and turns.

We try all sorts of things to control the mind—positive thinking, sleep, drugs.

Unfortunately, many of the things not only don't work, they create even bigger problems for us. Our inability to control the chattering monkey mind is exceeded only by the frustration and suffering it creates for us.

There are times, though, when the mind behaves perfectly, and seems to be under almost complete control. Remember when you became so focused on your work that even time seemed to disappear? Psychologists call this "task absorption," or a "flow experience." It often leads to a "peak experience," a time of great personal fulfillment and expression. During this time, the body and mind are completely coordinated. The mind is free of worry and unconcerned with past failures, and all of your attention is concentrated on the task at hand.

When you are totally focused, you do your best work, find creative solutions to vexing problems, and apply them effortlessly. When you are finished, you feel wonderfully alive, alert, and very relaxed. You feel positive about yourself as well as others. Even if the work was physically exhausting, you don't feel irritable or stressed. Instead, you feel the satisfaction of a job well done, and a rest well earned.

Now contrast this experience with the time when you had a lot of work to do, but sat around and worried. How did you feel after several hours of working like this? More than likely, you couldn't concentrate, your mind and body were out of sync, and you felt frazzled, tense, and irritable. Unfortunately, we have far more of these experiences than the peak experiences of task absorption. Work, relationships, and leisure activities don't always fascinate us to the point that we become completely focused on them. We need something for the times when we aren't completely absorbed in the task before us.

What if you had a simple, effective technique to control your mind chatter, one that could be used anywhere at any time, and was effective the moment that you used it? And what if this technique, when refined to a high degree of skill, would provide you with absolute control over your emotional reactions? Would you practice until you became very skilled in its use?

Well, get ready to practice because there is a technique that will provide all of this and more. The more skilled you become, the greater the benefits you gain. This technique is called Breath Awareness, and is one of the most powerful self-management tools that you will ever use.

Controlling Emotional Reactions: Breath Awareness

|||||||||| Watch your mind think for a few minutes. Don't get involved in the thinking, just observe the thoughts as if you were watching a train go by. Now, focus your attention on the *feeling* of the breath as it moves in and out of your

nostrils. When you inhale you will feel a slight touch of coolness right at the opening of the nostrils. When you exhale, you will feel a very subtle touch of warmth. You may have a little difficulty feeling warmth, but you will feel the air as it moves through the opening of the nostrils. Now don't *think* about the breath, concentrate on *feeling* it as it enters and leaves the nostrils. Whenever you find your mind wandering off into thought, bring your attention back to the feeling of the breath. At the same time, be aware of how you feel, and what happens in your mind. But keep your attention focused on the coolness of the inhalation and warmth of the exhalation.

What happens to your thoughts? Does your breathing change? Do you feel anything different in your body when you focus your attention on feeling your breath?

Three things happen when you focus on feeling your breath:

1. The chatter in your mind stops and your mind becomes clear and calm.
2. Your breathing slows and becomes more stable, creating balance in the autonomic nervous system.
3. You feel a slight release as your body relaxes because there are no longer any demands being made by your mind chatter. The body's natural state is one of relaxation. The more focused, calm, and quiet your mind, the more relaxed your body.

Think about the last time that someone started screaming at you. What was your initial reaction? If you are like most people, you reacted in one of two ways. Your mind may have said something like "You can't talk to me like that!" and you went on the attack and started screaming back. Or your mind said, "Oh my gosh, what's happening here? This is awful!" Intimidated, you back-stepped and tried to find a way to retreat. Or maybe you retreated by completely tuning the other person out and not even hearing what was being said. In any case, your ego was engaged and you reacted to the attack.

But what if you looked the screamer right in the eye and simply focused your attention on the feeling of your breath? By doing this, you maintain a calm, collected mind and prevent the emotional reaction from forming. Then you can usually count on one of two things happening:

1. The person attacking you becomes frustrated because you aren't reacting to his emotional attack. He may become even more intense. This is a clear sign that he is trying to intimidate or manipulate you with an emotional outburst. His frustration stems from the fact that it isn't working. Don't worry, just stay calm and focused. Sooner or later, he will calm down and probably end up feeling rather foolish for overreacting. When

you don't react, the screamer often backs off and gains respect for you because he can't manipulate you. At the very least, he learns he can't manipulate you in this way.

2. The person calms down because you aren't fueling his emotional reaction with your own. Usually, this person has overreacted, and isn't trying to manipulate. Often the individual is grateful that you remained calm.

In either case, by remaining in control of yourself, you take control of the situation. Your thoughts remain clear and focused, and you solve the problems presented to you more effectively and efficiently without giving yourself high blood pressure or an ulcer.

Let's take another common example. We're all familiar with traffic stress. For many of us, it's a daily event, and it's all too easy to become tense and angry. Your shoulders tighten, you begin to feel desperate about arriving on time, and your jaws clench in anger. Instead of a calm, relaxed ride to the office, you are riding with a monster, and it turns out to be you! By the time you reach your destination, you are in no shape to be productive or to lend a helping hand.

You don't have to create this tension and stress. The next time you are in traffic and feel the pressure starting to build, practice Breath Awareness. (Of course, don't close your eyes to do this!) Watch what happens to your tension and stress. You can't do anything about the traffic, but you can do a great deal about the kind of company you keep for yourself.

Managing Emotional Reactions: Damage Control

|||||||||| But what about the times when you lose control? There will be many times when you get your buttons pushed and react before you can remember to do Breath Awareness. Remember the last time you started screaming at someone who obviously deserved it? More than likely, it was over some trivial thing, but that final straw "broke the camel's back." Your anger welled up and you exploded. Afterward, you probably felt upset for several hours, maybe even days or weeks, as you kept thinking about what had happened, or couldn't resolve the difficulty to your satisfaction. You continued to upset yourself long after the disturbing event.

Even when we don't react so dramatically, we can still do a good job of disturbing ourselves. We get strong emotional surges, and don't know how to take effective damage control to stabilize our thoughts and feelings. We dwell on anger and hurts long after the initial event has passed. This is where Breath

Awareness can play a powerful role by preventing the secondary effects of emotional reactions.

Remember the example from Chapter 4 about walking into a room and seeing a person you dislike apparently talking about you? Your emotional habits usually have a field day with this one. You often can't prevent that first emotional rush that leaves you feeling paranoid, defensive, and hurt. But that first surge has only a limited impact. It's what you do next that really keeps you miserable. After the initial emotional reaction, your mind chatter takes off. You review your history with that person, justify your behavior, go over past arguments, and dwell on past hurts and injustices. We tend to take a singular emotional reaction from the unconscious and build a house around it. Then, not content with just one house, we build a village around the house. Some of us build an entire city. Now, however, we must pay rent for the whole city. That rent, of course, is not only a spoiled evening but the price we pay for emotional disturbance and stress.

Instead of allowing your mind to react and build all those scenarios and recall all those memories, what if you quickly refocus your attention on Breath Awareness to clear your mind? Then, once you feel balanced and calm, you can easily redirect your attention to a more useful task or a more pleasant person to be with. By not allowing your mind to travel down the path of disturbance, you stay calm, collected, and content. By taking control, you can refocus your attention on a more useful, creative, and productive train of thought. You end up in a very different place, and without the misery and unhappiness that your old habits would have created.

No one learned this better than Marge. She was a participant in a four-week stress-management training program sponsored by an agency of the Defense Department. As office manager, she was responsible for supervising seven people. She came to the seminar to learn how to relax, but what she really wanted was to find a way to avoid the stress she felt around her immediate supervisor, a difficult and demanding individual. By the end of the four weeks, Marge was able to tolerate her supervisor as long as she remembered to do Breath Awareness whenever he walked into the office. To help her, she kept a little card on her desk that had "Breath Awareness" printed on it. Every time she looked at that part of her desk, the card reminded her to practice. This early success made quite an impression on her, and she faithfully practiced many of the techniques she learned in the seminar. After several months, Marge became fairly skilled at using Breath Awareness and at staying relaxed. This had a calming effect on the entire office, and led to an unexpected outcome. The supervisor signed up for the next stress-management seminar, and after participating, sent every one of his staff to the following seminar. The last I heard from Marge was that she was promoted on her supervisor's recommendation, and both were sorry to have their working relationship change. She keeps that little card on her new desk just as a reminder.

Our emotional reactions follow our perceptions and thoughts. This process usually begins in the emotional habits in the unconscious. By the time we experience these reactions, we are already out of balance. Remember running down the hill? The stronger our reactions are, the more difficult it is to rebalance ourselves. But with Breath Awareness, we not only stem the tide of our emotional energy, we can often prevent the reaction from occurring in the first place. Of course, the more difficult the situation, the more skill it requires. It's usually easier to remain calm with strangers than with family members. The closer the emotional ties, the more practice it takes to maintain a calm, steady mind.

Conflict Management: Taking Out the Opposition

|||||||||| The more skilled we become with Breath Awareness, the more opportunities we find to use it. Just think of all the times you wish that you had been more in control of your emotional reactions. Such as the times when you got involved in a conflict situation, an argument with your boss or a co-worker, or with a member of your family. How differently would you have behaved if you had remained calm? Would that have changed the outcome? Using Breath Awareness, you can confront the issues without creating even more disturbance by overreacting.

In fact, you now have the tools you need to deal with any conflict situation without being disturbed. Let's put the elements together. The key element in any conflict is opposition. We may disagree and have different viewpoints, but unless we oppose each other, we don't have conflict. All conflict, whether it involves another person, a different ideology, or different wants and desires in our own minds, is created by opposition. If we understand this key element, we very quickly see that once we remove opposition and resistance, conflict cannot exist. This does *not* mean that we avoid conflict or become passive. Avoiding conflict is a sure way to lose self-respect and become a victim. Rather, it means that we take charge of the mind and direct the flow of energy instead of opposing it.

There are four key steps to effectively managing conflict and taking control of any situation. They maximize your ability to resolve difficulties or problems by helping you maintain a calm and clear mind. This is called the RARE model of conflict management:

1. Relax
2. Accept
3. Restrain
4. Explore

STEP 1: RELAX

|||||||||| The very first step in any conflict situation is to relax. Conflict generates tension very quickly. The more emotional the situation, the greater the possibility of tension. When we engage in conflict, the ego sees it as a battle. As part of the fight-or-flight alarm response, tension is the body's armor against physical attack. It is there to protect the body. However, when we are fighting ourselves, tension only serves to make the mind more rigid and create more work for the heart. In interpersonal conflict, our tension is a signal to the other person that a battle has been engaged. In turn, his unconscious mind reacts by increasing tension, and the emotional intensity builds. Instead of protecting us, our tension actually intensifies conflict and disturbance.

The first step, consequently, is to maintain a state of relaxed calm. This requires that you be skilled in deep relaxation. Of course, if you are only fighting yourself, you can relax anytime. But when you are face-to-face with an angry person who is emotionally out of control, it's a bit difficult to say, "Excuse me, I must go and practice my relaxation now."

If you are already skilled in deep relaxation, you can effectively use the technique of scanning anywhere, at any time. After scanning, you can maintain a relaxed state by making sure the frontalis muscles in your forehead feel smooth and even.

Your relaxation signals to the other person's unconscious that you are *not* trying to give him a hard time or create any resistance to his communication. More important, by staying relaxed, you maintain a calm and clear mind, which is more flexible and creative, and more able to find solutions to the problem in front of you.

STEP 2: ACCEPT

|||||||||| When you reject a part of your personality or repress certain feelings or patterns of thought, you create inner conflict. When you struggle with unwanted habits, feelings, and thoughts, trying to push them from your mind, the struggle itself is often more destructive than the "unacceptable" thoughts or feelings.

|||||||||| SCANNING EXERCISE ||||||||||

To scan, mentally go from the top of your head to your toes, and then back up, and quickly relax any tension you find. You can do this in just a few seconds. Practice it now. Start at your forehead, and then mentally go down through your face, your neck and shoulders, your torso, and then down your legs to your toes. Relax any tension you find. Then come back to the top of your head. Periodically check your habitual tension points—for example, jaws, shoulders, stomach, lower back—and relax any tension you find.

Scanning is a very useful technique to use when you need dental work. At the dentist's office, you can really notice the effect of tension. When you sit in the dentist's chair, your body touches the chair in only three places: the back of your head, your buttocks, and your heels. Everything else is suspended by tension! All this tension guarantees that you will experience pain. Pain is intimately connected with tension. The more relaxed you are, the less pain you experience. When you first sit down in the chair, begin systematically scanning and relaxing every muscle from the top of your head to your toes. By the time you have relaxed every muscle, the dentist will be finished, and you will have felt very little pain. Of course, the more skilled you are at relaxing, the greater control you will have over pain.

To accept something doesn't mean that you approve of or agree with it. When we accept our inner thoughts and feelings, that doesn't mean that we believe them to be true or helpful. You can immediately eliminate inner conflict by simply accepting negative thoughts or feelings that come to your mind. As we learned before, you can't fight with your thoughts and win. You don't have to, nor can you, prove anything to your mind. It is this struggle that creates inner conflict and weakens our will. Instead, be an observer and just accept the thought as a thought. Don't make any value judgments about the thought and don't invest it with any importance. By doing this, you rob it of its power to affect you. It can no longer create conflict or make you feel bad.

This same principle operates on an interpersonal level. Remember the time when you had something very important you wanted to ask of a friend or family member? But halfway through your first sentence, your friend looked at you and started shaking his head—no. How did that make you feel? Most of us get very angry when this happens. If you want to really anger someone, and create intense opposition, just refuse to listen. We do not get nearly as angry when someone disagrees with us as we do when we feel they don't listen.

If our goal is to eliminate opposition, we must facilitate communication, not block it. We can do this very easily in any conversation by nodding and saying "yes" or "okay." This does not mean that we agree with what is being said, only that we are acknowledging the other person's communication. Nodding your head up and down indicates acceptance and encourages the other person to talk.

When the other person is finished talking, you can disagree all you want. In fact, by not creating any resistance to the communication, you disarm the other person's resistance to your communication. Now whatever you want to say back will be heard, whether your listener likes your response or not. Some people will take your nodding and saying "yes" as an agreement to *what* they are saying. This doesn't have to be a problem. In fact, in a conflict situation, this is an advantage to you. It will often disconcert the other person and blunt his aggressiveness.

STEP 3: RESTRAIN

|||||||||| This is where being skilled in Breath Awareness pays great dividends. In order to take control of a situation, you must be able to keep your ego under control by restraining your emotional reactions. If you want to be effective and solve problems, you cannot allow emotional reactions to distort your perceptions and cloud your thinking.

In a conflict, the focus can very quickly shift from the problem at hand to the issue of personalities—particularly when the other person is reacting emotionally. The first thing he will do is reach out and try to grab you by the ego. This often takes the form of blaming and personal attack. Some people intentionally attack on a personal level as a manipulative technique. They try to control the situation by provoking an emotional reaction in you.

You can remain calm if you do only one thing: Breath Awareness. By practicing Breath Awareness while the other person is speaking, you perceive more clearly, maintain control over your emotional reactions, and remain relaxed and calm. This allows you the clarity and flexibility to take Step 4.

STEP 4: EXPLORE

|||||||||| Emotional reactions in conflict situations make solutions very difficult to come by. The more disturbed you become, the less you can solve problems, and the easier it is to become embroiled in further conflict. But if you stay relaxed, facilitate the communication by nodding your head, and practice Breath Awareness to keep your mind calm and clear, conflict situations can be productive. The emotional energy involved in a conflict situation can be redirected into an exploration of alternative viewpoints and solutions, creating mental flexibility instead of rigidity. The emotional energy now enhances the creative force of the mind instead of distorting it. By remaining open and accepting, we create an atmosphere that also allows the other person to be more flexible, to explore and accept alternatives. But we only gain this benefit when we remain in control of ourselves and allow our creativity to flow in a productive, nonfearful way.

Language: The Power of Creative Reality

|||||||||| Once we take command of our creative forces and stabilize our emotional reactions through Breath Awareness, we can take the second step and learn to use the powerful function of language. We have already seen that words define our personal sense of reality, and they trigger our emotional reactions. Once we take control of our language, we have the means to starve fear and self-hatred.

When we become sensitive to the words we use, we can choose words that create positive, stress-free moods and attitudes. Toshi is a young woman who has always shown an uncanny ability for self-control and inner strength. I have never heard her use the word "failure." She will talk about mistakes, and the lessons that she has learned, but failure isn't part of her lexicon. Once she and one of her friends were working on a class project. Toward the end of the time allotted for the project, they suddenly realized that they had mistakenly done the wrong assignment. The other girl was in tears, saying over and over again how she couldn't believe that they had made such a stupid mistake. After about fifteen minutes, Toshi told her friend to go on home and that she would try to find a way to fix the problem. After her friend left, Toshi sat back and calmly thought about what they had done, and the assignment they were supposed to do. After a few minutes, she made a few changes in their project and was able to present it as a novel approach to the assignment. Later she told me that she asked her friend to leave because she couldn't think clearly while this girl was talking about how awful the problem was. *By taking control of her thoughts and imagery, she was not only able to salvage her work, but also earned high marks for her creativity and ingenuity.*

Here again, the key is self-awareness. Often we aren't very sensitive to what we are saying and how our own words affect us. My Master was skilled in making me face the consequences of my own words. On one occasion, he called me and another psychologist into his room and started teasing us. After a few minutes of small talk, he suddenly said, "You people [meaning psychologists] talk funny." And he began to imitate the way I spoke—the professional jargon I used, the tonal qualities, even the facial expressions were perfect imitations of my own speech patterns. As he spoke, I saw myself in his words, and could feel how those words affected me. The entire event didn't last longer than a few moments, and I was laughing so hard that I had tears in my eyes. But I remember clearly how those words felt, and ever since then, I have been much more careful of the words I use and much more sensitive to how they create my emotions and reinforce my habits.

It isn't difficult to take charge of this powerful function. As we learned with the Green Frog Exercise in Chapter 3, the first step is to stop believing what your mind says. The next time that voice says "You are really second rate," follow it immediately with another thought that says "Okay, somebody has to be. What's next?" Then clear your mind with Breath Awareness and refocus your attention on something more useful. You have the power to determine your emotional states *by consciously choosing what to attend to, how to describe or talk about it, and what to dismiss as an unproductive line of thought.*

The language we use can interfere with our ability to understand what is going on. There is an ancient Chinese proverb that warns us of the deceptiveness of words:

If you wish to see the truth, then hold no opinion for or against anything. To set up what you like against what you dislike is a disease of the mind.

Practice using nonjudgmental words. Instead of "good" and "bad," use words that have less emotional charge, such as "helpful" and "not helpful." Play with your language. Use different words to see what kinds of changes they create. Instead of saying "That is awful," use the phrase "That's an interesting development." Instead of telling yourself you can't do something, say "Let's see what I can do." By stepping back and experimenting with the words and phrases we use, we learn how to use language as a tool rather than be abused by it.

By using Breath Awareness and taking charge of our language, we take the power back from the dragons and redirect our energy into far more useful and productive channels. With these two skills as the foundation, we are ready to confront the dragons. We can now directly attack the two dragons—fear and self-hatred—and dramatically minimize their impact. We won't win each battle. There will be many times that the dragons are more powerful and more sneaky than we anticipated. But it doesn't matter. Each time we become worried and afraid, every time we abuse ourselves with self-contempt or guilt, we have an opportunity to practice our techniques and become a little stronger. In this way, we use the dragons to make ourselves stronger. Instead of obstacles to self-mastery, they become our means.

Confronting Fear: Steps to a Life of Freedom

|||||||||| Once we stabilize our emotional reactions and take control of our language, we can begin to develop effective strategies to eliminate fear and self-hatred. We should never accept them as part of life. We have all the resources we need to be so strong that fear and self-hatred play no role in our lives. This is evident in times of crisis when suddenly we call on reserves we never realized we had. Our problem is not one of lack, but one of access. As we shall see and experience in the next chapter, we have all the confidence and strength we need. But first we have to confront and tame our dragons. We must prevent the sensory mind from creating these destructive beasts we call fear and self-hatred.

We begin with the fantasy we call fear. The next time you begin to worry, step back and examine your thoughts, images, and feelings. Pay close attention. Is what you are worrying about *actually* happening to you, or is it something that you *think* might happen to you? Is it an actual event, or just a picture in your mind? Then pay attention to how you deal with an actual dangerous or potentially harmful situation. What are your feelings and thoughts when you are actually taking action? You will notice that when you are attentive and involved, you do not feel fearful.

This is the essence of martial arts training. In martial arts, you don't anticipate the future, you are fully attentive to the moment. You are so focused that you become sensitive to the subtle thoughts and movements of your opponent. In karate, this advanced state is called *mu shin* or *mu no kokoro*, the "empty mind" or "the mind of nothingness." It indicates a mind so free of conceptual thought, worry, and concern that it accurately reflects the perceptual reality around it. It is an active, all-embracing state of mind in total harmony. By focusing on the present, you prevent your mind from anticipating the future, and you remain free from fear. Your body is relaxed, your mind is responsive to its environment, and your movements are coordinated and graceful.

Even if you don't practice martial arts, you can learn how to eliminate fear. You can practice confronting your fears and living in the moment. To do this, you need a simple strategy to follow. The following has been very helpful to many people. Why not give it a try?

STRATEGIES TO CONTROL FEAR

1. *Take control of your mind chatter.* Use Breath Awareness to clear your mind of everyday fears and worries. Don't allow your mind to build a city of disturbance where you are forced to pay the rent. It doesn't matter if you have to clear your mind a thousand times to get past a worrisome situation. Each time you do so, your habit of Breath Awareness gets a little stronger. The more you use Breath Awareness, the more control you have over your mind chatter, and the less fear it can produce.

Taking control of your mind chatter doesn't mean that you don't think; it means that you become skilled in directing your thinking. Make sure that the words you use help you remain strong, and don't create weakness or fear for you. Reframe (reinterpret) a worrisome situation, using words that are descriptive rather than judgmental, that offer options rather than only one way of doing things. For instance, any difficulty can be defined as a "disaster," a "problem," even an "opportunity." When you find yourself starting to worry, take a few moments to clear your mind, then redefine using different words.

Whenever you face a problem that includes a personal threat, depersonalize it so you can maintain mental clarity. Focus on the problem to solve, and avoid being part of it by imagining all the terrible things that will happen to you. In Chapter 8 you will learn centering techniques which will enable you to clear your mind deeply, to refocus your attention, and to allow your unconscious mind to present you with a creative alternative.

2. *Be present-centered, focus on your strengths, and take action.* Once you clear your mind of chatter, focus your attention on the problems that you face now, not what might happen in the future. Remember, fear doesn't exist in the present, it exists only in relationship to a future event. If we pay attention to what is happening now, we prevent the mind from creating fear and we are more aware of the choices available to us now. To paraphrase a famous advertising slogan for wine, make sure that you "solve no problems before their time."

You must take action to solve any problem. You solve problems by what you do, not by what you can't do. Focus your mind, energy, and effort on the strengths and the resources you have available to you and on the actions you can take. Every time you act on your strengths, you are literally practicing to be strong. This reinforces both your strengths as well as the habit of using them.

On the other hand, every time you act out of weakness, you are practicing weakness and become weaker.

Action also completes the circuit between mind and body. By taking focused action, by doing something, you coordinate body and mind and prevent fear from forming. Many people resist taking action because they are afraid of making mistakes. Doing nothing reinforces this fear and builds barriers to success. This loss of confidence leads to even greater fear. Mistakes provide the opportunity to make adjustments and corrections that will eventually lead to a solution or resolution of the problem. If you keep a clear, calm mind, you will always learn from your mistakes and avoid making the same mistake twice. But if you sit and worry, nothing is resolved, nothing is learned. The only result is that you become more skilled at worrying.

3. *Face your fears directly.* When fear, worry, or anxiety grips the mind, most of us engage in avoidance behavior: we find friends to console or reinforce us, we sleep, go shopping, we eat or drink. Avoidance behaviors are distracting; they do not allow an understanding or resolution of fear. Instead of trying to get rid of the fear, sit quietly and examine it as if you were a court reporter. Where do you feel the fear? What color and shape is it? Then completely examine the assumptions your mind makes. Follow through with each consequence, and don't allow your mind to stop until you've reached the very end. Bring everything out in the open for your observation: *If this happens, my boss will be mad at me. What then? . . . Well, she will chew me out. What then? . . . I'll lose her respect, and feel bad and stupid What then? . . . I may get fired, not be able to make my mortgage payments, and lose my house. What then? . . . Oh, I probably wouldn't lose my house, I'd just have to find another job, which might be tough going for a while, but I'd get through it. What then? . . .*

As you follow each of these thoughts and force them to a conclusion, watch what happens to your fears. Then use the other strategies to maintain your calm and steady mind.

Fear, as powerful as it is, is only a habit of your mind. To have strength and courage doesn't mean that you don't have fears, it means that you confront them and do not allow them to make decisions for you.

You can free your mind of petty fears, worries, and anxieties. Of course, the stronger and deeper your habits, the more effort and training it takes. But you gain an added benefit. The same methods also free your mind of the habits and patterns of self-negation.

Letting Go of History:
Facing the Dragon of Self-Hatred

|||||||||| In Richard Bach's book *Illusions: Confessions of a Reluctant Messiah*, there is a phrase in the Handbook for Messiahs which states, "Argue for your limitations, and sure enough, they are yours." Many of us do this. We constantly remind ourselves of our mistakes, our weaknesses, and our shortcomings. No wonder depression is so prevalent in our society.

Every human being makes mistakes, feels rejected, and experiences hurt and failure. Our childhood experiences often leave scars that are deep and painful. We develop self-destructive patterns in the mind that become a false identity, ones that lead to self-hatred, guilt, and hopelessness. We never allow ourselves to experience the power and beauty of our personalities because we spend so much of our time looking only at the pain and negativity. This, of course, creates enormous unhappiness and stress for us.

A dangerous condition comes from self-hatred—feeling hopeless and helpless, that nothing you do will ever make a difference, and that you are completely out of control of your life. A large body of evidence clearly shows that people who feel hopeless, helpless, and victimized slowly but surely destroy their immune systems. Animal research by C. P. Richter in the late 1950s, and Martin Seligman and Bruce Overmeir in the late 1960s, showed conclusively that animals will learn helplessness. When this happens, the animals lose motivation, stop making effort, and even die. The clinical research in cancer by O. C. Simonton and Lawrence LeShan in the late 1970s showed that a sense of helplessness in people is a consistent pattern prior to the development of cancer, depletes the immune system, and can lead to premature death. Current research in psychoneuroimmunology all points to one and the same conclusion: depression, hopelessness, and helplessness depress immunity functioning and lead to serious disease states such as cancer, as well as to premature death.

Clearly, when you spend a lifetime arguing for your limitations, it can cost you your health, your happiness, and even your life. We can, and must, put an end to this self-inflicted disaster. We can only do this by no longer allowing ourselves to be victims of our own emotional habits and mind chatter. Medication can be somewhat helpful for various forms of depression. But in the end, we still must help ourselves. We must take charge of our own minds and find ways to access our inner strengths. We begin at the level of the sensory mind by taking these four steps:

1. *Develop response ability by giving up the role of victim and taking back your power.* When we blame ourselves and/or others for our circumstances, our

feelings, or anything else, we deny our own inner strength and power. We can never be free of self-hatred as long as we don't take full response ability (remember, the word "responsibility" is best understood as two words, "response" and "ability") for our thoughts, feelings, and actions. Others may harm us, but they cannot make us feel a certain way. You may have the power to take my life, but you do not have the power to make me fearful. You may condemn me, but you do not have the power to make me condemn myself. Only I have the power to do these things.

We develop response ability by accepting full responsibility for our thoughts and feelings. Try this exercise once and see which feeling you prefer to have. The next time you become angry at someone, blame them by saying, "You make me angry." Pay attention to how it feels to give someone the power to make you feel a certain way. Notice if you experience any sense of helplessness or powerlessness. Also pay attention to the other person's reactions.

Then, the next time you get angry, change the words you use. Say to that person, "I get really angry when you do that." Is there any difference in how you feel about yourself? Which way of speaking leaves you with more self-respect? Which way feels more powerful and satisfying? What was the impact on the other person?

We don't always make the best choices when it comes to our feelings, but we are still the ones who choose. It is our unconscious habits that make us react, not someone else's. No one has the power to manipulate our glandular responses or our neural synapses. When we deny our power by blaming others or ourselves, we become victims, lose self-respect, and begin to feel hopeless and helpless. At that point, we start to damage our immune systems. As long as we continue to deny our own choices and power, we continue to create stress and disease.

Those who are successful and in command of their lives, who feel self-respect, don't begin with any more control over their circumstances than those who feel hopeless and helpless. They simply do not allow themselves to feel victimized by their circumstances. Successful entrepreneurs must believe in themselves, or they can never take the risks necessary to build a business, or a career. A close friend of mine, Oded Lurie, president of Gray Matter Inc., is a good example of perseverance. He had a successful career as senior executive for several major corporations. He decided to begin his own consulting firm, using technology and information to help small companies compete more effectively. For several years, it seemed as if every move he made ran headlong into poor economic conditions. After years of financial hardship, during which he even had to give up his home, the tide began to change. Today, he has a thriving consulting firm and has developed a unique computer program that promises to revolutionize management decisions. More important, Oded trusts his own strengths, and doesn't depend on fate to create opportunities for him. People like Oded hold firm to the conviction that whatever happens, they can learn from it, and use it for growth and benefit. They carefully build this attitude through constant practice of taking full response ability. In so doing, they actually gain control of their lives, while those who live their lives as victims lose it.

2. *Practice forgiveness (patience and acceptance).* An important step in developing our full response ability is to free ourselves of guilt. Guilt is entirely useless. It enslaves the mind and reinforces the very behavior we wish to avoid. The simplest way to free ourselves from guilt is to practice forgiveness. Forgiveness consists of two elements: patience and acceptance. We can learn to be patient with ourselves and others if we don't judge ourselves or others. Acceptance is the ability to separate the behavior from the individual. We may think the behavior is wrong, even destructive, but we can still hold on to the value of the individual. Forgiveness is one of our greatest virtues, but we must begin by forgiving ourselves. Once you develop your power of forgiveness, it becomes easy to recognize and learn from mistakes, so you don't keep repeating them.

I remember one incident that taught me a great lesson. I was involved in helping stage a large international congress. On the opening day, I was running around taking care of final details. In typical Type A fashion, I was busy directing and giving orders. As I walked into a large room, I saw an old friend whom I hadn't seen in years. He cheerfully greeted me and extended his hand. Instead of returning his greeting, I (again in typical Type A fashion) said, "Oh, Larry, quick, go into the front office and do such and such." Without another word, I continued on my busy way. About forty-five minutes later, Larry caught up with me and confronted me. He said that he was very angry and didn't like the way I had treated him.

I had no idea what he was talking about. As he explained his anger about the abrupt and off-hand way in which I had greeted him, I realized that he was absolutely correct. I quickly and sincerely apologized. He was surprised that I was willing to admit my mistake so easily and very quickly forgave me, and our friendship continued to grow and deepen. I recognized my mistake, corrected it, and moved on without any guilt. Because it was such a clear lesson for me, I am much more careful about letting my Type A qualities override my love for my friends. When you accept yourself, it's easy to apologize for, and correct, the inevitable mistakes you make.

One of the best ways to practice forgiveness is to let go of the need to be perfect. It's amazing how much disappointment we create for ourselves because we never measure up to some fantasy. Create psychological space to grow by giving yourself permission to be yourself. By constantly wishing you were different, you create a continual rejection and depression in the mind. You don't have to puff up your ego, simply stop telling yourself what a jerk you are. If you don't create the negative, you don't have to compensate by creating the positive.

3. *Focus on the here and now.* It's not hard to banish the negative when we use Breath Awareness to clear the mind. Like any other mind chatter, we can quickly eliminate self-negation if we focus on the here and now. Be on full alert with your mind chatter. As soon as your old habits surface telling you that you are a terrible person, how you will never change, or whatever your mind does to punish and blame you, go immediately to Breath Awareness and clear your mind. Then redirect your attention to the task in front of you. Again, it doesn't matter if you have to use Breath Awareness a thousand times a day. That just means more opportunities to become skilled. Never give up on yourself, and never give up on Breath Awareness. It has taken your whole life to build the habits you have now and it will take time to replace them.

4. *Use language carefully.* Avoid language that involves blame and self-pity. For instance, the punitive use of the word "should" strongly reinforces guilt feelings. We repeat "I should [or shouldn't] have done . . ." or "You should [or shouldn't] have done . . ." over and over until we have ingrained the pain of failure into our or someone else's mind. When we make a mistake, it's appropriate to recognize what we should or should not have done. But the second or third time we repeat the phrase, we aren't recognizing a mistake, we are beating up on ourselves (or someone else). This damaging habit leads to a great deal of stress, resentment, and unhappiness.

The next time you find yourself repeating a "should have" statement, try this should-stopper exercise. After the third repetition, walk over to a window and look up into the sky. If you do *not* see the hand of God writing in indelible gold letters "You should not have done that!" then you can figure that what you did or didn't do was okay. If God doesn't personally punish you, why do it to yourself? Accept the mistake, learn from it, and move on.

The physical action of walking to the window, along with the mental action, helps weaken the neural synapses in the brain that structure the habit. About the third or fourth time you do this exercise, you will find that the habit of "shoulding" yourself has weakened. Now you can successfully replace it with a more productive pattern of behavior, such as paying attention to the task in front of you.

Fear and self-hatred slowly but surely destroy our capacity to freely express ourselves and experience the self-respect and feelings of power and confidence that this engenders. We begin to avoid the challenges of life and become indecisive and weak. We lose our self-respect, leading to even more self-negation. It becomes a vicious cycle, and the only outcome is stress, unhappiness, and disease.

Perception: The Basis of Knowledge

|||||||||| But there is far more to Breath Awareness than just controlling emotional reactions. It is also the most effective way to develop perceptual sensitivity, to become more aware of the world around us. By keeping the mind clear and calm, we become more sensitive to the subtle cues in our environment. We begin to notice things that we hadn't paid attention to before. Now we begin to master the fourth step, refining perceptual sensitivity, and using the power of the sensory mind in a more useful and effective way.

We can see just how useful Breath Awareness is when we understand that the sensory mind does only two things: it either thinks (chatters) or perceives. But it doesn't do both at the same time. It seems that we are doing several things at once as our attention shifts rapidly back and forth. Our focus can shift so fast (yoga science claims that this shift occurs in approximately 1/485th the time it takes to utter a single syllable) that we aren't aware of it, so it seems as if we are doing several things at once. But actually the mind engages only one process at a time.

We can become so distracted by our thoughts that we stop paying attention to the world around us. Remember the last time someone was talking to you and you became preoccupied with some thought in your head? Suddenly, you realized that you hadn't heard a word the other person was saying. You were distracted, too busy talking to yourself to listen. Or the time you got into your car and suddenly found yourself at your destination without even realizing how the journey went?

We don't often realize that the foundation of our knowledge is what we perceive. The act of perception is the primary process. That means that the basis of our information about the world comes through our senses. The collection, organization, and interpretation of sensory input is a perceptual process, not an analytic one. Thinking is abstract, a secondary process based on our perceptions. If we are too busy thinking, we aren't doing a very good job of perceiving. There are times when we want to tune out the world and focus on our own thoughts. But all too often we get lost in our thoughts when what we really need to do is pay attention. When we want to know what is happening in the world around us, when we want to see the whole picture and not just analyze its parts, we use perceptual sensitivity.

Just as we stop perceiving by focusing on our thinking, we can also stop our thinking by focusing our attention on the perceptual process. Instead of reacting, we find ourselves using even more information and making better decisions for ourselves. Now we are using the creative force of the sensory mind to help us instead of creating dragons.

Creativity: Changing the Rules

||||||||||| Many of us don't feel very creative. We think that creativity is something that only a lucky few are born with. We don't realize that creativity is a natural function of every human mind. The mind is busy at every moment creating a personal reality and making sense of the world. It is the sensory mind's natural ability to organize perceptual data into meaningful categories. Unfortunately, if we aren't aware of this organizing function of the mind, we never learn how to take control and use this creative force as a conscious skill. As a result, our creativity is constricted by habits, and we get locked into seeing things in the same old way.

These habits are like rules. When we always follow the rules, we never have the opportunity to develop new perspectives. One of the most succinct statements of creativity was made by Admiral James T. Kirk in the movie *Star Trek II: The Wrath of Khan*. Kirk was approached by a lieutenant about a training simulation that was contrived so that no matter what the trainee did, she would always lose. Angered by the impossibility of the simulation, the lieutenant had been told by Spock that the only person to beat it was Kirk. Asked how he beat the simulation, Kirk responded, "I changed the rules." Creativity is all about changing the rules. When we aren't sensitive to our own creative forces, it becomes difficult to change the rules and express our natural creativity.

If we feel we aren't creative, it isn't because we lack creative capacity. It's because we unconsciously limit the inherent and spontaneous creative power of the sensory mind through fears and habits, or because we narrowly restrict the input to the mind. These limits or rules on creativity are entirely self-imposed. Our environment may reinforce or inhibit our creative expressions, but our environment has no power to limit the creative nature of the mind. Only we can do that.

We engage the creative force at every moment as we continue to bring new meanings, interpretations, and reactions into existence. Our personal reality is a product of the fertile and imaginative mind, which constantly creates, sustains, and destroys a vast number of interpretations, realities, behaviors, and events. The entire dance of the sensory mind is one continuous creative movement that either reflects spontaneity or becomes restricted by rigid repetitive behaviors.

It isn't hard to experience this creative movement. It simply takes a little reflection and attention to your mind chatter. You can easily watch the creative process if you step outside of it and become a witness. Try the following exercise in Creative Thought. First read through the exercise, then close your eyes, do the exercise, and watch your mind work.

Throughout the exercise, your mind created images, thoughts, and feelings. Some could lead to action; some could interfere with action. Your habits structured some of the images, thoughts, and feelings that arose, while others were spontaneous, leading to feelings of anticipation and joy. The problem is not

||||||||| A BRIEF EXERCISE IN CREATIVE THOUGHT |||||||||

Sit back in your chair, get very comfortable, and close your eyes. For a few moments, focus your attention on Breath Awareness, clearing your mind of extraneous and unnecessary thoughts . . . . As you do this, you will feel yourself relax, and your attention will direct itself inward. Next, visualize yourself in your ideal vacation setting . . . . Imagine as clearly as you can what it feels like to be there . . . . what you are wearing . . . . the weather . . . . Be as complete as you can . . . . Enjoy this vision for a few moments . . . . You have always wanted to live and work in this setting; now is your chance. What must you do to transfer your job and family here . . . . Mentally go through all the steps it will take to do this . . . . What does your office or work station look like? Surely, it's quite different than what you have now . . . . How will you go about conducting your affairs? . . . . . . What will you need to do to bring about this ideal setting and these work conditions? . . . . . . Observe your feelings as you allow your mind to create possibilities for you . . . .

Now, think of all the reasons why you can't possibly do this, why it wouldn't work . . . . the company won't move, you can't earn a living, your family doesn't want to move . . . . Let your mind create all the reasons why it won't work . . . . Be aware of your feelings as you allow your mind to create obstacles for you . . . . Then open your eyes.

can you be creative, but rather *how* you use your creative force. Through self-mastery, you learn to consciously take control of the creative force, and use it to your benefit instead of allowing your habits to choose for you.

If you learn how to consciously direct your mind to create scenarios, you can stay more relaxed, feel more in control, and become more sensitive to all the possibilities that your mind will offer. Remember, the tendency of the sensory mind is to follow its habits. If you simply react to a problem, your mind takes the path of least resistance provided by old habits and you will lose touch with the creative process. These old habits are the rules of the mind. Automatic reactions diminish your creative capacity and your effectiveness at solving problems. By maintaining a calm and reflective attitude, your mind can play, and the creative force will work for you. Like Admiral Kirk, you can change the rules.

Listening with the Whole Mind

|||||||||| When we use Breath Awareness to calm the mind, we become much more sensitive to all of our sensory input. We don't just hear a conversation with our ears, we also see the person's face more clearly and feel his emotional energies more acutely.

In my seminars, the participants pair up and practice listening to each other. While one partner talks for several minutes about a problem he is involved in at work, the other must listen without responding, using Breath Awareness to keep her mind clear of inner chatter. One of the most typical reactions is for the person listening to say, "This is uncomfortable. I want to respond back, and help my partner solve his problem." It's very difficult to listen with full attention. We are too practiced in talking to ourselves. Often, the person who does the talking will say, "I didn't want you to solve the problem, I just wanted you to listen. By talking to you, I get a chance to be more objective as I listen to myself, and that gives me my own insights into how to solve the problem." If we constantly solve other people's problems, we rob them of an opportunity to develop their own creative insights. The most important thing we can do is simply listen, but do that with the whole mind.

After a few minutes of conversation, I ask the one who is listening to focus on what she feels as she listens, what thoughts pop into her mind, even to name the talking partner's favorite color. It's often quite shocking for the listener to find out that she knows far more about her partner than what she heard in the words. When we listen with the whole mind and body, we experience the emotional states—the doubts, worries, happiness—that the other person is experiencing as he talks. This information is the basis for real understanding. It allows us to make better decisions for ourselves and for others, to avoid unnecessary conflicts, and to be more clear in our communications—all of which helps reduce the misunderstandings and mistrust that so often lead to stress.

For example, one of the classic conflicts between men and women is directly related to listening. When a woman is talking to her husband about the frustrations of her day, he is busy trying to solve her problems. In all likelihood, all she wants is for him to really listen to her. She is quite capable of solving her own problems; she simply needs him to listen to her, to give her his attention. The real message is "Honey, I need your attention," not "Please solve this problem for me." Meanwhile, instead of really paying attention and listening, he is busy thinking about what she should have done. Worse, out of good intentions, he will probably tell her what she should have done. This can start a chain reaction where each is not listening to the other and each is frustrated with the other for not understanding.

Learning to listen with the whole mind is not difficult to do. The best time to practice is in social situations where there is no pressure to solve problems or gain information. The next time you find yourself chatting with someone, practice using Breath Awareness while she is speaking. Don't try to solve her problems, or add to her story, simply listen. Be aware of the thoughts and feelings that pass by as you listen. You might be surprised by how much you learn about that person in just a very short period of time.

When we listen with the whole mind we become aware of enormous amounts of information that we never noticed before. This information comes to us through all our senses, not just our eyes or ears. There are times when we enter a room full of people and the tension is so thick that you could almost see it. We don't go around assessing each person individually in the room to see if he or she is angry or upset. We feel the tension the moment we enter the room. Our kinesthetic sense warns us very quickly and accurately of trouble. And while there isn't an instrument in physics that can measure that atmosphere in the room, the mind knows it instantly and accurately. This sudden recognition is a powerful form of knowledge called instinct.

Instinctual Knowledge: Nature's Gift

||||||||||| Instinct is a perceptual event, not an analytic one. Instinctual knowledge doesn't come from thinking about something, but by being aware of what already is there. The sensory mind has the capacity to know immediately what will hurt us or harm us without having to analyze or think about it. As you clear

your mind of unnecessary and destructive chatter, you will become more sensitive to your environment and to the subtle behaviors and moods of those around you. The more focused you are, the more clearly and deeply you understand the events and circumstances around you.

Instinct, a powerful form of knowledge based on sensory input, depends heavily on perceptual sensitivity. Instinct is part of the primitive urge for self-preservation which tells us of potentially harmful or helpful elements in our environment. Instinct protects us from danger, provides an unerring sense of timing, and allows us to be sensitive to the subtle thoughts and feelings of others. We must be sensitive to the dangers that we face, but we don't have to worry and create more dangers than those which already exist. Nor need we be afraid of these dangers once we recognize them. The sooner and more clearly we recognize dangerous situations, the more effectively we can deal with them, as long as we don't become afraid.

We all experience times when instinct warns us about danger. We may be driving along and, suddenly and unexplainably, we have a strong sense that we had better slow down. As we slow our speed, the driver next to us suddenly changes lanes without any warning. We are often very instinctual about our children. But because of our close emotional ties to our children, our fears interfere with our instincts and often tell us to be concerned when no real danger exists.

When we become skilled at listening to the whole mind, we find that instinctual feelings are quite different from fear. Like anyone else, I can worry about my children being hurt. Recently, I had to leave town on a business trip the same day my oldest daughter participated in a canoe race on the river that runs through our town. The river level was high and the current very swift because of snow melt and spring rains. Since this was only her second time in a canoe, I was concerned for her safety. I agreed to her participation, but as I drove to my destination I spent several hours worrying about her. After over twenty-five years of practice listening to my inner voices, it was quite obvious to me that my worry was rooted in my concern for her safety, not in an instinctual response to the reality of her canoe trip. With practice, we can learn to make the subtle differentiation between what our fears are telling us and what our instincts are telling us.

Unfortunately, most of us must relearn how to really listen to ourselves and trust our senses. The sensory mind and body act like a radio receiver, constantly pulling in and responding to information. As we take in information, the unconscious part of the sensory mind processes it and immediately communicates any vital data back to the conscious mind. Our instincts, tied to the primitive drive for self-preservation, communicate to our conscious mind through the emotional message path of our feelings. If we aren't aware of our feelings and sensations, we can't use our instincts effectively. They often become confused with the fears and desires that are also in our unconscious.

The more skilled we are with Breath Awareness, the more sensitive we are to these subtle feelings and sensations. We can use any activity, even the way we walk with someone, to gain insight into their personality and the nature of our relationship with them. Try the following Walking Exercise, then practice

|||||||||| THE WALKING EXERCISE ||||||||||

The next time you go for a walk by yourself, be very sensitive to how this feels. The purpose is to establish a baseline of information about your own inner feelings. Do this several times, noticing the difference in how it feels to walk in different situations—for example, when you are in a hurry, when you are relaxed and comfortable, when you are worried about something.

After establishing a baseline about your own inner feelings, use it as a reference to study what you feel when you walk with someone else. As you walk with this person, be aware of how you walk, how you hold your body, what it feels like to walk with him. How does it differ from when you are walking by yourself? How do your feelings differ? Are you more tense or less tense? Do you have feelings of anticipation or of lowered energy? What are the differences between walking with this person and walking by yourself?

Do this with different people. How do your inner feelings and reactions differ from person to person, or from when you walk by yourself? What does this tell you about how you feel about each of these individuals, about how they react to you, or about the nature of your relationships with them? Does anything else come to your mind?

You might think you walk differently with other people because they have a different stride. But they also walk differently with you than by themselves or with someone else. After your walk, write down your feelings and any insights you might have had during it. Use this record to see which feelings gave you accurate information and which ones misled you. Doing this allows you to recognize the difference between your emotional projections and genuine instincts.

using it when you are with different people. See what your feelings tell you about that person. This exercise provides an opportunity to practice listening with your whole mind, and helps you to become more sensitive to the subtle perceptions that form the basis of instinct.

Instinct and creativity are natural resources of the sensory mind. If we learn to keep the mind clear of the noise and distortions created by fear and self-hatred, we discover an increased ability for creative problem solving, we understand people more completely, we find that our instincts are more refined, and we have a more effective sense of timing. When we are under attack from the dragons in the mind these resources are buried by the mind's noisy chatter. The more calm and focused we become, the more information and knowledge we have, and the better choices we make. As we make better choices, we create fewer problems and less stress for ourselves.

The Next Step: Reaching for the Power

|||||||||| By taking control of your sensory mind, you begin to take control of your life. Once your mind is calm and clear, you can use an almost endless number of techniques—language and reframing, imagery and affirmations, the RARE model to control conflict, or creativity techniques for effective problem solving—to redirect the creative force of the mind. The more sensitive you are to the subtle perceptual events of your mind, the easier it is to use your instincts, and the better decisions you make.

As we become more fearless and less abusive to ourselves, we must now face the final dragon, loneliness. It takes more than balance and clarity to vanquish this dragon. We must travel beyond the busy sensory mind, beyond the limitations of our habits and language, beyond the influence of our emotions, to the most subtle dimension of the mind, and cross this barrier into the unlimited spiritual Self.

But before we can solve the problem of loneliness, we must become strong enough to take on the ego, the most powerful and generalized function of the mind. To do this, we must tap into and refine the power behind the creative force of the sensory mind. We do this through our conscious ability to pay attention, to concentrate. Unless we develop and refine our inner concentration, we cannot access and use our inner strengths and wisdom as conscious tools, nor can we reach into the experience of the spiritual Self. These are our next steps, to move from balance and clarity into power, and from power into strength and wisdom.

CHAPTER 8

MOVING FROM POWER TO WISDOM

Tell me Master, What is the great secret?
"Attention," said the old man. "Attention, attention, attention!"
—Zen Story

|||||||||| Of all the different personal qualities that you bring to your work—creativity, experience, knowledge, communication skills, sense of humor, organization skills, persistence—which one would you choose as the most important? What is the one skill or quality that makes you successful in your work?

I have asked thousands of people this question, and the answers vary from person to person. But no matter how creative you are, how well you communicate with or manage others, or how well you solve problems, the day you go to work and cannot focus your attention, you cannot do anything well. The single most important skill that we have as human beings is the ability to focus our attention, to concentrate. When we concentrate, we coordinate mind and body, think more clearly, work more efficiently, and achieve peak experiences. Our ability to learn and to remember depends entirely on concentration. Through concentration we alter our experience of time and space and become more sensitive to our environment. The greater our power of concentration, the more effective we are at everything we do.

Yet, for all of its importance, very few of us ever train our powers of concentration. Nor do we find concentration training in our educational systems. For most of us, concentration is a haphazard event. Sometimes it happens and sometimes it doesn't. Our ability to concentrate varies from day to day, even from moment to moment, and whatever skill we have is accidental. And yet, it is critical to everything we do.

Mind Power—Synchronized Energy

|||||||||| If we recognize that the mind is an energy field, then it's not difficult to understand concentration. As we interact with our environment, mental energy takes different forms—thoughts, images, and sensations (feelings), which we experience as knowledge. But these patterns stimulate others and the mind constantly moves from thought to thought, from image to image. It becomes difficult to keep our focus on any one thing for a period of time.

When we focus our attention and concentrate, however, we begin to synchronize the mind's energy. As the mind becomes more synchronized and less distracted, we find a greater ability to think clearly, and to understand. In other words, the greater our power of concentration, the more powerful the mind will be. A distracted mind is weak, open to suggestion, and under the domination of its habits and emotions.

The difference between a distracted mind and a concentrated mind is like the difference between a normal lightbulb and a laser. Light consists of individual units of energy called photons. These photons are given off by a light source and travel through space until they strike a surface. In a normal lightbulb, these photons scatter and weaken as they interact with other subatomic particles on their journey through space.

In a laser, instead of being dissipated, the photons are synchronized. They are compressed into a cohesive flow, and all move in the same direction at the same time. They become a light so powerful that it can penetrate steel plate, or so delicate and precise that it is used for eye surgery. Just as we make a light powerful by synchronizing and focusing its energy, we make the mind powerful by synchronizing and focusing its energy.

The Benefits of Concentration

|||||||||| The power of the mind is the ability to focus mental energy and to concentrate. The greater the skill to concentrate, the more powerful and penetrating the mind becomes. As we concentrate and synchronize the energy of the mind, we gain several benefits:

- Concentration enhances coordination between mind and body, which leads to greater inner balance, the deepest level of relaxation, and a healthier mind and body.

- Concentration quiets and calms the mind, expanding our awareness, which allows greater perceptual sensitivity, enhances our instincts, and provides greater clarity of thought.
- Concentration leads to a greater ability to form accurate and penetrating knowledge, which allows more effective learning and provides access to our power of discrimination and intuitive knowledge.

RELAXATION: THE DEEPEST LEVEL

‖‖‖‖‖‖‖ The first and most immediate benefit of concentration is enhanced inner balance. As we concentrate, we minimize the crosscurrents of the conscious and unconscious mind. This reduces the demands on the body, which in turn creates a deeply relaxed body. The stronger the concentration, the greater the coordination between mind and body, and the deeper the state of physiological balance and harmony. This is why the deepest level of relaxation is created through concentration.

One of the most important relaxation exercises is called "61 Points." This exercise creates a very deep and profound state of relaxation, which is why we use it when working to control high blood pressure. No other relaxation exercise can reduce vascular tension as completely. In this exercise, you concentrate on 61 points within the body, visualizing a blue star or blue flame at each point. If you have difficulty visualizing a blue star or blue flame, you can concentrate on feeling a spot of warmth at each point. The exercise is very systematic and easy to learn. Figure 8.1 shows the 61 points, and general instructions are provided in the accompanying box. Detailed instructions for taping are provided in Appendix D.

EXPANDED AWARENESS: THE FOUNDATION FOR CHOICE

‖‖‖‖‖‖‖ It's easy to see how concentration creates relaxation and balance. The more focused we are, the fewer instructions are sent to the body, and the more relaxed we become. But relaxation is only the tip of the iceberg. An even greater benefit of concentration lies in its ability to expand our awareness. It may seem contradictory, but the more focused we are, the more aware we become of everything related to our point of focus.

Concentration is a conscious, intentional action. Daydreams, trance states, subliminal learning, even hypnosis may have some value, but they do not strengthen the conscious mind. They do not synchronize mental energy. Only by focusing our conscious attention do we achieve this.

Concentrate on either a blue flame or a blue star at 61 different points in or on the body. Choose one or the other, but don't switch them around. The star should look like an actual star in the sky, while the flame should look like the small blue flame used in natural-gas commercials on television. The color blue provides a restful focus for the mind. Do not substitute colors; doing so will change the effect. If you cannot picture any light at all, concentrate on a point of warmth, about the diameter of a pencil.

1. Begin by clearly deciding to remain awake. Then lie on your back on a pad or carpeted floor. Place your feet about 12–18 inches apart, and your arms and hands slightly away from the body, palms facing up. Use a small pillow to support the curve of your neck.

2. Concentrate on smooth, even diaphragmatic breathing. Picture your body like a hollow reed, breathing as if you are inhaling through your toes and filling your body with breath to the top of your head. Then exhale back down to the toes. Continue this until you can feel as if your whole body is expanding when you inhale and contracting when you exhale. (This is the Sweeping Breath Exercise.)

3. Visualize a blue star or flame at each of the 61 points as shown in the accompanying diagram. Begin with the first point and let the star or flame be as clear, as small, and as perfect as your mind will allow it to be. Hold the image in your mind for 10 to 15 seconds. (As you become more skilled, gradually increase the time to at least 20 seconds.) Then visualize this star or flame at each of the other sixty points in the body as shown in the accompanying figure, focusing on only one point at a time and spending the same amount of time on each one. Follow the diagram and instructions exactly, as this is a very precise exercise.

4. Finish with the Sweeping Breath, and be aware of your body. Before opening your eyes, slowly bring your hands up, being aware of every movement from the inside out. Then, holding the palms of your hands about 4 inches from your face, open your eyes to the palms of your hands. After your eyes are open, you can bring the hands back to your side, and get up whenever you are ready.

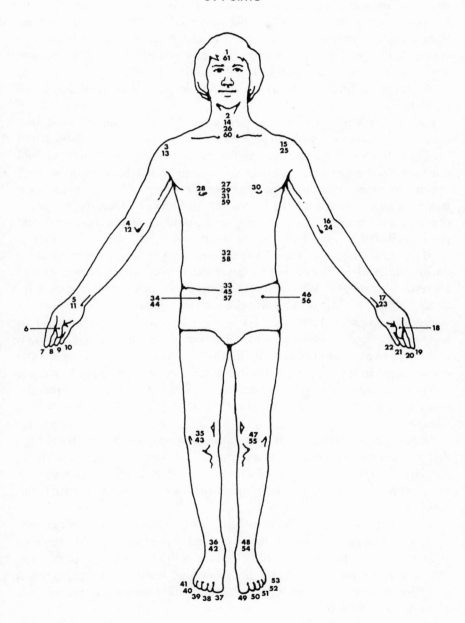

FIGURE 8.1

61 POINTS

We pay attention for two reasons: interest and fear. Both focus our attention, but each has a dramatically different impact on the mind. With interest, our awareness expands, and we become more sensitive to everything related to the object of our attention. The more interested we become, the more intensely we pay attention, and the more synchronized the mind's energy becomes. As the mind becomes stronger, our awareness continues to expand, and we find even more to be interested in. We initiate a positive cycle of interest, awareness, focus, and more interest, leading to deeper and deeper states of concentration.

For instance, writing is part of my profession. When I start an article, or work on a book, it takes me a while to get into what I am doing. If I get distracted in the first half hour or so, it takes longer. But if I can really focus on my work, and don't get distracted by a phone call or someone in my family asking questions, I become more and more involved. After an hour of focused work, it takes much more to distract me. My writing begins to flow, I make connections and think of examples more easily, and I am much more productive. I become more and more fascinated by what I am writing about, and more interested in doing a good job. Once I become really focused, even my breaks become productive, creative times when I let my mind explore alternatives and create new ways of expressing my subject. At the end of the day, I am in a great mood, ready to interact with my family or do whatever else is on the agenda.

Fear also focuses our attention, but our focus becomes fixated on the problem, and we find it harder and harder to come up with creative solutions and alternatives. Instead of calming the mind, fear intensifies the emotional crosscurrents in the unconscious mind. Instead of synchronizing, fear is disrupting, preventing genuine concentration. What we end up with is pseudo-concentration—the conscious mind is focused, but the unconscious mind is disorganized.

All of us have experienced times when we were so worried about something that we just couldn't seem to find a way out. Then someone else comes along and says, "Why don't you do this?" The answer to our difficulties was right before our eyes, but we couldn't see it because our awareness was so limited to the problem.

Along with creating the fight-or-flight alarm reaction, fear constricts our awareness. The greater our fear, the more limited our awareness. We begin to suffer from "tunnel vision," and all we can see or think about is the problem itself. In pseudo-concentration, the body becomes tense; thinking is clouded and grows more rigid; we behave in compulsive and erratic ways; and even our physical movements become awkward, jerky, and unbalanced.

On the other hand, self-hatred prevents concentration because it takes away the energy. Depression and withdrawal significantly reduce the energy available for concentration to occur. The more depressed we feel, the harder it is to think about anything, let alone do it properly.

By eliminating fear and self-hatred and becoming interested in what we are doing, we create an entirely different condition for ourselves. The greater our concentration, the more calm and sensitive we become, and the greater the power of the mind to penetrate and understand the realities we face. The bridge between the inner world and the outer world is secure.

INTUITION: DEVELOPING INNER WISDOM

|||||||||| It is through concentration that we access and take command of our deeper, more powerful inner resources. As we refine our inner concentration, we discover the power of discrimination, the fourth dimension of the personality. You will recall from Chapter 2 that discrimination is the mind's ability to discern subtle cause/effect relationships and understand the true nature of things. In yoga science, this dimension is referred to as *buddhi*, or pure intellect.

The power of discrimination is very subtle, and involves the very core of how the mind forms knowledge. Although it is the basis for rational analysis, it is not an analytic function. This dimension of the mind is free of the limitations of time/space and pain/pleasure which shape the patterns of the sensory mind. The power of discrimination, and the knowledge it forms, is unaffected by conditioning, or habits. It is also free of the powerful influence of our emotions. Because of this, its voice is subtle and quiet, easily buried beneath the noisier, more demanding distractions of our habits and emotional reactions.

When we use the power of discrimination with the sensory function, we think things out, analyze, and make conscious decisions. The more skillfully we use our discrimination, the greater our capacity for rational thought, and the more clearly we think about things.

The real power of our pure intellect, however, lies in the fact that it is not dependent on sensory information and its limitations. Through discrimination, we discern subtle critical elements as they now exist, as well as their outcomes. We experience this as intuition, the ability to "see into the future." This is not fortune-telling, nor is it intelligent guessing, but a clear recognition of cause/effect relationships.

There are many different techniques to develop your intuition, and all depend on your ability to concentrate. When we pay attention to something, it is as though we've inserted a disk into a computer to copy a program on it. If we add extraneous data during copying, such as a computer virus, it interferes with our ability to run the program. When we are distracted, we are adding extraneous data to our inner programs. The more distractions we have, the more difficult it becomes to form accurate knowledge. The more concentrated we are, the more perfect is our knowledge.

Simply collecting information does not lead to intuitive insight. We need focused involvement—concentration—to generate relevant information. *The quality of our concentration is far more important than the amount of information we gather.* Studies of executive decision-making clearly show that successful executives can make decisions based on far less information than is available to many executives who aren't successful. Likewise, studies of scientific insight show that reverie and daydreaming are more important than the amount of information. Information is useful, but more important is our ability to discriminate and comprehend intrinsic connections and cause/ effect relationships.

An essential element to using intuition skillfully is the ability to witness the subtle thoughts and images in the mind. This is called reflective attention. Letting the mind focus in an untroubled manner on the problem, and then clearing the mind completely, allows the unconscious processes to form knowledge. Learning to listen, to focus without strain, without the struggle of "trying," takes a degree of skill. The more relaxed you are and the less troubled your mind, the greater your ability to concentrate and the more sensitive you are to your own innate intuitive wisdom.

Along with reflective attention, the following are crucial elements that help develop and enhance intuition:

- Self-Awareness: Perceptual sensitivity and skill; the ability to quiet the thought processes and become aware of the more subtle skills of the mind and body. We gain sensitivity to subtle feelings as a source of information, an awareness of the subtle thoughts that often seem to be merely passing thoughts, and an enhanced awareness of inner strength and knowledge.
- Fearlessness: A calm and tranquil mind, free of fears and anxieties; non-judgmental attitude, skilled in the practice of non-attachment. Genuine self-confidence.
- Concentration: Committed, fully involved, and concentrated on the task; inner concentration leads to direct awareness of intuitive knowledge; external concentration leads to task absorption and intuitive insight of work.
- Playfulness: Willing to experiment, learn from mistakes; creative, open to new ideas, new ways of doing things.
- Incubation Periods: Stillness is very necessary for inner awareness and developing intuitive knowledge. A busy and/or stressed mind is seldom intuitive.
- Flexibility: Physical, mental, and emotional flexibility leads to enhanced intuitive knowledge and personal effectiveness.

- Openness, Receptivity, Courage, and Love: Respecting oneself and others; compassion; a willingness to listen and learn from others; a sense of humility.

The Insight Exercise that follows is a very useful technique for developing intuitive insight. Like many exercises of this type, it involves becoming relaxed and being receptive to whatever your mind presents.

ⅢⅢⅢ INSIGHT EXERCISE ⅢⅢⅢ

Use this simple exercise after you have already come to some conclusions, but are not sure which one would be best. The key is to empty the mind completely, allowing your conscious effort to be submerged into the imagery of the exercise, clearing the mind of all conscious thoughts and concerns about the problem. The quietness of the mind will allow a greater wisdom and a new perspective to develop.

Sit back comfortably in your chair, closing your eyes and relaxing as completely as you can. Let your breath become smooth and even, and picture your forehead as smooth as a piece of silk. Now visualize a beautiful blue mountain lake, surrounded by evergreens and snowcapped mountains. Focus on the blueness of the lake, until you feel that you are completely surrounded or submerged into that blueness. Now focus your attention on the base of the largest snowcapped mountain. Imagine yourself becoming that mountain emerging from the lake. Your seat is the base of the mountain. Slowly bring your attention up to the top of your head as you visualize yourself at the snowcapped peak. Allow your arms to be the sides of the mountain. Let yourself become the mountain, with the deep blue lake before you. You feel deeply restful, at peace with yourself and the land around you.

Spend at least a few minutes just enjoying the stability, tranquillity, and peace of the mountain and the blue lake before you. After a few minutes, gently bring your attention to the problem you face, and examine the different choices you see. The best choice will most likely feel that way to you. An obvious choice may be apparent, but if not, choose the one that seems to fit with the stability and peace of your mind.

Things to Watch For

Becoming skilled with intuition takes some practice. You can be misled by subtle fears or desires, mistaking them for insight, or you can have an intelligent hunch, which is still not using your intuition. Be aware that the following factors can mislead you:

- *Not everything that we think, imagine, or feel is an intuition.* A close friend of mind woke up with a clear thought about betting on a particular horse. He kept thinking about that horse the entire morning. Finally, he rushed over to the track just in time to bet on the horse. He lost. Not everything that comes to your mind is wisdom. Maybe it's just a desire, some need or want. This is particularly difficult to distinguish when you are just beginning to develop your intuitive sense. The mind is quite capable of fooling us, as my friend who bet on the wrong horse found out. You can quickly train yourself to differentiate between real intuition and everything else by taking notes. Every time you think that you have an intuition, write it down. Note everything that you observe about the intuition—how you felt; whether it was an image, thought, or feeling; what was your reaction; how strong or clear it seemed. Then, later on, indicate whether or not it was accurate, and note any benefit you gained from the insight. This forces you to pay attention, and it's your attention that will develop your sensitivity to genuine insight.
- *Imagery may not be clear.* Because the images that come from our unconscious are almost always symbolic, they must be interpreted and understood in context. Always cross-check your understanding of your insights by checking out how it feels to your body. Was the insight comfortable or uncomfortable? Was there an emotional component? If so, be careful. True insight is free of emotional content, and feels like a simple statement of fact. We may get excited after the insight, but the insight itself is characteristically clear. We can often validate whatever thoughts and images the mind generates by consulting our feelings about them.
- *Intuition does not always give a complete answer.* Often, intuition only points us in the right direction. We will not always know how things will turn out. But if we continue to pay attention as we act on our insights, we can self-correct and can take advantage of new insights and developments. Periodically check your feelings and thoughts about your direction. This helps keep you on the right track, even when your intuition is incomplete and partial.

It isn't difficult to develop your power of discrimination and intuition. It simply takes practice. A number of excellent books, such as Philip Goldberg's *The*

Intuitive Edge and Frances Vaughan's *Awakening Intuition,* provide a variety of techniques to help access your intuition.

Developing Concentration

||||||||||| There are a number of ways to develop concentration. One way to start is by using the body to train the mind. There are good reasons for this. First, we are usually more familiar and more comfortable working with the body than with the mind. Second, the body *needs* exercise and stretching to minimize muscle tension and maximize flexibility. At the same time we are minimizing stress in the body, we can be training the mind in concentration. Again, Eastern traditions lead the way in using the body to develop concentration.

Traditional schools of martial arts, such as karate, tai chi chuan, and Aikido, use the body and breathing to train concentration skills. A traditional approach focuses on self-development through concentration and self-discipline. True martial arts are built on self-respect and respect for others. The training develops mind and body as a way of eliminating fear and developing an awareness of the underlying unity of life.

The most sophisticated approach to using the body to train the mind is hatha yoga. The postures are designed to work with the body to expand awareness of both mind and body. It systematically proceeds from physical exercises to breathing exercises to mental exercises—all to achieve a higher level of awareness. In particular, the balancing postures, which require your full attention to accomplish, help refine your concentration.

The best way to develop concentration is to use what is most natural to the mind. That's why Breath Awareness is such a useful tool. Sitting quietly, focusing on the feeling of the breath, and not allowing your attention to wander is a very simple way of training concentration. We are using kinesthetic sense to train the mind to be one-pointed. But you don't have to sit still to use Breath Awareness to help you focus. The practical usefulness of this tool is that anyone can use it at any time or anywhere.

Twelve-year-old Sam has learned to use his breathing to focus his mind during basketball. Like his two older sisters, Sam loves to play basketball. Very early in his life, Sam was taught how to use his breathing to focus his attention. When he was five years old, he also began training in Washin-Ryu karate. Because of his karate training, Sam has a great deal of poise and balance. When he plays basketball, he is aggressive, good at defense, and rebounds very well. His shooting skills, however, weren't quite as developed.

About halfway through this past basketball season, Sam discovered that he could use breathing and concentration to improve shooting foul shots. Normally, Sam would make only about 50 percent of his foul shots. Now when he comes to the line, you can see him briefly close his eyes, focus on his breath awareness, and then concentrate on the ball going through. His foul-shooting average has shot up to over 85 percent. This change has given Sam a great deal of confidence in his ability to solve any problem through concentration. He brings this same concentration to his homework, to the woodworking he loves to do, and even to video games.

We, too, can use our vision. Since we depend so heavily on the sense of sight, it is a natural tool for training the mind. In yoga science, this is called *trateka*, or gazes. When we hold a gaze, the eyes are not allowed to move off the target object or even blink, and the body is very still. We focus all of our attention on the object, ignoring all thoughts and sensations, until our eyes begin to water or our concentration is involuntarily broken by blinking. At that point, we can close our eyes and rest, or visualize the object internally.

One of the simplest exercises is the Candle Gaze. We can use the natural attraction of light to strengthen our concentration. We can either focus directly on the flame or gaze at a reflection of the flame in a mirror. Direct light creates a heating sensation in the eyes, while indirect or reflected light creates a cooling sensation. If you are light sensitive, you may wish to use reflected light. The goal is to slowly increase your capacity to gaze at the light without blinking or distraction for increasingly longer periods of time. Don't wear glasses or contact lenses when you practice a gaze.

From Power to Wisdom

Where there is peace and meditation,
there is neither anxiety nor doubt.
                    —St. Francis of Assisi

Concentration leads to a powerful mind. But even a powerful mind can be tormented by loneliness and grief. We must take the final step and use our power to live with inner strength and wisdom. We cannot escape from ourselves through power, but we can use it to discover the spiritual Self. We must find a way to live in today's world with strength—a way in which we can stay balanced, use our power to fulfill our obligations and desires, and use our wisdom to create the joy, peace, and fulfillment we know is possible.

We are citizens of two worlds: our external reality and our inner reality. To be effective in both without destroying ourselves in the process, we must bridge

⊔⊔⊔⊔⊔⊔⊔⊔⊔ CANDLE GAZE EXERCISE ⊔⊔⊔⊔⊔⊔⊔⊔⊔

Do this exercise in a dark, quiet room. The candle should be an even-burning dinner candle, placed approximately an arm's length in front of you. The flame should be level with your eyes so you can hold your head steady and gaze straight ahead. To use reflected light, place the candle behind you so that you see the reflection in a mirror directly in front of you, at the proper height.

1. Sit quietly, and for a few moments close your eyes and focus on Breath Awareness to clear your mind and steady your concentration.

2. Open your eyes and gaze without blinking at this steady flame (or reflection). If you blink very soon after beginning the gaze, ignore it and continue to gaze. Focus your attention on the flame, ignoring all other thoughts, sensations, and feelings. Keep your gaze steady and unblinking.

3. When you blink, or your eyes begin to water, stop the external gaze. Close your eyes and visualize the flame in the center of your mind as long as you comfortably can. The smaller, clearer, and more defined the image of the flame, the better the training for concentration. Don't worry if at first the image of the flame is undefined or vague. With practice, the image will become clearer and more defined. By internalizing the image, you change the exercise from a concentration exercise (external orientation) to a meditation exercise (internal orientation).

Keep a daily practice, and let your capacity slowly expand until you can hold the external gaze for at least 20 minutes. If, at any time, you get a headache, reduce the time you spend gazing. Headaches are an indication that you are pushing too hard and going beyond your natural capacity. After reaching this 20-minute capacity, maintain at least a weekly practice of 20 minutes. You might notice an increase in both the intensity of your dreams and your ability to recall them.

these two worlds successfully. We can do this if we develop our inner strength and utilize our deepest resources. But we must use all of the mind, not just part. Once we know how to create inner balance and power, we must continue to expand our awareness, discover our more subtle resources—intrinsic wisdom, genuine self-confidence, and the unlimited power of the spiritual Self—and become skilled in using the innate power of our mind and spirit.

Meditation creates this bridge between internal and external reality. It is the finest tool we can use to develop awareness of our inner strengths and the resources of the mind. It is a practical, systematic method based on refined concentration that allows us to

- become aware of and understand all dimensions of our personality;
- understand our environment completely, without emotional bias;
- eliminate and prevent inner conflicts, distortions, and disturbances;
- create an alert, tranquil mind that is fearless, joyful, and compassionate.

Meditation is not an act of magic, but a process to access and refine the power of the mind. If we systematically develop and command this power, we can use it to achieve whatever we choose, and do it without creating unhappiness, stress, and disease.

Meditation: Misperceptions and Misapprehensions

|||||||||| In the past twenty years or so, much of the silliness first attached to the term "meditation" has dissipated. Still, many people think of meditation as strange and foreign, and are misinformed about what it is, prejudiced about its origins, and ignorant of its power and simplicity. They often associate it with a foreign religion, or funny-looking people who have shaved heads and wear orange-colored clothes, or people trying to float in the air. Others simply confuse meditation with hypnosis, or closing the eyes and fantasizing about New Age angels, guides, and other spirits. Unfortunately, many of those who practice, and even teach, meditation have only fragmentary knowledge about it.

One of the most common mistakes is to confuse meditation and religion. Meditation is not a religion, nor is it a philosophy. It is a tool that has been used by all major religions, including Christianity, as well as by agnostics and atheists. Likewise, meditation has no intrinsic link with any particular culture. Meditative techniques are found in all areas of the world. Eastern methods, particularly yoga, have been more completely and systematically developed than others, and thus they often serve as models.

Many people mistakenly think of meditation as a kind of trance state or hypnosis. It is neither, although all three share one basic characteristic—you must be relaxed to do them. The similarity stops there. In trance states, you lose awareness as you surrender to a sensual experience. In order to be hypnotized, you must focus your attention on a suggestion (either your own or the hypnotist's) and comply with it. Unfortunately, most of us are already hypnotized, in the sense that we are always following others' suggestions (we call it peer pressure or advertising).

Meditation, on the other hand, is a process of *conscious observation,* a condition of heightened awareness; it is self-directed and can never be other-directed. Concentration on a single point such as the breath, or a mantra, should not be confused with suggestion, for suggestion implies action taken. Observation means only observing—there is no judgment or action. The difference between observation and suggestion is like the difference between watching a particular horse (observation) and getting up on the horse and riding away with it (hypnosis) or focusing on the pleasure of the ride (trance). They are different actions, and they have radically different outcomes.

In hypnosis you surrender control to the suggestion, and in trance you surrender to the feelings. In meditation you expand conscious self-control and awareness. Research shows that you gain no significant changes, either physically or psychologically, after the long-term practice of hypnosis, other than what you can achieve by simply practicing relaxation.* On the other hand, if you practice meditation over a period of time, you significantly reduce the physiological parameters of stress and significantly increase psychological maturity. New hypnotic techniques now blend observation and hypnosis and appear to approach the meditative state. However, if suggestion is followed, it is still hypnosis and thus limited in scope and power. Only when you change your perspective from involvement with the hypnotic suggestion to pure observation will meditation occur.

Meditation and drug use are not at all compatible. So-called teachers who advocate the use of psychedelic drugs to enhance meditation are ignorant of the meditative process. Drugs don't expand awareness, they explode it, and the collapse which inevitably follows leads to confusion rather than clarity. Meditation is a systematic, controlled expansion of consciousness that takes place totally under your own control. Drugs are antithetical to the development of self-control and lead ultimately to internal chaos.

---

*Changes resulting from hypnosis are specific to the hypnotic suggestion only, and are not lasting. This includes the use of hypnosis as a part of therapy, for in this case hypnotherapy is part of the overall process that induces personality change.

Another common misconception concerns the lifestyle necessary to do meditation. First of all, meditation does not create instantaneous personality change. Change occurs naturally as we become healthier and more mature, and we make better choices for ourselves. There is no meditative profession or lifestyle, but there are lifestyles which will prevent you from meditating. These also prevent you from growing in any direction. Meditation is as useful to the executive as it is to the plumber, and to the housewife, and to the student. Meditation is a tool; it is not a way of life. Everyone can benefit from it. Not everyone will (or can) utilize the same form of meditation, but there are many different methods—and they all work. The tool can be adapted to any personality with any reasonable lifestyle, at any time.

Finally, there is a confusion between meditation and certain brain-wave patterns. Many people, especially research professionals, associate meditation with particular brain patterns, such as alpha or alpha/theta brain waves. Researchers identify certain brain waves that arise when you sit quietly with your eyes closed, focusing your attention inwardly. The psychological states of reverie produced during alpha and theta waves, as beneficial as they are, are not necessarily part of meditation. They are generally desirable states, associated with creativity, inner balance, and peacefulness, and produce healthy and beneficial outcomes. *But meditation is not a psychological state or a physiological event*; it is a *conscious process* which leads to a fourth state of consciousness beyond the three familiar states of waking, dreaming, and sleeping. Highly skilled meditators can meditate in any of the three states, including deep sleep. Meditation is a process which involves expanded awareness and a condition of high potential energy created through concentration. These conditions are not dependent on any particular brain-wave pattern.

Meditation as Refined Concentration: Creating the Laser Mind

||||||||||| So what is meditation? In three words, it is *refined inner concentration*. If you understand why concentration is so important, it is easy to see why meditation is such a critical tool. By intensifying our concentration, we create an even more powerful state of mind. As we refine our skill, we synchronize more and more of the mind's energy until we are deeply concentrated. Now the mind becomes like a laser, burning away the remaining distractions. Any distractions left are inactive, and no longer influence the mind.

We make our conscious mind strong through the discipline of deep concentration. We have seen how our unconscious emotional habits and patterns can create fear and other problems for us. But they have little power against the "laser-strong" power of a trained conscious mind. This is the consequence of the practice of meditation.

This refined state of concentration is not easily achieved. Nor is it something that anyone else can do for you. Like any skill, it takes effort and practice. But neither is it something magical or esoteric. It is practical, available to anyone who puts forth the effort, and requires only sincere effort and the right techniques. It does not require a college degree, a particular religious belief, or subservience to a teacher.

The Elements of Meditation

|||||||||| Relaxation, often confused with meditation, is only the first step toward meditation. It is a very important step, however, for unless mind and body are relaxed, concentration becomes difficult and meditation is impossible. Of course, the more concentrated you become, the more relaxed you become.

Proper breathing is another critical element in meditation. We know that we must breathe with our diaphragm if we want to balance our autonomic nervous system and eliminate stress. But there are more subtle aspects of breathing that are important if we want to refine our concentration. We must also create balance between the activity of the two hemispheres of the brain. This balance is indicated by an even, steady flow of breath through both nostrils. Recall from Chapter 6 that ordinarily we breathe primarily through one nostril, and that nostril dominance shifts on a cyclic basis. When the flow of breath is even through both nostrils, we create balance between the two hemispheres of the brain. This balance is necessary if we are to deepen concentration. This is the application of *sushumna* mentioned in Chapter 6, without which meditation cannot occur. With a little effort, we can learn to consciously control the flow of air. The Alternate-Nostril Breathing Exercise given in Chapter 6 develops our ability to consciously control nostril balance.

After we calm the body, stabilize the breath, and create complete neurological balance, the next step is to calm and focus the mind through inner concentration. This final element in the process of developing meditation is often mistaken for meditation itself. In yoga science, inner concentration is the necessary stage before meditation and, if properly developed, leads to meditation.*

---

*Most of the research on "meditative" states has really been made on inner concentration, not meditation. This does not deny the usefulness of the research, it only points out an incomplete state of knowledge about meditation.

Most of us can concentrate to some degree if we focus on an object or event in the external world. We can concentrate on our work, our play, or a book, particularly if it captures our interest. But if we have to concentrate on an internal process, most of us quickly find that we have little capacity for it. We are a determinedly materialistic culture, focused almost exclusively on what our senses tell us. Our culture is not familiar with the inner world, nor does it encourage much exploration. Our education and training involve the external world of facts, figures, and objects. We are taught to study the objects of our senses but not the filter mechanism—the mind in which the sensory data are collected, organized, and given meaning. It is no wonder that we can focus easily on the external world but find it difficult to do so inwardly.

When we first try to meditate, we find we have very little skill. Our attention is pulled here and there by competing thoughts and feelings, and we seem to have very little conscious control. For instance, if we are worried about something, the mind returns to the problem over and over, generating even more fear. When we want to sleep, the mind chatters on and on, preventing us from falling asleep. The harder we try to focus, the more insistent the disturbances become. All of us suffer from this monkey mind to some degree. Very few of us have the ability to choose the focus of the mind, to choose what and when to think. As a consequence, very few experience genuine tranquillity and calmness.

Remember, control doesn't mean that we suppress or repress our thoughts. This only leads to even greater dis-ease and stress. Real control is the ability to consciously choose which thoughts we think and how to use our emotional energy. As we saw in Chapter 7, we begin this process of choice by controlling the inner dialogue of the mind.

But our ability to choose depends on how aware we are of our habits and other patterns in the mind. This awareness comes from the ability to focus the attention, to concentrate on an inner point. If we aren't skilled at inner concentration, we will have little ability to choose which thoughts and feelings we want. Our choices will be made from our unconscious habits and emotional reactions. As we become more and more skilled in meditation, as we focus our attention on one thought, image, or sound, all others are brought under control and become quiet.

Meditation expands our inner awareness. Picture the mind as a very large, very hard block of ice. We can easily see what's on the surface and just below the surface of this block of ice. But the deeper we go, the less we can see. This is the same with the mind. The conscious mind is what we are aware of at any moment. We are also aware of thoughts, feelings, and memories that are just below our normal awareness. But the deeper parts of the mind remain unknown to us. We have a sense that something is there—emotional habits, knowledge, feelings—but we aren't conscious of what that something is or how it affects us. This unknown part of our mind we call the unconscious mind.

Like the deeper part of the mind, we can't see into the center of this large block of ice. We know something is buried in the center, but we can't quite see what it is. In order to get to the object buried in the ice, we must break through it. If we take a flat, wide board and beat on the ice, the force of the blow is dispersed over the flat surface, and we have very little power to penetrate the hard ice. It is the same with the mind. We have very little power to penetrate the unconscious because our attention is distracted by all sorts of thoughts, feelings, sensory inputs, and reactions. On the other hand, if we use a sharp ice pick so that all the force of the blow is focused on a single point, we can very quickly break through to the buried object. If we train our concentration to be one-pointed, like the ice pick, we can penetrate our unconscious and become aware of our habits.

We often speak of the unconscious mind as if there were no way to directly apprehend or understand it. Western psychiatry and psychology, with their focus on pathology, have instilled in us a fear of the unconscious that is both unreasonable and ill-founded. Our so-called unconscious mind is not out of reach of conscious awareness. In reality, "unconscious" simply means that we haven't paid attention. We can indeed begin to know the total mind, with all of its habits and talents, if we use our attention to penetrate it. This is the task of inner concentration and meditation.

If you want to understand your spiritual Self, there is no alternative to inner concentration, to sitting very quietly, still and focused. Systematic methods for training inner concentration and meditation are given below. Once you become skilled in relaxation, you shouldn't spend more than five minutes on this preliminary stage. The more time you devote to training your power of inner concentration, the better. The concentration itself will lead to deeper relaxation, and as you become more focused and develop greater awareness, your ability to command your inner resources increases. More important, as you become more skilled in inner concentration, you are preparing yourself to use the most sophisticated tool for self-knowledge and self-control available—meditation.

Meditation: Pathway to Freedom

|||||||||| Meditation is not a state or a condition, but a process by which we achieve ever deeper levels of awareness. According to the Masters of yoga science, meditation is a technical term indicating a highly refined inner process.

Meditation is a continuous stream of effortless concentration, on a single point, over an extended period of time.

The phrase *continuous stream* indicates an uninterrupted flow of concentration. Your attention never wavers or wanders. This also characterizes your breath, which must flow evenly, without pause. Pauses and stops in your breath actually reflect pauses and halts in the mental processes going on in your mind. Uneven breathing means uneven attention. The entire process of meditation is directly related to an even, steady flow of breath. Until you have learned breath control through Diaphragmatic Breathing and Breath Awareness, you cannot meditate.

Effortless concentration defines the quality of the inner concentration — the flow of concentration must be effortless, without any struggle. If there is a struggle, if you are *trying* to meditate, you aren't. For example, you are concentrating on the breath and suddenly your mind begins to wander off. You immediately restrain the mind and bring your attention back to the breath. The very effort required to refocus your concentration prevents meditation from occurring. Meditation is not thinking about meditation, or trying to do meditation; it is the process of the concentration flow itself. The word *effortless* also points to another difference between concentration and meditation. Concentration evolves into meditation when the faculty of attention is so highly trained that effort is no longer required to focus it.

The next phrase, *on a single point,* means that the mind does not wander here and there but remains focused on the object of observation. This is more difficult than you might suspect. Try for a few moments to concentrate on only the word *blue.* What happens? If you observe carefully, you will see all sorts of thoughts come into your mind, associations based upon the word *blue.* Or you might have felt an itch somewhere on your body, or moved in order to get more comfortable. It takes time and practice to create single-minded, one-pointed concentration, and gain mastery over the wandering mind.

The phrase *on a single point* also differentiates between meditation and contemplation. In contemplation you focus on a word or concept and then attempt to understand and experience it in all its aspects. The mind is trained to fully understand its core meaning as well as all its relational meanings. In the meditation process, on the other hand, all relational (and, of course, nonrelational) aspects of your focus point are purposefully and systematically excluded. You do not "think about" anything. You focus only on the one thought, image, or sensation in order to make your concentration one-pointed.

Finally, the phrase *over an extended period of time* indicates that the flow of effortless, uninterrupted, and one-pointed concentration must be more than momentary. Concentration must be unbroken and maintained for some time. This is difficult; even two or three minutes is quite an accomplishment.

Don't be alarmed or discouraged about how difficult this might seem. It takes time and effort to develop and refine your power of inner concentration, but the dividends are great. The journey itself is rewarding and brings about many of the changes you need to achieve self-mastery. If you look upon the practice of inner concentration and meditation as an investment in personal growth, then you minimize both your impatience and discouragement.

As you become more skilled with inner concentration, it slowly expands itself into meditation. Even as a beginner, you will have rewarding moments. And the process is evolutionary. The more skilled you become, the more benefits you have and the better you feel. When your skill becomes sufficient, and your inner concentration becomes effortless, unbroken, and sustained, then you will feel the full power of meditation. You will have no question about whether or not you are meditating; the process is complete in and of itself. You will know through your own experience.

The Two Forms of Meditation

|||||||||| There are an infinite variety of meditation techniques, but there are only two basic forms of meditation—inclusive and exclusive—which are like two sides of a coin. We use these terms for categorical convenience, as both involve concentration and observation. The primary difference lies in the focal points.

The exclusive form of meditation is what most people think about when they hear the word *meditate*. To become skilled at meditation, your mind must first become still and calm. To accomplish this requires consistent daily practice—sitting quietly, closing the eyes, and bringing full attention to the flow of the breath, then to a particular center, and then observing the flow of your mind chatter. Sitting quietly, with eyes closed, you focus your concentration on a single point. When other thoughts, feelings, and sensations arise, you simply allow them to pass and return your attention to the focus point. In this way you gradually train your mind to remain focused on a single point.

There are three types of content in the mind: thoughts, images, and sensations. Any one of these can serve as the focus point. In meditative traditions, when thoughts are used as the focus point they are called *mantras*. A mantra is a syllable, sound, word, or set of words that has a particular effect on the mind. Different sounds create different effects. When you are initiated into a particular meditative tradition, the mantra is chosen by the teacher to fit your particular nature. All mantras calm the mind and allow your awareness to penetrate into deeper levels of the mind at a gentle, controlled rate. As you become more aware of the subtle dimensions of your mind, you gain access to their powerful functions, such as your intuition and inner strength.

Images serve as another focus point for meditation. Light is a common focus point in all meditative traditions because the human mind has a natural affinity for it. If you are walking down a street and someone strikes a match or shines a light, it immediately draws your attention. We can use this natural affinity to train the mind in meditation. Still another focus point is a sensation, such as Breath Awareness, focusing attention on the feeling of the breath as it passes in and out of the nostrils. As you concentrate more deeply on Breath Awareness, you gradually become aware of more subtle sensations, until you achieve awareness of the energy (prana, chi, or ki) within the breath.

You must use care in choosing a focus point because many can lead to negative states. Not all thoughts are beneficial, nor are all sensations and images helpful. An anxious person concentrates on his thoughts, but they only lead to more compulsiveness, pain, and suffering. Concentration on the wrong images can easily lead to fear. All of us know someone who concentrates on the wrong sensations—like the hypochondriacs who take hours to answer the question "How are you?" In all meditative traditions, such as yoga science, the mantras, images, and sensations have been researched and verified for their usefulness for thousands of years. They are carefully selected for their known benefit to the meditator.

Meditation in Action

|||||||||| In inclusive meditation, the focus point is the stream of consciousness itself. No object, perception, thought, feeling, or image is excluded. All the activities of the mind are included in the observational field. The critical factor here is that you as the observer remain an observer. You don't allow yourself to be caught up in the mind's events. Everything that happens in the mind is noted with the same neutral equanimity that you would experience when watching the flow of water under a bridge. When you get caught by a thought or emotion, then concentration is broken.

You get caught when you identify yourself with the thought or emotion. Instead of observing the mind feeling anger, and noting it, "I" get angry. Of course, once "I" get angry, "I" also experience all the feelings, disturbances, and tension that accompany the anger. Instead of remaining calm, "I" get excited and upset. By losing awareness, by no longer remaining a witness, you become the emotion and must travel with it wherever it goes.

The primary tool for meditation in action is Breath Awareness. The purpose of meditation in action is to gain complete knowledge of the mind and its contents, and to place yourself in a position of choice rather than be controlled by the mind's compulsive habits. By remaining an observer, you can actually experience what the mind is doing. You don't have to figure it out, the mind presents it to you directly. It's like sitting on a fence watching the horses in a corral. If you continue to sit on the fence, eventually you will see all of the horses in the corral as they come by. In this way, you will come to know the entire contents of the corral. But if you become attracted to a particular horse, jump on that horse and ride away, you no longer see the other horses in the corral. By learning to watch the mind, you will eventually know its patterns and habits. This gives you a greater opportunity for choice.

Both inclusive meditation and exclusive meditation are needed if we want to understand the power of the mind and use it effectively. If the mind is cleared for thirty minutes each day with exclusive concentration, then muddied up with uncontrolled or habitual reactions for the next twenty-three and a half hours, the odds of developing powers of self-mastery are not favorable. But if we practice both forms of meditation, we gradually develop the skill to maintain equanimity for those twenty-three and a half hours. Then the thirty minutes of deep, one-pointed concentration quickly evolves into meditation, and we access the power of the mind and spirit.

Learning to Meditate: Methods and Techniques

||||||||||| Many effective techniques train the mind and open the door to our inner resources. We already have the basics—relaxation, Diaphragmatic Breathing, and Breath Awareness. Now we need to learn how to enhance our concentration and develop the skills which lead directly to meditation.

Many of the techniques we have already learned, such as "61 Points," can easily be used to develop concentration. After several months of practice, the Alternate-Nostril Breathing Exercise (Chapter 6) can evolve into a sophisticated Breath Awareness exercise. To do this, you stop using the fingers to control the flow of breath and use only your mind. This takes some skill and practice, but it is a powerful technique for enhancing concentration. The simplest concentration exercise is Breath Awareness. It is easily used, and will reinforce your skill for meditation in action.

Success Insurance: Knowing How to Practice

|||||||||| The purpose of practice is to gain skill. We want to become skilled human beings, in control of our resources. Trying to use the mind in a sophisticated way without a systematic approach involving all dimensions of the personality is like trying to play championship tennis without learning how to serve. All concentration and meditation practices should be done very systematically. We build success from preparation. The stronger the foundation, the easier it is to develop the power of the mind. Following are a number of foundation builders that we must consider:

1. *Commitment—Dedicating Time to Personal Growth and Development*: Find and dedicate one fifteen-minute period a day to developing your internal skills. It should be a time, and place, when no one will disturb you. Early morning is an excellent time to practice. Your mind is fresh and rested, and concentration is easier. However, any time that is free of distraction and allows you to practice regularly is fine. Avoid times when you are tired or have just finished eating. Concentration takes energy and alertness, and if you are tired or digesting food, you will not be very successful in your efforts.

2. *Start from a Position of Balance:* Concentration requires a mind free from worries, anxieties, and fears. If you are uptight or upset, it is difficult to clear your mind and focus your attention. Practice relaxation and diaphragmatic breathing before each meditation session. The more skilled you become at relaxation and inner balance, the easier it is to increase your power of concentration. Once you are skilled, never spend more than a maximum of five minutes practicing relaxation. The time is far better spent in concentration exercises.

3. *Use the Correct Posture:* Posture can either facilitate or interfere with concentration. If you slump while seated, or walk with your shoulders hunched, it creates a neurological imbalance and interferes with diaphragmatic breathing. All of this creates noise in the mind. For practicing concentration, the most helpful posture is an erect, seated one, with the head, neck and trunk in proper alignment. A natural S curve of the spine keeps the trunk of the body erect without any muscle tension. This upright posture allows you to breathe easily with the diaphragm, properly aligns the neural pathways of the spine, and allows the muscles of the upper body to relax. With few exceptions, such as the "61 Points" exercise, always practice concentration in this erect, seated posture.

4. *Make Transitions Gently:* Whenever you close your eyes to practice an inner exercise—relaxation, imagery, concentration, or meditation—do not open your eyes abruptly when you are finished. Doing so creates a subtle shock for the nervous system, similar to awakening to a shrill alarm clock. The sudden rush of sensory data to the mind also creates a momentary confusion. In-

stead, before opening your eyes, slowly bring your hands up, being aware of every movement from the inside out. Then, holding the palms of your hands about four inches from your face, open your eyes to the palms of your hands. This eases the transition from one level of awareness to the other, and prevents any shock to your nervous system.

Breath Awareness as a Meditation Exercise

|||||||||| As mentioned above, Breath Awareness can also be an effective concentration technique. To practice, close your eyes and sit in the erect, seated posture. Relax the body and focus the mind by using the Alternate-Nostril Breathing Exercise (page 155). Then focus your attention on the feeling of the breath as it enters and leaves the nostrils. For the first few moments, just center your attention on Breath Awareness. Then, by paying attention to the feeling of the breath going in and out of the nostrils, determine the dominant, or open, nostril. This is the one through which the air flows most easily. Don't use your fingers; use only your sensitivity to determine which nostril is dominant. After determining the dominant nostril, focus your attention on it for several breaths.

Now switch your attention to the passive, or closed, nostril, the one where the air flow is blocked or diminished. Concentrate on this nostril until you begin to feel the air moving freely through it, and it becomes the dominant nostril. After the air flows freely through this nostril for several breaths, bring your attention back to the first nostril, the one originally open. When you begin to feel the air flow freely through this first nostril, shift your attention to the center between both nostrils. Concentrate on the air flowing freely through both. (Remember, air flowing freely through both nostrils indicates complete balance in the autonomic nervous system and between the hemispheres of the brain. During this time, your concentration can deepen and intensify.)

Whenever your mind wanders to thoughts or other distractions, bring your attention back to the feeling of the breath. Sit very still, maintaining this focus, for as long as you comfortably can. When you are ready to finish, gently wriggle your toes and fingers. Slowly raise your hands to your face. Holding the hands about four inches from your face, open your eyes to the palms of your hands.

A Meditation Practice

‖‖‖‖‖‖‖‖ Once you become skilled in using Breath Awareness, shift the focus point from the breath to a deeper mental image. You can begin by using the image of a candle flame as a focus point. The Candle Gaze (page 209) will help develop this focus point because it is a concentration exercise. After a few minutes, close your eyes and visualize the flame in the center of your mind, directly behind the point between your eyebrows. Creating an internal image turns this concentration exercise into a meditation exercise.

Using the flame is often a good way to begin practicing meditation. But eventually, after several months of practice, learn to use a thought as the focus point. This leads you to the most subtle levels of your mind. When using a thought as the concentration point, the key is to learn how to *listen* to the thought, and not "think" it. The thought becomes a sound of the mind. Listening trains your power of observation as well as your power of concentration. When you become skilled at observation, concentration becomes effortless and evolves into meditation.

You can use the sound of your breath to provide a useful, neutral thought. If you listen carefully to your breath, you can hear the sound of "So" on the inhalation and "Hum" on the exhalation. Converting these sounds to thought, focus on the thought "So" during the inhalation and "Hum" during the exhalation. These two thought forms, So and Hum, are neutral to the mind, and free of any unconscious associations. They provide a useful focus point for training the mind even at the most subtle levels of the unconscious.

We will break the meditation exercise into two parts. The first is a Centering Exercise which brings you to the fifth dimension of the mind, the balanced mind, a center of quietness and stillness. Centering is a crucial step in meditation, but it can also be used as a first step in a number of different exercises, such as regaining self-confidence and resolving emotional conflicts with others. The second consists of a meditation exercise using the words *So* and *Hum* as the mantra.

When you first begin, you will be thinking *So* and *Hum*. After some months of practicing, learn to *listen* to the mind think instead of doing the thinking yourself. In this way, you train yourself to become the observer of what the mind *does* instead of being the one who thinks.

Sit for as long as you comfortably can, letting your own capacity be the determining factor. But do so on a daily basis, for regularity is essential in order for you to increase your capacity. It will also help if you select a specific time, and do your practice at that time every day. This helps establish the habit of sitting to meditate, and the time becomes associated with a relaxed, peaceful state of

|||||||||| CENTERING EXERCISE ||||||||||

Begin this exercise in the erect, seated position with your eyes closed. For the first few moments, mentally scan the body, relaxing any tension you may find. Then for a few minutes, practice Breath Awareness until you feel both nostrils open. After a few moments of concentrating on both nostrils flowing freely, follow the next inhalation up as if you are following it into the center of your mind. It is as if you are turning your eyes inward and looking toward the very center of your brain. Then picture yourself sitting in the middle of the mind, watching the body breathe around you. At this point, experience the body like a shell around you. After a few more moments, be aware of the center of the mind, and the inner space around it. Notice that there is an inner space where thoughts, images, and sensations seem to be, and an outer space, outside the skin of your body. Your body is like the dividing line between the outer space and this inner space.

Within this inner space, you will find a center of quietness. When you become aware of this center, your body will become effortlessly still, and the mind very calm. You will notice that thoughts, images, and sensations seem to revolve around this center, but within the center itself it is very quiet and peaceful. Enjoy this calm center for a few moments. Learn to watch the thoughts and other activities passing by. You are only the observer, the witness to these activities of your mind. Don't get involved in thinking, just observe, and enjoy the calmness of this center. Whenever you find yourself being distracted, come back to this calm center.

mind. If you have difficulty using a mantra, use the Candle Flame or Breath Awareness as your focus point.

With these exercises you can begin practicing inner concentration. If you practice them systematically and consistently, you will find them very effective. It is very helpful to find a competent teacher or guide, and learn the basics of meditation. An experienced, skilled teacher can point out the pitfalls and provide the fundamental skills and tools you need to refine the process. Remem-

############ **MEDITATION EXERCISE** ############

When you are centered, bring your focus of concentration either to the space between the two eyes, the mind center, or to the space between the two breasts, the heart center. If you are more intellectual than emotional, you should center your focus on the mind center. If you are more emotional than intellectual, you should focus your concentration on the heart center. Either concentration or focus should be on the space within the body, not on the surface skin area. Now focus your attention on the sound of the breath. On the inhalation you will hear the thought (sound) of *So*, on the exhalation the thought (sound) of *Hum*. Try to focus on exactly where the thought arises in your focus space (mind center or heart center). Don't try to anticipate or remember, but stay focused on the thought itself as it exists at this moment. All sorts of thoughts will come to your mind. Let them come and go. Whenever you find your thoughts wandering, or off on a tangent, bring your attention back to the *So* and *Hum*. Don't struggle or fight with your mind, simply come back to the focus point.

When you are ready to finish, direct your attention to the flow of breath through the inner space of your body. Follow the next exhalation out the nostrils, and focus your attention on the feeling of the breath for a few moments. Now wriggle your toes and fingers gently. Slowly, being aware of every inner movement of the body, bring your hands up to your face. Holding your hands approximately four inches from the face, open your eyes. The first thing you should see are the palms of your hands. Maintain the inner calm and stillness you feel as long as possible throughout the day.

ber, though, that your goal is independence and freedom. A teacher or guide cannot do your meditation for you, nor can the teacher be responsible for your health, your choices, or your life. Only you can do that. *You must take your own response ability!*

Practical Applications

||||||||| During meditation, don't try to solve problems or work out personal is-sues. Keep meditation reserved only for meditation, concentrating on your focus point. As you become more skilled, you will find that the practical bene-fits of meditation happen outside of the meditation process. But you can and should use the Centering Exercise for a number of different inner-work exer-cises, such as creative problem solving, imagery exercises to develop insight and intuition, and even conflict management. One of the most powerful appli-cations is to use it to resolve disputes and conflicts that leave you feeling upset and disturbed. The steps are very direct and simple. The key to using centering as an effective conflict tool is to remember that you cannot control someone else's behavior, but you have unlimited opportunities to choose other behaviors for yourself.

You can use the Centering Exercise in a number of different ways. The more you use it, the more skilled you become. But it cannot and should not re-place the consistent practice of meditation. Without the refined concentration established by the practice of meditation, the Centering Exercise lacks power and effectiveness. The effectiveness of centering *depends* on the quality of your concentration. The most important example of this relationship between med-itation and centering is found in the access and use of our innate self-confi-dence.

Unlimited Confidence

||||||||| Underlying much of our fear and unhappiness is a subtle lack of self-con-fidence. We hold ourselves back, feel anxious, delay decisions, avoid difficul-ties, accept unnecessary limitations—all because of self-doubt. When push comes to shove, most of us lack genuine self-confidence. Even those who ap-pear confident, when faced with the possibilities of failure—losing their job, not making enough money, having their boyfriend or girlfriend "fall in love" with someone else—are racked with anxiety, indecision, and self-doubt.

Most of us build self-confidence by being successful in the world. As long as we are successful, we feel confident. But what happens when we aren't suc-cessful? By depending on success, we depend on what happens in the world around us. No matter how much effort we expend, we can never control all the events in the world around us. No one can ever be certain that they will suc-ceed. So we are building confidence on a bed of shifting sand. Even when it

Use the Centering Exercise to establish a calm, clear mind after being drawn into a conflict situation that was not resolved and left you feeling angry and/or upset. Once centered, you can use the calmness of your mind and your ability to observe to minimize your emotional disturbance and find effective ways to achieve your goals. Two principles are involved:

- First, when we operate from a clear, calm mind, we operate from our strength. When we are emotionally upset, we operate from weakness.
- Second, it is far easier to create options for your own behavior than to try to change the behavior of another. By changing your behavior, you create different outcomes.

When you find yourself upset owing to a conflict situation, take the following steps:

1. *Centering Exercise:* Find a quiet time and do the Centering Exercise (page 223) to create a calm, clear mind free of any emotional upset.

2. *Observe:* Once you are centered, re-create the situation in your mind. Observe both your behavior and the other person's behavior with a clear sense of detachment. If you feel any emotional hook as you review the incident, return to your Breath Awareness and repeat the Centering Exercise until your mind is calm and clear. Then again review the incident. Continue to re-center yourself whenever necessary until you can review the entire incident without any emotional attachment and without any judgment about what occurred in the incident.

3. *Review:* Study your behavior in the situation, but do so without any judgment about right or wrong. Is there anything that you could have done differently to create a positive outcome? It is important that you not justify or criticize your behavior or the other person's.

4. *Visualize:* See yourself performing these alternative behaviors, and experience the positive outcome that this new behavior brings. Practice the new behaviors and the positive outcome in your mind until you are confident that you will use these new behaviors at the next opportunity.

5. *Observe:* Review the other person's behavior, with particular attention to their emotional compulsion. Understand how their emotional reactions determined their behavior, and they had no real choice. If you feel any negative emotional reaction, any hint of anger, resentment, or intimidation, clear your mind with Breath Awareness and again re-center yourself. When your mind is calm and clear, again review the situation until you can watch the other person's behavior without any negative reaction.

6. *Visualize:* Visualize this person's face surrounded by golden light or a blue light, whichever comes easier, until you feel a sense of compassion for this person.

7. *Centering:* Return to the clear, calm center of your mind, then practice Breath Awareness for a few moments, and open your eyes to the palms of your hands. Now you can resolve this conflict from a position of strength rather than weakness brought on by your emotional reactions.

works, the uncertainties leave much to the imagination, and confidence is seldom complete.

You don't have to live very long before you experience a fundamental rule of life, the 10–80–10 rule:

- 10 percent of the time, no matter what you do, you are successful.
- 80 percent of the time your ability to influence events varies. You have some input or control over what happens, but the outcome is indefinite.
- 10 percent of the time, no matter what you do, you fail.

As a consequence:

- 10 percent of the time you have absolute self-confidence.
- 80 percent of the time you are insecure, with some doubt coloring your level of confidence.
- 10 percent of the time you have no confidence at all.

When we rely on success to build self-confidence, we unknowingly stack the odds against ourselves. At the subtle level of our discriminating mind, we recognize that success is fickle, and that we really don't have control, no matter how much insurance we buy, how many contracts we sign, or how much money we save. We all feel the insecurity that being subject to the fickle finger of fate creates. We see ourselves as victims and talk about chance and luck, hoping that the fates will be kind.

Negative self-concepts are even more destructive to our self-confidence. In early childhood, the pain of "failure"—people laughing at us, calling us names, telling us that we are inadequate or not good enough; hearing constantly words such as *no, don't,* and *you can't*—has a stronger impact on the mind than whatever success we achieve. By the time we enter adulthood, these patterns have a powerful influence. Even though we may compensate by making a fortune or being the big shot, our inner world is full of self-doubt and stress because we really don't feel genuinely confident.

There are ways to help unwrap your confidence:

1. Use Breath Awareness to clear your mind whenever your mind chatter starts "bad-mouthing" you. Don't allow the mind's habit of name-calling and disappointment to remain unchallenged.
2. Take control of your language. There is no such thing as failure, only premature quitting. Reinterpret the situation in terms of cause/effect. Whenever you take any action, you always get some results. Instead of labeling them as good or bad, successful or unsuccessful, examine how they came about. Spend your time and effort understanding cause/effect relationships instead of creating mind pollution.
3. Evaluate how you produced these particular results and modify, if necessary, whatever actions you took. Then take the necessary actions to produce different results, using what you have learned from the last time.
4. Any time you find yourself focusing on what you can't do, immediately clear your mind with Breath Awareness. Refocus your attention on what you can do. Keep doing this until it becomes your mind's habit.

All of this will help, but it still won't lead to unlimited self-confidence. Genuine, unshakable self-confidence has nothing to do with the world at all. It is a natural part of every human mind. Unfortunately, we are so busy talking to ourselves, feeding our dragons, and paying attention to *outside* events that we ignore this inner reality.

The problem we face with self-confidence isn't one of acquisition. We already have everything we need, including unlimited self-confidence. The problem is one of access. It has nothing to do with "positive thinking." In fact, it has nothing to do with thinking at all. Remember the experience when you feel that "God's in his heaven—All's right with the world"? This sense of genuine harmony and contentment is the natural expression of our balanced mind, the fifth and most subtle level of the personality. This inner balance is the source of our genuine self-confidence. We access it through a deeply quiet and calm mind, the kind of mind created by meditation. *The most effective and efficient method of achieving unshakable self-confidence is the consistent practice of meditation.* The more skilled at meditation you become, the more confidence you gain. You will experience this as:

- an increase in mental calm and clarity, the ability to focus on what's important and to ignore distractions;
- greater emotional stability—things just don't bother you as much;
- clearer thinking, more perception, understanding cause/effect relationships more clearly;
- greater effectiveness as you focus your energies more efficiently and waste less time disturbing yourself.

Meditation leads to a gradual overall increase in your ability to access your innate self-confidence. As you become more aware of this subtle core within

|||||||||| A CONFIDENCE EXERCISE ||||||||||

Begin with the Centering Exercise (page 223). When you feel centered, observe whatever thoughts arise in your mind. Notice how these thoughts appear around the center of your mind, but never occur in the center. Then direct your attention toward the problem you face. As disturbing thoughts or feelings arise, clear your mind with Breath Awareness and re-center yourself. Keep returning to the problem until you can watch your mind think about the problem without feeling disturbed or worried. As you remain calm, you will notice that you feel more confident about handling the problem. Once you can observe without any emotional reactions, let your mind play with the problem, allowing whatever creative solutions to arise without judgment. You can now use the creative force of your mind to find a solution. After choosing the solution you want, visualize yourself solving the problem, and allow yourself to feel the success of the solution. Then clear your mind with Breath Awareness, open your eyes to the palms of your hands, and go to work.

your balanced mind, you can use the Centering Exercise to access this experience and train your mind to remain calm and confident whenever difficult situations arise.

Meditation: Using Power to Gain Strength

|||||||||| Meditation is the finest tool we have for personal growth and development. Through meditation, we systematically expand our inner awareness and become conscious of our true inner potential. In this way we gradually transform the entire personality. Meditation enhances and promotes the evolutionary growth process, and since this takes place as a natural consequence of our own efforts, it remains under our control. As we grow in inner strength and independence, we are able to give more freely to others without resentment, without fear, and without manipulation.

The consistent practice of inner concentration and meditation provides specific benefits to physical, mental, and social health:

- A gradual change in the physiology of the body reflecting a significant and permanent reduction of stress—a slower pulse rate, a lower and more stable blood pressure, a more stable galvanic skin response, deeper and more even breathing patterns, and lower blood lactate levels.
- A corresponding increase in self-confidence and self-acceptance as well as an overall increase in self-actualization (a strong indication of increasing maturity and personal fulfillment).
- Less need for and less use of alcohol and drugs of all types, prescription and nonprescription.
- A gradual change from compulsive and rigid behavior (which results in negative outcomes) to more helpful, thoughtful behaviors (which are more satisfying and productive).
- Increased powers of concentration leading to greater personal effectiveness.

But the most important benefit is the change in how we experience ourselves. Meditation is an introduction of ourselves to ourselves. Our personal sense of I-ness undergoes a gradual transformation as we slowly become aware of the deeper resources of the mind—our innate strength and wisdom and the very essence of life, the spiritual Self. We begin to view the world from a dramatically different perspective. Change no longer frightens us, and we no longer need to be perfect or punish ourselves for not being perfect.

As we grow in mastery and knowledge, we gradually dis-identify with those aspects of ourselves which we considered for so long to be essential to our sense of identity—our thoughts and ideas, our emotions, our bodies and behaviors, our roles and social attachments. As we develop our skills in inner concentration and meditation, we put our old self into a new and more useful perspective. We grow out of self-imposed limitations, and as we gain emotional distance, we see things with greater clarity, become less reactive to stressful situations, and take command of our habits and actions. As we refine our mind power, we increase an evolutionary movement that leads us to our most potent resources: an unlimited inner strength that we experience as a genuine self-confidence.

But most important, we experience the spiritual Self, the unlimited core of our humanity. We do not reach this transpersonal Self through therapy, drugs, reading books, or even having wonderful parents. It cannot be gained through intellectual discourse or by going to college. It is already deep in our minds, it is who we already are. With meditation, we access and refine the power of the mind. With this refined power, we take the final step to access our spiritual strength and free ourselves from the dragon of loneliness.

CHAPTER 9

SPIRITUAL STRENGTH: THE END OF LONELINESS

Shall I at least set my lands in order?
—T. S. Eliot in *The Waste Land*

||||||||||| Our success and self-confidence shouldn't depend on external forces we cannot control, but on the inner ones we can. As we practice meditation and refine the power of the mind, we begin to experience our real inner strengths. Self-mastery is not a matter of becoming or acquiring something; it is a matter of becoming conscious of the strengths we already have. It is a process of transformation, not change. With the proper tools—diet, exercise, relaxation, and breathing—we transform a weak, rigid, and stressed body into a balanced, flexible, strong and stress-free body. By developing and using our natural resources, we end up with a healthy body. The same is true of the mind. With the proper tools—Breath Awareness, imagery, reframing, concentration—we transform a fearful, self-hating mind into a clear, flexible, creative, and insightful mind. By developing and using our natural resources, we end up with a powerful mind.

With these two instruments, a healthy body and a powerful mind, we complete the journey to self-mastery. Just as we refine concentration to achieve meditation, we refine our meditation to achieve awareness of the spiritual Self and experience yet another transformation—one that is deeper, more profound and complete. It is the blossoming of our spiritual strength, and the resolution of all loneliness. This experience of the spiritual Self is a mystical experience, yet it is the most practical way of life. It is called a mystical experience because the intellect cannot quantify or qualify the experience. Any words we use to define or explain the experience are not the experience itself, but only a shadow of the truth that we experience. While the mind does not comprehend, the heart knows it completely. This is not the physical heart, but the spiritual heart, the soul-Self which lies at the very core of the personality. It is practical because it frees us completely from the dragons of the mind and limited ego and returns to us our full capacity to love.

This experience is called by different names. In Zen it is called *satori*, or enlightenment; in Taoism it is referred to as living the Tao; and in Tantra it is called *samadhi*. In Western traditions, it is referred to as a mystical experience. Whatever the name, it is this experience alone which completely frees us from loneliness and the other dragons of the mind. And it does this through love.

We may have a powerful mind, even a powerful will, but unless we reach into the very core of our being and experience our spiritual Self, we have not yet completed our journey to self-mastery. How we first experience this Self varies from person to person. There are, however, universal qualities—timelessness, unsurpassed peace, a blissfulness that transcends any experience of pleasure—that are part of almost every mystical experience. For many, it is a timeless experience of an indescribable light. Listen to the words of the mystical poet T. S. Eliot:

> *At the still point of the turning world. Neither flesh nor fleshless;*
> *Neither from nor towards; at the still point, there the dance is,*
> *But neither arrest nor movement. . . .*
>
> *I can only say, there we have been: But I cannot say where.*
> *And I cannot say, how long, for that is to place it in time. . . .*
>
> *The inner freedom from the practical desire.*
> *The release from action and suffering, release from the inner*
> *And the outer compulsion, yet surrounded*
> *By a grace of sense, a white light still and moving . . .*

For others, it is a recognition that this Self is eternal, a part of the Universal One, free of all disease, all suffering, and all limitations.

Different minds translate this mystical experience into concepts that are limited by culture, beliefs, and traditions. There can be no argument about which experience is correct, as they are all "correct." Nor can the intellect find a logic to explain it. This experience has nothing to do with the mind, so the mind cannot fully comprehend it. At best, the mind can only define our experience through different words. The only way to understand, to comprehend the experience, is to have the experience itself. This mystical experience is the core of all meditative and spiritual traditions. Without it, we cannot know our full capacity for love, and we cannot be completely free from loneliness and the other dragons.

Although a mystical experience can happen spontaneously, these events are rare. Consequently, the great traditions of self-mastery systematically develop the capacity for mystical knowledge through the consistent practice of meditation. In Tantra, the task is to refine meditation so that all the power of the mind is focused on a single point. Like the point of an ice pick penetrating a block of ice, the awareness of the meditator penetrates the density of the mind and opens into the spiritual realm. It is this awareness that opens the spiritual heart and frees us of our physical and mental limitations.

The End of Ignorance . . .

|||||||||| This singular experience need only happen once, and the entire personality is transformed. You don't become a different person, you experience a new identity. You no longer think of yourself as the habits and patterns of the ego-mind. However brief this one experience may be, you know beyond a shadow of any doubt that this personality that represents you is not who you really are, but simply your tool. The ego can claim no longer to be the owner of the personality. The tantrics have a saying: "If a fool enters into deep sleep, he awakens as a fool. If a fool enters into *samadhi*, he awakens as a sage."

In Tantra Yoga, this mystical experience is considered to be the beginning of the end of ignorance. Recall from Chapter 3 that in the meditative traditions, ignorance means to ignore, to be unconscious of. When we are unconscious of the spiritual core, we identify with the ego-self, the material personality. Instead of seeing the mind and body as the tools they are, we come to believe that our thoughts and our physical experiences are all that we are. Consequently, we define ourselves by whatever thoughts and feelings come to mind, not realizing that we are the witness, the observer, the spiritual Self that uses thoughts and feelings to interact with the world around us. This confusion of identity lies at the root of our loneliness, fear, and self-hatred.

When we finally experience our spiritual Self directly, this experience awakens us to the fact that we are much more than our thoughts and feelings, much more than a physical presence. It is not an understanding, but a realization. No matter how intellectual we are, or how many degrees we earn, thinking about the spiritual Self is not at all the same as having the experience. Just as thinking about eating is not the same as eating, reading about mystical experiences is not the same as having one. The proof of the pudding, the power of the experience, is in the experience itself.

Although our first mystical experience is indescribably powerful, it does not mean that we will be skilled in maintaining this spiritual awareness. In fact, we may even spend quite some time agonizing why we cannot go back to the mountaintop. The task we face after achieving *samadhi*, or the mystical experience, is to become skilled at maintaining that awareness. This is precisely why there are traditions of self-mastery. They provide the systematic methods that not only lead us to the mystical experience, but also develop the ability to maintain this spiritual awareness and knowledge as the foundation for the rest of our lives.

. . . And the Opening of Love

|||||||||| The power of this mystical experience lies in a very simple reality. It is called love. For the tantric Masters, love is considered to be the most ancient of all travelers. It is the power of Consciousness itself. Or said in more Western terms, it is the very nature of the soul. Almost every account of a mystical experience speaks of this transcendent experience of love as the core quality of the experience. But it is always spoken of as a force that flows through and from the individual, not something that is received. This is quite different from the emotional experience that we often call love in poetry and songs. There is no longer a sense of "me" or "mine," no sense of a small ego-self taking something in. It is this defining quality of selflessness that puts an end to the dragon of loneliness.

This makes sense if we understand something about our emotions. When we examine the nature of our emotions and emotional energy carefully, we see why this change of identity from the personality to the spiritual Self brings about an end to the emotional disturbances that we suffer.

Emotional Energy: The Source of Power

|||||||||| Much of the power that we command through concentration and meditation has its source in our emotional energy. When we don't understand this energy, we unknowingly use it to create conflict and disturbance, harming ourselves and others. In our ignorance, we have even come to believe that an emotional person is a weak person when, in truth, our emotional energy is the power behind our actions.

All the exercises we have learned are designed to help us balance and direct emotional energy. But how is this energy channeled into emotions? What are our emotions anyway, and how do we create them? Unfortunately, modern psychiatry and psychology have only a superficial view of emotions. They do not have a systematic science or technology that provides the tools we need to command and direct this powerful energy. They do know how to label emotions. There are diagnostic manuals that have labels and categories for any and all behavior. In fact, if you look at these books you begin to think that everything we do can be labeled as some emotional disorder. But nowhere do we find a clear understanding of what emotions are, or how they arise in the mind and body. Since our emotions impact every aspect of our lives, it is foolish not to have at least some understanding of how we create emotional disturbance.

The Four Primitive Urges

||||||||| In yoga science, there is a clear distinction between negative emotions, which lead to imbalance, stress, and suffering, and positive emotions, which lead to freedom, balance, and harmony. These two categories of emotion have two very different sources. Our negative emotions are a distortion of very powerful and primitive drives which are part of the physical body. Yoga science points out that there are four instinctual urges, or primitive drives, inherent in our biological structure: self-preservation (which we have already talked about in Chapter 3), hunger, sleep, and sex. We share these four primitive urges with all other members of the animal kingdom. The purpose of these primitive drives is to ensure both the survival of the individual and the continuation of the species. These drives motivate us to protect ourselves from danger, to seek out food for nourishment, to give ourselves adequate rest for revitalization, and to participate in the creation of new life so that the species may continue. They are the source of energy for our emotions, but they are not the emotions themselves. They are the primary unfocused fountains of energy which supply power to the emotions.

When one of these primitive urges is stimulated, such as self-preservation when we face danger, it generates energy. This energy is quickly directed to a specific goal or object that in the past has satisfied the underlying urge or drive. When this energy is given a specific direction, or goal, it is called desire, and becomes a very powerful motivating force. All of our behavior is motivated by a desire of one kind or another. We may have lots of wants and wishes, but we won't be moved to action until there is a desire, enough energy to move us toward achieving some goal.

From a yogic perspective, animals are controlled by their nature. Whatever primitive urge is strongest at the moment dominates the actions of the animal. It will eat any food available, run or fight if threatened, find a den when rest is needed, and engage in sex during the mating season. Unfortunately, human beings can also be dominated by urges and desires. But we can also refrain from acting, no matter how strong the desire. Through the power of *reflective awareness*, human beings can step back and observe their urges, they can postpone their desires, they can go halfway around the world to pick a mate or find a specific food. In other words, we can complicate our world. We can find a seemingly endless number of objects that can satisfy (at least temporarily) any one basic urge. As a consequence, we can, and have, created an almost endless number of desires.

Notice that the phrase is *reflective awareness*, not thinking. Thinking is a different process. Thinking is using the mind to collect sensory data, to analyze, to reflect, to make a discrimination, however well we do so. Animals also clearly think. They solve problems, they use language, they also show emotions. But there is no evidence that animals know they are thinking. It is this power of reflective awareness, the ability to observe the mind work, that provides us with response ability, the capacity to free ourselves from the compulsion of our primitive drives, to have the freedom to choose something different. This is the human difference—not that we think, but that we can step away from the mind and its compulsions and see it from the perspective of our spiritual Self. This is why meditation is so necessary—it develops our capacity for reflective awareness.

If the object of our desire satisfies us in any way, the connection between the urge and the particular object is reinforced, and the desire becomes stronger. It's as if desire is a channel of energy which deepens if the chosen object satisfies the desire. Every time we satisfy a desire, it becomes stronger, and we increase the probability that this particular channel will be utilized again. Soon, that particular choice becomes a powerful habit in the mind. If our choice is painful or uncomfortable in any way, we quickly learn to avoid it. Then that avoidance becomes the habit. In many ways, pain conditions the mind even more powerfully than pleasure. We act as much from the need to avoid unpleasantness or pain as we do to find pleasure.

The connection between the desire and the object can become so strong that the desire and the object come to be seen as one. The more often we successfully use the object, person, or situation to satisfy a desire or avoid pain, the stronger the connection becomes. After a while, we become dependent on that particular object, and become convinced that only that object will make us happy, secure, fulfilled, satisfied, and/or protected. By this time, we have developed a very strong habit in the mind.

This is where we begin to get into trouble. Up to this point, we are in harmony with ourselves. Neither the basic urge nor the desire, in and of itself, creates imbalance and unhappiness. The danger lies in our dependency relationship to the object of our desire.

Let's take a simple example. When we start running out of fuel for the body, we begin to suffer from a nutritional deficiency. At this point we begin to feel hungry. But we don't stay with a vague sense of hunger for long. We quickly begin to think about specific foods that will satisfy us. While there may be plenty available, we begin to "hunger" for a particular dish—cherry pie, for instance. Hunger, the urge, is now directed to a particular object; we desire the cherry pie even though it may not provide the nourishment we really need, the absence of which is the real cause for the hunger.

Let's say that you had a long morning at work, missed taking your break, and by the time 12:30 or 1:00 rolled around, you were really hungry. What made you even more hungry and eager for lunch is that a colleague with a reputation as an excellent baker had left a message that there was a piece of homemade cherry pie waiting for you in the staff refrigerator. It was yours to have on your break or at lunch.

Your mouth watered as you thought about that piece of pie. You quickly shuffled papers off your desk and went immediately to the staff lounge. As you walked into the lounge, you saw another colleague finishing up a piece of cherry pie. You opened the refrigerator, and all you saw was an empty paper plate with your initials on it, and an apple sitting next to it.

The more you wanted that piece of pie, the stronger your reaction would be to the "loss" of that pie. If your frustration was so strong that you lost your balance and perspective, that other person in the room finishing a piece of cherry pie was definitely in danger. The apple could certainly assuage your hunger just as well as the cherry pie, and, in fact, would have done a much better job of it. But under the power of your attachment to the pie, you would look at the apple and not even see it.

It wasn't your hunger that caused your emotional reaction. It wasn't even your desire for the piece of cherry pie. What made you angry was your "need to have" that piece of cherry pie. It is our "need" for a specific object that leads to a negative emotion. In *Creative Use of Emotions*, Swami Rama and Swami Ajaya state, "It is in seeking to obtain and keep objects of our desire that we become emotional in one way or another. Thus it is said that desire is the mother of all emotions." Emotional disturbance somehow always involves our relationships to the external world. Not a single negative emotion has an exclusively internal source; they always arise from our dependency, our attachment, to a desired object, situation, or person.

It doesn't have to be a piece of cherry pie. We get attached to just about everything—belief systems, ideas, people, causes, automobiles, gems, income, spouses, children—the list is as endless as our desires. And every dependency has the power to create a negative emotion.

We become emotionally disturbed whenever any desire is unfulfilled, blocked, or somehow threatened. When someone or something prevents us from fulfilling our desire, or threatens to take away an object of our desire, we become disturbed. This emotional disturbance creates patterns in our mind that distort our perceptions and our thinking, inhibit our creative force, and force us into more rigid forms of behavior, which leads to imbalance and stress. Even though we may express our emotion, such as anger, and relieve some pressure, the damage (internal imbalance) has already been done. The best we can do now is to clear the mind and rebalance as quickly as possible.

As we have already seen, fear is a distortion of the urge for self-preservation, and is one of the dragons we face. We set the conditions for fear whenever we feel that our physical self and/or our ego-self (our sense of self-worth, importance, and so on) depend upon a specific event or condition, object, or person. After all, our greatest attachment is to our lives, which certainly includes our physical bodies. When we *anticipate* harm to the body, or to the ego-self, through loss, a change in events, or the inability to gain what we think we need, the inevitable outcome is fear. As the authors of *Creative Use of Emotions* point out, "Without the habit of dependency there could be no fear." The authors list other negative emotions such as jealousy (or envy), greed, depression, and pride. Each and every negative emotion is based on an attachment, a condition of dependency. And all of them are powerful habits in our mind.

Building Helpful Habits

|||||||||| Satisfying all our desires, even if it were possible, is not the answer. It doesn't take long before we realize that sometimes satisfying a desire leads to even greater difficulty. For example, greed, another negative emotion, arises when we already possess the objects of our desire. But this possession only feeds the desire further. Instead of just one piece, now we want the entire pie. Many of us never have enough no matter how much we get. Life becomes a rat race, a futile attempt to get enough to make us happy. This is the hidden trap of materialism. We always want something a little bit better. We always strive to raise our standard of living. We must have a little more than last year or we think we are not doing well. We lose any sense of sufficiency as we become driven to have more and more and more.

As we become focused on satisfying our desires, we lose sight of any consequences until after they happen to us. For example, eating the piece of cherry pie would satisfy a desire, but what would happen to the digestive system? The pie, loaded with sugar and white flour, creates an imbalance in the digestive process, and we end up with another kind of problem. Or we "fall in love," marry, and find out that the person we married is definitely not the person we thought we married. How many times have you heard that love is blind? That isn't true at all. Love isn't blind, it is undemanding. What is blind is our emotional attachment.

Nor will we gain much ground by trying to regulate each emotion or reaction. Our negative emotions are symptoms, information resources that tell us when we are out of harmony with ourselves and our environment. Negative emotions are the result of misdirected energy. To take control, to consciously direct our energy skillfully so that we can use it to create a strong will, we must go to the source, the four basic urges. We must discriminate between the emotion (such as anger or fear) and the emotional power behind it. By regulating and directing the emotional power (the primitive urge), we free ourselves from emotional disturbances and the problems and stress they create.

If we have a body, we have emotional energy. The challenge we face is to channel it constructively. If we remain unconscious and allow our old habits to continue to direct this energy, we continue to suffer from negative emotions and related diseases. But if we take charge, develop new patterns and channels, new habits of thinking, speaking, and behaving, this energy will flow smoothly, satisfying the primitive urges and leading to healthy, creative living and a powerful will.

Regulating the expression of our energy by building helpful habits is the first level of self-mastery. For instance, we already know that fear is a distortion of self-preservation, and that by taking charge of our mind chatter we can prevent fear. We also know the impact of diet and the necessity of regulating the "what, when, and how" of food intake. We can satisfy this primitive urge by taking nutritionally useful food at proper times and in a proper way. By regulating food intake, we control the difficulties related to food intake (such as compulsive eating, indigestion, and obesity) as well as associated emotional disturbances (such as guilt, fear, and self-hatred). Practicing good dietary habits also leads to the desire for healthy food, thus channeling this urge constructively.

Knowing how to sleep is as important as knowing how to eat. If you regulate your sleeping habits and train yourself to sleep properly, your life force is revitalized, and you don't feel tired and cranky at the end of the day. Too many of us simply collapse into bed and fall asleep. Even if we sleep through the night, our sleep is disturbed from tension. The key is to systematically relax before going to sleep, and prepare both the mind and body for a restful sleep. The Sleep Exercise (Chapter 6), for instance, quiets the unconscious and allows for deep and peaceful sleep. You will spend less time sleeping as the quality of your sleep increases. In this way sleep becomes truly revitalizing—an important element in a healthy lifestyle.

The fourth and final primitive urge, sex, is different from the other three. In yoga science, the primitive drives of both food and sleep are considered to be subservient to the primary drive of self-preservation. Sex, however, is considered to be unique, and serves a unique function. Contrary to popular opinion, sex is necessary for the species but not necessary for the survival of the individual. Because sex is extremely pleasurable (or painful) both physically and emotionally, it creates very strong attachments. In addition, since it involves another person's needs and moods, its satisfaction becomes highly unpredictable. As a consequence, sex is extremely fertile ground for developing negative emotions such as jealousy, greed, anger, and fear. Therapists will tell you that sexual conflicts are by far the most prevalent emotional disturbance in any society.

Yoga science has studied sexuality as intensively as it has studied all inner events. In yogic traditions, sexual management doesn't necessarily mean abstinence. But it does require that we take control of both the mental and the physical aspects of sexual activity. The word *control* does not mean to suppress or repress sexual energy. This inevitably leads to disease and emotional pathology. Control means conscious, skillful choice, not compulsive action.

There are a number of steps we can take to make sex a very powerful and satisfying experience. Two essential elements are to limit the frequency of the sexual act and to develop a stable sexual partnership. This is not a moral position, but a recognition of the specialness of sexual energy, and the need to develop its full power and potential. If we simply react every time we feel the desire, we only build the habit of reaction. Sex becomes commonplace and habitual. Along with this comes a whole host of problems—guilt, fear of loss and rejection, disappointments, even disease—leading to ever-increasing dysfunctional states of mind. The attention created by specialness is lost as quantity replaces quality. Having a stable partner does much to eliminate the risk of disease as well as insecurity.

The purpose is to make the sexual act very special, and to free it from compulsion and guilt. One of the most productive ways to do this is to limit sexual activity, to consciously fix the time and place for sexual expression with a chosen partner. This makes sex very special, which, in return, generates even greater attention and concentration. It also leads to control of this powerful source of energy. The greater our control, the greater our use of sexual expression to gain genuine union. As we alter our attachments to old patterns of behavior, our control over the expression of this energy flow also increases.

Physical exercise, such as hatha yoga, helps redirect our energy away from troublesome desires toward a more general expression through physical activity and involvement in the world around us. At the same time, breathing exercises and meditation help maintain a calm mind and allow for increased self-awareness. These all help in developing control. The sexual urge then becomes an extremely important ally in creative work, loving relationships, and expanded levels of consciousness.

Nonattachment: The End of Ownership

‖‖‖‖‖‖ If we accept that the root cause of our negative emotions is dependency, then building healthy habits can help regulate our emotional energy. But the key to self-mastery is to put an end to our dependencies. That doesn't mean that we can't satisfy our desires, or that we no longer have any pleasure. Obviously we aren't going to stop eating, sleeping, having sex, or protecting ourselves. Nor does it mean that we become passive and accept whatever happens to come our way. Through self-mastery we put an end to dependency and the suffering it causes by becoming more skillful in creating happiness, having pleasure, and satisfying our desires.

The process for letting go of our dependencies is called nonattachment. If you were nonattached to that piece of cherry pie, you could have still enjoyed it if it had been waiting for you. But you would not have had the emotional reaction when you found it missing. Instead of being angry about someone eating *your* piece of cherry pie, your mind would have appreciated having the apple to eat. You still would have liked to have had the cherry pie, but you wouldn't be disturbed by its absence.

Nonattachment doesn't mean noninvolvement. It means that our involvement is clear of dependencies which muddle our thinking and prevent us from understanding the reality around us. Nonattachment means that we don't "need" a particular thing, person, or event in order to be content and secure. It stems from a recognition that things and people do not make us secure or happy, the realization that the source of our happiness, joy, security, and strength is within ourselves.

We cannot achieve this awareness as long as we remain locked into our identity with the ego-self. Here again, we discover the power of the mystical experience. But even before we reach this level of awareness, we can experience some degree of freedom from the need to have things. Close your eyes and do the Centering Exercise from Chapter 8. Once you feel centered, then explore what it feels like to be in the center of your mind. Do you find any disturbance there? Is there anything wrong with you? Is there anything lacking here at the center? Notice that if any negative thoughts do arise, they seem to come up around that center, but not from the center itself. Be aware of the contentment you feel in the center of your mind.

Doing this Centering Exercise gives us some idea of what we experience as we gain freedom from the need to have objects. When we become so focused that we penetrate the veil of the mind and have a mystical experience, we find that we are already complete and whole, that nothing more is needed. Nonattachment arises naturally from the recognition of our spiritual Self as our true identity and the experience of our own wholeness. As the realization of our spiritual Self dawns, there is a corresponding decrease in our dependency on things in the world to make us feel whole, complete, and secure. This is true nonattachment. Until we have this realization of our spiritual Self, and the inner strength that it brings, we are not yet free.

Spiritual Desire: The Wellspring of Inner Strength

IIIIIIIIIII We know that desire is powerful, and is the motivating force of all our actions. Not all desires, however, spring from the four urges. Yoga science points to another desire which does not stem from the primitive urges—the desire for higher knowledge. This has its roots in our spiritual nature. It is what leads us to explore both the external universe and internal truth, and it can become so powerful that even the primitive urges will come under its control.

The desire for higher knowledge lies at the heart of a meditative discipline. It provides an unlimited source of emotional energy, giving us the strength to complete our journey. Meditation is the release mechanism for this force. As our meditation deepens, the positive emotions of love, joy, and tranquillity emerge without effort, and we experience their power to change our lives. With this driving force gathering strength behind our meditation, we achieve the mystical experience and complete the process of transformation.

Love: The Freeing Force

IIIIIIIIIII The first and most powerful positive emotion is love. Love plays a vital role in our life, but most of us have a limited view of it. We aren't talking about the emotional attachment of so-called love songs. This form of love is polluted with emotional need and attachment to someone who satisfies our needs and desires. In its pure form, love is the expression of selflessness, the ability to give to another. Love is the force that flows from us and releases us from the limitations of our ego. The more loving we become, the less limited we are, and the less pain we experience in life.

Whenever we experience pain, we experience a boundary or a limit. By refusing to accept limitations or the habitual characterizations of ourselves that we learned in early childhood, we begin to free ourselves from them. But our greatest limitation is our own ego. If we believe that all we are is the personality, then we are stuck with whatever habits constitute it. It's easy to gauge the degree of neuroticism and unhappiness a person feels. Simply count the number of times he uses the words *I*, *me*, and *mine* in a conversation. The equation is very direct: the more self(ego)-centered you are, the more pain you create for yourself. This ego-centeredness is the sole cause of loneliness.

A friend and I were in a deep discussion about her life. She was very unhappy and dissatisfied with the way her life was going. She was in another relationship that was not meeting her emotional needs. Kae had been practicing meditation for several years, and I knew that her greatest fear was being alone. I asked her to name a famous individual that she felt would be free of the loneliness that so plagued her. After several moments of thought she said, "Mother Teresa." I was a bit surprised because that was the choice that I had in my mind. So I asked, "Why did you choose her?"

"Because she gives so much love that it must always be coming back to her."

Kae's answer reflected her own need to have someone love her. If she could only love enough, then someone would love her back. And if that happened, then she wouldn't be lonely anymore. So Kae would always find someone who needed a lot of love and set off to make him her life's work. Unfortunately, these people were unable to give enough love back to make the relationship really work for her. When the relationship ended, Kae would declare, "I always seem to choose the wrong person."

I asked Kae who was it that was getting love back? She looked at me rather peculiarly, probably thinking that somewhere I had lost a little bit of my sense. "Mother Teresa was getting it back," she replied.

"No, no, who was there to get it back?"

"Mother Teresa. If she was giving all that love, it was all coming back to her."

"Look, Kae, if Mother Teresa was giving love, there was no little ego there to demand love back. There was no little 'self' to be lonely. Her strength doesn't lie in all the love she receives, but in all the love that she gives."

The secret of spiritual strength is that we are able to transcend our ego needs. Literally, when we are truly loving, there is no little ego, no sense of "me," to be lonely. Love allows us to break free from the boundary of our small self and experience our great Self, the spiritual Self that is unlimited, timeless, and universal.

When we are loving, we aren't even thinking of ourselves. Just remember the time you were shopping for gifts during the holiday season. Suddenly, you saw the perfect gift for someone. You could feel their surprise and happiness as you imagined them opening the gift. Just look at how this simple act of giving made you feel. No matter how pleased they were, you already had most of the benefit.

To become skilled at loving, practice selflessness. This doesn't mean sacrifice. Service doesn't mean resentful giving. If you have a martyr complex, you are not loving. If you feel like you are making a sacrifice, you are not loving.

Graham Greene once described a martyr in the following way: "Alice lived her whole life for others. You could tell 'the others' by the haunted look in their faces." We all know, or have met, someone who lives only to help you, and you better damn well be grateful. This isn't loving, it's manipulation. Doing favors to gain favor, using guilt to ensure payback, and creating dependencies have little to do with genuine love.

When we are truly selfless, we feel free, not imposed upon. Others feel our compassion and love; they don't feel haunted and smothered. They experience the same freedom we experience as we love. The more we practice selflessness in daily life, the more freedom we all gain.

Joy: The End of Expectation

IIIIIIIII Joy, the second positive emotion, is what we experience when we love. Joy arises out of a natural and unrestrained expression of who we are. Spontaneous and unrehearsed, it is found in the experience of being one's self without pretense or apology. The greater our integrity, the more consistent our inner thoughts, beliefs, and values are with our outer behavior, the more joy we experience. It is joy that both reflects and maintains our inner and outer harmony in life.

We increase our joy through laughter and our sense of humor. Simple, spontaneous laughter is one of the best techniques for stress management available to us. If we understand laughter, we will understand joy. We laugh at a joke because the punch line is unexpected. The third or fourth time we hear the joke, it's no longer funny. It is the unrehearsed, spontaneous punch line that breaks through our expectations that creates our laughter.

Now, let's take the analysis one step further. The opposite of life is death, right? Wrong. Death is the opposite of birth. In this world of duality, the one reality that has no opposite is life. It changes form, it changes from gross to subtle, from seen to unseen, but life continues on and on. Life is complete in and of itself. Life itself is joy. But when we impose our expectations on life, we miss the punch line. When we greet life as it is, without expectations and demands, we experience joy. Expectation is the mother of suffering. The more dearly we hold on to our expectations, the more dearly we suffer.

Our joy, as it expresses itself in laughter, is the light that illumines our path through life. We cannot cultivate joy by seeking our own happiness, but we will always find it as we help others find theirs. When we are loving, when we express ourselves without limitations, when we stop creating expectations, when we accept life as it is, we cannot help but experience joy. When we stop disturbing ourselves, when we stop being ego-centered, joy is spontaneous and natural.

Tranquillity: The Calm of Self-Acceptance

|||||||||| The third positive emotion, tranquillity, or inner peace, is the expression of complete self-acceptance. Just as we experience joy when we lose our expectations of life, we experience tranquillity when we lose our expectations of ourselves. This doesn't mean we become passive or apathetic. It is rather a state of tranquillity that characterizes a balanced mind. This inner peace allows us to fully enjoy and engage the turns and tumbles of the world without being disturbed. Instead of withdrawal from the world, we enjoy complete and skillful participation in it. It is a calm, peaceful mind that comprehends the absolute fullness of life and can participate in it. The deeper our inner concentration, the deeper our inner balance and tranquillity. *Meditation is the most powerful tool to achieve inner peace and tranquillity.*

Our spiritual desire for higher knowledge is our most powerful aid in becoming free from the dragons of the mind. In the final analysis we alone are the source of our own suffering. We are also the cure. Only we have the power to alter those habits of behaving, perceiving, and feeling that result in fear, self-hatred, and loneliness. They were not acquired overnight, nor will they be magically altered overnight. There are no fast and easy answers, only the promise of continued evolution and growth. In the mastery of skillful living lies our freedom. Self-mastery and inner strength are the consequence of skillful living, and just as any skill development takes time and training, learning to live skillfully requires patient self-training.

Will: Directing the Power of Your Mind

|||||||||| As we touch upon the strength of our human spirit we discover all the elements of a powerful will: a relaxed, calm mind, free of stress and disturbance; an enhanced power of concentration; the ability to resolve conflict; and access to our inner strength.

Using will is quite different from using what we call willpower. When we get caught up in conflict, we typically try to use our willpower to solve the problem. This is particularly true when we deal with inner conflict. One part of the mind wants one thing, another part wants just the opposite. We get into a battle with ourselves, and try to overpower any resistance. Unfortunately, what we overpower is only another part of our own minds. Instead of focusing on possible solutions, we are involved in a struggle. No matter which side wins, we lose since the mind becomes the battlefield. The only sure outcome is misery, stress, and more conflict.

Before I was really able to stop smoking, I quit a thousand times. I would throw away whatever cigarettes were left in the pack, and tell myself that I would not smoke again. Ten minutes later, I would remind myself that I quit smoking. And again, a little later on, I would tell myself again that I quit smoking. I would tell myself at least a hundred times a day that I quit. But I really wanted that cigarette. The more I told myself that I quit, the more I wanted the cigarette. I became preoccupied with not smoking, so smoking was always on my mind. Finally, I would find a cigarette, light up, and say to myself, "Maybe next month." I wasn't really ready to quit, and all I did was create conflict for myself. And when I did finally give in and smoke, no matter how much I rationalized, I felt like a failure.

Will is the conscious ability to focus all of the energy of the mind toward a single direction. We use will when our thoughts, emotions, and actions are consistent. When this happens, our determination is complete (no internal conflict), and the mind's energy is one-pointed. I was able to quit smoking when I was sensitive to the pain that smoking caused for me, and decided that I would have nothing to do with cigarettes, one way or the other. I never allowed my mind to even think about quitting. I kept my focus on anything else but smoking or stopping smoking. Since there was no conflict in my mind, stopping was very simple. With willpower, we have only partial commitment, whereas when we use our will we have total commitment. We use doubts and worries as motivation, and we direct all of our desires toward achieving our goal.

To create a powerful will, our values and beliefs must be fully in accord with our actions. Those who have a powerful will are committed to their value system. They function with integrity; there is no conflict between their inner thoughts, emotions, and beliefs and their outer actions. They are true to themselves.

One of the most subtle and unrecognized causes of stress is when our actions are inconsistent with our true beliefs. This causes a subtle (often unconscious) but powerful conflict in the mind that, if not remedied, leads to feelings of guilt and powerlessness and damages our will. Along with refining concentration, meditation plays a powerful role in developing our integrity in two ways:

1. Through meditation we gain the self-awareness and knowledge necessary to realize and examine our values and beliefs, and the sensitivity to realize when we are inconsistent with ourselves.
2. Through meditation we gain awareness of the spiritual Self and the innate harmony and values that arise from it. This leads to enormous strength of character and integrity, which in turn provide for a powerful will.

Most of us spend very little time thinking about the purpose of our lives, or seriously examining our beliefs and values. All too often, we simply repeat what we learned as children, incorporating the values and beliefs of the culture in which we grew up. Unfortunately, much of what we learn is inconsistent with our real nature, and includes contradictions, fallacies, and mistakes that often lead to cynicism, inner conflicts, and self-doubt. These all become incorporated at an unconscious level into our personal values and belief systems. As a result, our personal philosophies become a source of weakness instead of strength, of stress instead of harmony, and of conflict instead of will.

As we become more skilled at meditation, our increasing awareness of our inner resources and the experience of our spiritual Self allow us to create a personal philosophy consistent with our true nature. When we act with integrity, when we are consistent both inside and out, we are in harmony with ourselves and with the world around us. We may not be understood, we may not be in agreement with some of society's beliefs and values, but we will be in harmony with our own nature. The difficulties in life cannot affect us. This is self-mastery—to live life fully and completely, to become a complete human being and experience the love, joy, and tranquillity that are our own spiritual Self.

Self-Training: Developing Personal Response Ability

||||||||||| A world-class personality requires world-class training. We know that to develop into a skilled tennis player, surgeon, or musician takes a great deal of training. But what does it take to become a skilled human being? We seldom, if ever, even think in terms of becoming a skilled human being, and yet freedom and personal fulfillment demand exactly that.

The training we need is self-training. Externally imposed discipline is based on suggestions and information from others. This can be useful, and we can gain a great deal of information, methods, and techniques through it. But if this is all we do, it leads to an "ignorant" or "blind" mind because it doesn't require that we fully understand what we are learning. This training builds habits, but they remain unconscious and unexamined. When we are asked only to accept, believe, and/or behave in a certain way, no matter how beneficial the intent, it leads to a constriction of awareness, dependency, and inner conflict. As a result, we lack genuine self-confidence and suffer from indecision, which leads to conflict and stress. Then, when the mind is divided and our habits in conflict, we end up doing what we really don't want to do, and rarely do what we want. The mind is too scattered, awareness is limited by the suggestions we accept, and the will is weakened.

Self-training, on the other hand, is based on the expansion of awareness and the increasing ability to guide or direct that awareness. In self-training, you do not accept suggestion (someone else's experience) as the basis for decision. Instead, you seek to discover your own inner reality through directing and examining your own experience. In this way you gain self-confidence and develop the power of will, the ability to discriminate, to decide, and to carry through that decision in thought, speech, and action. Self-training involves all aspects of your life, from self-study and relaxation to regulation of the four primitive urges.

Relaxation training provides a concrete example of the two different approaches to training. As noted earlier, external training utilizes suggestion and autosuggestion to create a state of relaxation. This method, usually used by psychologists, psychiatrists, and other therapists, is effective to a limited degree. In self-training we use the Relaxation Posture, Diaphragmatic Breathing, and observation of a smooth, even flow of breath. We direct our attention toward what is taking place in the body. This expands our awareness, providing greater control. You can easily tell the difference between relaxation based on suggestion and relaxation based on diaphragmatic breathing and direct awareness. The first leads only to a state of relaxation; the latter leads to a state of inner knowledge and balance—as well as to a much deeper state of relaxation.

The purpose of self-training is to develop the self-mastery that comes from self-knowledge and self-control. In this way we increase our capacity to consciously direct the mind, speech, and actions. When we no longer create inner conflicts through indecisiveness, we control and direct the flow of emotional energy and achieve balance. Once we free the mind of the dragons, we can use our inner resources to become more successful, gain deeper knowledge, and develop our creative abilities.

There are several positive attitudes that not only are essential for good health, but facilitate our efforts at self-training. There are certainly more than discussed here (and you can add as many as you wish), but the following play a major role in determining our success. They are not moral absolutes, but practical guides to day-to-day life.

SELF-RESPONSIBILITY

|||||||||| By now you should realize that you have sole responsibility for yourself and your world. This doesn't mean blame. As discussed in Chapter 1, responsibility is really response ability. There is no room for blaming others and becoming a victim, or blaming ourselves and becoming depressed. Practice taking responsibility for your feelings and actions without blaming yourself for mistakes. Remember, it's when we make mistakes that we pay closest attention and learn the most.

The outstanding characteristic of self-responsibility is personal strength. The choices we make for ourselves allow us to go through life without feeling resentment toward others. Those who interact with us feel comfortable and enjoy our company because they know that they won't be blamed for how we feel. Even if they disagree with us, they respect us because we act with integrity and responsibility.

SELF-ACCEPTANCE

|||||||||| This doesn't mean a pat-on-the-back, "I'm okay no matter what" attitude, nor is it self-serving egotism. True self-acceptance allows us to look at all aspects of ourselves and to recognize their fundamental unity. It is the recognition that mistakes and failures are opportunities for learning and growth, not whipping posts for self-punishment. It is also the recognition that one's intrinsic value is never altered by petty stupidities.

To the degree that we condemn ourselves, we create unnecessary suffering. To the degree that we condemn ourselves, we also condemn others. Self-acceptance leads to acceptance of others. The biblical commandment "Love thy neighbor as thyself" is not a hopeful injunction, but an accurate description of reality. You can only love others to the extent that you can love yourself. This isn't an egotistical and selfish concern for your personality; it is a deep and abiding respect for the universal consciousness, the spiritual Self that is inherent in all of us.

Both self-acceptance and self-responsibility are extremely practical. Most of us focus on only part of the truth about ourselves, the part which satisfies our emotional need or condition at a given time. It's very easy to focus on negativity when we feel depressed, or "down on ourselves." Then all we can see are our mistakes, our petty faults and stupidities, and the consequence is more suffering and depression. Or perhaps we do something marvelously well, and we become big-headed in our egotism. Both attitudes are based on a partial understanding, an incomplete awareness of the truth about ourselves.

Through meditation, we begin to see ourselves in a calm, detached way—we observe the personality, the workings of the mind and body, from a neutral viewpoint. This sharpens our discrimination, our ability to discern clearly cause/effect relationships without judgment. Judgment implies a right or wrong, good or bad value placed upon the cause/effect relationship, and this leads to emotional involvement. To understand our inner workings clearly, we must be able to experience them directly without interference from our emotions and defense mechanisms. This awareness enables us to alter the habits and patterns we decide are not helpful. If we judge instead of discriminate, we obscure this knowledge by our emotional attachment to a "good" or "bad" outcome. It is very probable that our judgments would then be wrong, as they would be based on inaccurate information.

Self-acceptance, on the other hand, allows us to experience the truth about ourselves. The very practical consequence of this knowledge has been stated in many ways, and for thousands of years. In the Western world it is reflected in the biblical statement "The truth shall set you free." In the Eastern world it is reflected in the Vedantic statement "Knowledge is that which liberates."

The outstanding characteristic of self-acceptance is humility. Genuine humility has little relationship to meekness or passivity. It arises from inner strength and health. It has its origin in the sense of awe that we experience upon the birth of a child, when we look at the starry heavens on a clear, dark night, or experience the power of a thunderstorm. When we see all of the personality, and the spiritual Self that lies at the heart of it, we experience an inner sense of awe as we recognize that we are one small but integral part of a reality that is far larger, more profound, and more mysterious than our ego. This natural sense of humility stimulates our curiosity and allows us to learn, to appreciate other ways of living, and to be attuned to the rhythms of life around us.

SKEPTICAL CURIOSITY

||||||||||| If you really want to learn about yourself, develop a very healthy skeptical curiosity. Obviously, curiosity is necessary. If it only feeds a superficial analysis, it will impede your ability to discriminate, to observe your mind with detachment and dispassion. You need to be skeptical about whatever answers your mind presents to you. Your mind never tells you the truth, it only tells you what it needs to say to maintain its own integrity and patterns.

If you remember that your purpose is not to find answers, but only to observe, you facilitate the natural evolutionary process of inner transformation and growth. Direct, experiential knowledge does not require that your mind analyze itself; it requires only that you become aware of what the mind is doing at the time it is doing it. Constantly free yourself from preconceived notions about what should be. This can be done easily as you develop your skill with Breath Awareness.

Remember that beliefs are guidelines, not gospel truth. They are structures that help us organize our experience. But when they become rigid, when we allow ourselves to be trapped into "only one way" thinking, we stop growing and create fear. As long as we remain flexible and willing to entertain new ideas, alternative ways of viewing life and the world, we will continue to grow and expand.

These three attitudes—self-responsibility, self-acceptance, and skeptical curiosity—are integral to achieving self-mastery. The practice of meditation develops and strengthens them. When you practice you set in motion a circular reinforcement system. Self-training and meditation help develop these attitudes and these attitudes strengthen your practice.

Building Skills

|||||||||| You have the basic information, now you must establish your own self-training program. There is no other way to gain mastery, strength, and freedom. Only you can do the necessary breathing and relaxation, as well as practice concentration and meditation. Only you can regulate your diet and exercise. Remember, the whole person needs to be trained. If you do a partial job, you only obtain partial results. To this end there are a few points that you should keep in mind when establishing your own program:

1. *Begin with the practice of diaphragmatic breathing.* Proper regulation of the breath is of primary importance in stress management. In fact, you must breathe diaphragmatically in order to eliminate unnecessary levels of arousal in the body. If your breathing rate is "normal" (if it is between sixteen and twenty breaths per minute), you can be sure that you suffer from stress.

A minimum practice is ten to fifteen minutes twice daily. This can easily be done when you go to bed at night and right as you awaken in the morning. Daily practice gradually reestablishes diaphragmatic breathing as your habitual pattern. It will also reduce the accumulated stress in the body and prepare the mind for concentration exercises.

2. *Begin your self-training program very gently.* Don't expect yourself to start an all-out program, spending an hour or two every day on it. You will tire of this superficial discipline very quickly—and decide to stop doing anything. The most successful programs are those that are built slowly and methodically. De-

cide what you can do on a daily basis that will not interfere with your essential duties. Then make sure that you practice according to that schedule every day.

When one exercise, or period of practice, has become habitual, then add on to it. For example, once you have become accustomed to spending five or ten minutes on Diaphragmatic Breathing every morning, add five minutes of concentration on Breath Awareness. Then slowly expand that period of concentration to your capacity. If there are times when you feel that you can't concentrate, simply practice your breathing. Keep practice time for practice. Don't do something else with the time you have set aside for it.

Apply this same method of scheduling to your physical exercise. If you do five minutes of stretching, slowly expand the time and the amount you exercise after the first five minutes has become routine. Self-discipline is a matter of slowly acquiring the habits you want to have. It should not be self-punishment. Avoid sudden and dramatic changes, as these most often lead to resistance and problems. Study yourself; learn to understand your needs, and gradually shape your behavior to satisfy those needs in a systematic and regulated way.

3. *Be consistent.* Even if you do only five minutes of diaphragmatic breathing daily, do that every day. Consistent practice develops skill. The more systematic you are, the greater will be your progress. It definitely helps if you set aside a specific time every day in which to practice. This helps establish the habit. You will also find that this daily time period becomes a stimulus for inducing a state of relaxation and calm. The same is true if you select a certain room or place to do your practice. This place becomes associated with relaxation and further reinforces your practice. In this vein, it is important that the place be quiet, clean, and well ventilated. Don't expect to gain skill in inner concentration and relaxation by practicing in the corporate cafeteria or some other noisy place.

4. *Be flexible and work within your own capacity.* Your goal is increased awareness, not a particular state or exercise ability. Learn to let your concentration flow; it should not be forced (forced relaxation or concentration only creates tension). You create more tension when you try to beat the clock or set some kind of record. Remember that you are an explorer, discovering the truth about yourself at this moment; you are not trying to become an expert at anything. By working consistently and systematically within your own unique capacity, you will definitely expand it.

5. *Be patient.* Allow time for progress to take place. Be gentle with yourself; trust in your innate capacity for growth. Trees, flowers, plants, and animals all grow to fulfill their innate potential. You have that same capacity. You create tension when you try to control instead of allowing your innate capacity to unfold in its own natural, inevitable way. Trusting yourself helps you grow and

creates a minimum of stress. Above all, your program must be very practical. Each time that you practice, it is an excursion into awareness and tranquillity—so enjoy what you are doing.

I strongly recommended that you work with a competent meditation teacher, preferably one with years of training in breathing and meditation techniques. While this book gives you sufficient information to begin your practice, meditation is best learned directly from a good teacher. When selecting one, examine both his training and experience as well as his students. The biblical phrase "By their fruits shall ye know them" definitely applies in this situation. The teacher should also be inspiring and should exhibit some degree of self-awareness and self-control. Real teachers aren't hunting for mindless followers. They work to instill independence and self-respect in their students. Real teachers will be demanding, pushing you to your limits, testing your strengths, and helping you become stronger. But most of all, does the particular path really appeal to you? Does it fit your heart?

Becoming Fully Human

|||||||||| Of all the sources of stress, fear, self-hatred, and loneliness are the most destructive. These are the "will-killers" that cripple us, prevent us from being creative, and destroy our human potential. When we objectively examine our dragons, we discover an untapped capacity for life that we had only vague notions and dreams of before. Just as the calm depths of a lake lie hidden beneath its turbulent surface, so does our true potential lie hidden by the sound and fury of our dragons.

It is not by accident that the same tools which eliminate the dragons also lead us to experience, directly and consciously, our true selves. In a very real sense, self-mastery, taking charge of the personality, is also Self-Mastery, the fulfillment of our spiritual heritage. This has been known to yoga science for thousands of years. By learning to regulate your breath and develop your powers of inner concentration and meditation, you take the first steps on a wonderful journey to fulfilling your inner potential. Each step, however small, brings greater understanding and increased capacity for living life in all its fullness and richness. Our dragons allow us to be only partly human. To become fully human is to discover the peace within and to live using our full capacity.

We call this personal empowerment. Empowerment doesn't depend on external conditions. It can't be earned through university degrees or granted by government decree. Many of us think that if we become rich and famous, we'll be happy and content and personally fulfilled. It doesn't work that way. Personal empowerment is exactly that—personal. It arises out of the innate resources found in every one of us. When we discover these inner resources and turn them into conscious skills, we empower ourselves, become effective human beings, and create the life we choose.

Throughout the book, we spoke of various innate abilities, such as instinct, intuition, and genuine self-confidence, that emerge from within the different dimensions of the personality. Now we will put them all together to see what the road map of personal empowerment looks like.

The ultimate skill is refined concentration, which we achieve through the practice of meditation. When we use meditation we achieve awareness and skill in the following areas:

• Balance—We develop health and wellness. These are the skills of *body/mind balance, optimism/joy,* and *contentment* that lead to a healthy mind and body, free from stress and disease. Through self-control, we face the world with equanimity, free from fears, worries, and compulsive wants and needs. Optimism and joy are inner qualities that arise naturally from a balanced mind.

• Perceptual Sensitivity—We develop *instinct, creativity,* and *imagination.* As we have already seen, our instincts are a powerful source of information. As we weave the patterns of our lives, our creativity not only solves problems, but adds color and beauty. When we remove the dragons from the mind, our imagination becomes a powerful tool to direct our creativity and the power of the mind to accomplish what we choose.

• Insight—We develop *intuition, reasoning,* and *decisiveness.* These visionary skills allow us to create our future. Intuition, the knowledge of cause/effect relationships, provides both insight and wisdom. It is our true conscience, telling us what will benefit us, and what we should avoid. Our power of critical thinking, or reasoning, allows us to understand and solve the problems we face. When we come to trust the mind, making decisions is not any more difficult than paying attention. We already know what to do, and even how to do it. Decisiveness is a natural function when we eliminate self-doubts, anxieties, the fear of making mistakes, or the fear of what others will think of us.

• Power—We develop *genuine self-confidence, will,* and *self-discipline.* Through self-confidence, we can turn any obstacle into an opportunity. When we act with integrity, when we are consistent with who we are, we develop a strong will, the ability to consciously direct the power of the mind. Above all, life demands self-discipline. For those who understand the mind, self-discipline is simply doing what you really want to do. The mind has an infinite capacity to form habits. By taking charge of this capacity, we can consciously build the habits we choose, and act in the ways we want to act.

• Harmony—We develop a sense of *wholeness and community* and the spiritual skills of *cooperation, humility,* and *love.* We know that fear and self-hatred are two of the greatest sources of stress. But there is another, even greater, and that is loneliness. Of all the conditions that we face as human beings, the greatest unhappiness is loneliness. We make friends, get married, have families, and yet we remain lonely. The only solution to this deep-seated isolation is to discover the friend and lover within, the spiritual Self. The experience of this spiritual Self allows us to be whole and ends our loneliness forever.

Spiritual skills arise from the successful practice of meditation. As we discover the power of our human spirit, we realize that the fundamental law of life is not "survival of the fittest," but cooperation. Our personality is a cooperative effort. All levels, functions, and systems of our personality work together, doing whatever is necessary to maintain the personality. Each part, organ, and function serves the whole. Our personality is a model of interdependency and cooperation. When these don't cooperate, the result is stress and disease.

When we realize our spiritual Self, we understand that all living creatures are a part of the whole. We experience a sense of community that destroys all vestiges of mistrust, isolation, loneliness, and fear. In their place is the natural awe and humility that spiritual realization brings. The final skill, love, is the expression of the spiritual Self in our daily life. The more we give of ourselves, the greater we become. If we give respect, we gain respect. If we give power, we gain power. By giving of ourselves, we overcome all self-imposed limitations.

Fulfilling the Promise

|||||||||| Why be content with just a little relaxation or a healthier cardiovascular system? These you can have—and much, much more. Experience your true nature directly. Calm the body; then calm the mind through self-training. Allow no movement of body or mind to disturb the clarity of your inner perception. Meditation will lead you to fulfill the most meaningful question of all "Who am I?"

It is important to remember, however, that we are talking about self-mastery—not religious ritual. They should not be confused. Meditation is a practical technique for understanding human nature at all levels. This is the most important thing we can do. The great sages of all cultures have been very practical men and women who, through meditation, have sought for and discovered genuine and lasting release from fear and suffering. What they discovered may be found in many languages, in many religions, in many cultures. It is found in Sophocles' statement "Know Thyself"; it is "Be still and know that I am God" in the Jewish tradition; it is "The kingdom of God is within" in the

Christian tradition; and in the Vedantic tradition it is "That I am." Every culture expresses this one great truth in some way. It is the same truth that you must, and will, discover in your own practice.

Nothing is more practical than the freedom of self-mastery. Nothing is more powerful than the direct and joyful experience of the inner spiritual Self, and the discovery that it has always been there. As T. S. Eliot said at the end of his last and greatest work, the *Four Quartets:*

> *We shall not cease from exploration*
> *And the end of all our exploring*
> *Will be to arrive where we started*
> *And know the place for the first time.*

ON THE WAY TO SELF-MASTERY: STARTING YOUR SELF-TRAINING PROGRAM

If you always do what you always done,
you always get what you always got.
—Anonymous

|||||||||| To build a successful self-training program takes commitment, care, and attention. When we were children, we were told what to do, when to do it, and even how to do it. As adults, we often find the same conditions—either someone telling us what, when, and how or we struggle with conditions that dictate to us our what, when, and how. Self-training programs are different. You are in charge; you and you alone decide what is to be done and what is not to be done.

The great beauty of self-training is that you get out of it exactly what you put into it. You alone decide how important it is to develop your inner strengths. You alone decide the amount of time and effort. You have the freedom to make excuses, you can find any number of valid reasons for not taking the time to practice. But in the end, it is your life and what you make of it is up to you. You end up with what you take the time to create.

Inspiration and Commitment

|||||||||| Obviously, the key is your commitment to your own self-mastery. What you need to know is that commitment is an emotional process based on inspiration, not facts and information. Remember from Chapter 9 that desire is the motivating force. Very little desire comes from facts. My Master always spoke of

progress as being 90 percent inspiration and 10 percent perspiration. When you are inspired, effort becomes effortless. You can do a number of things to maintain your commitment to your own self-mastery.

1. Maintain a high level of inspiration. Read books, talk with others who are engaged in developing self-mastery, listen to inspiring lectures, do whatever you need to keep your level of interest high in your practice and in your goals.

2. Enjoy whatever exercises you do. We make a great mistake when we look upon self-mastery as "work." It isn't. It is experimentation, it is exploration, it is having fun with your mind. When it becomes a burden that you "must do" along with all the other things you "must do," then your practice is definitely in danger.

3. Strive to create "beginner's mind." Don't let routine dull your attention. In karate, we strive to achieve "beginner's mind." When we first learn something that we are interested in, when we are beginners, our attention is really focused. As we become more familiar, we lose this capacity for attention, and we lose our capacity to learn. In doing your exercises, don't let them become routine in your mind. Pay attention, learn to watch for the subtle changes that are always there.

4. Your mind can provide powerful motivation and encouragement through affirmations. An *affirmation* is a mental/emotional confirmation of your own power or of the reality you want to bring about. You create affirmations with thoughts, images, or feelings. The greater your concentration, the more effective the affirmation. To be effective, affirmations must be made with a strong desire and in accordance with what you really believe and value.

There are no magic affirmations; there are only thoughts or images that the mind empowers. Below are a few affirmations that I have found particularly helpful:

- I should do it, I can do it, I will do it.
- I am full of confidence, free of worry and doubt.
- I am responsible, able to learn from any situation.
- Fear [or doubt] is a thought. I will face my fears [or doubts], let them pass through without resistance, and when they have passed, only I will remain.

To do an affirmation, begin with the Centering Exercise in Chapter 8. Then focus your attention on the affirmation. Allow your entire mind to be filled with the affirmation until you actually feel the confidence and calm indicated by the words. Once you feel the emotional aspect of the affirmation, clearly picture yourself going through the day, doing your tasks in this calm and focused state. If the affirmation is specific to a particular task, clearly picture yourself completing the task.

Some Basic Principles

- Build with simplicity: keep your program very simple and direct. Make only one or two small changes in your daily routine, and practice these changes until they become habits.
- Don't try to change the world or yourself in a day. Make a reasonable time commitment. Keep in mind that you earn depending on what you invest. A five-minute investment is not a large investment. In my experience, progress demands that you make at least one fifteen-minute commitment where you work only on building inner skills.
- Consistency is important. A fifteen-minute commitment done consistently provides real benefits whereas an hour done haphazardly will lead to little skill development. Every day do something to become stronger, wiser, and more capable.
- Persist until you have the habit or skill established. If you finish the smallest of tasks, you strengthen your will. On the other hand, if you do not finish a self-assigned task, you subtly weaken your will.
- Build on a strong foundation, and continue to build it. You won't be able to meditate if you can't breathe properly and have chronic tension in your body. Start at the beginning, build your skill at relaxation, and establish diaphragmatic breathing as your moment-to-moment breathing pattern. Then your practice at concentration and other exercises will be successful.
- Develop an attitude of experimentation and playfulness with your self-training program. Once you begin to work with your mind, you will discover a wide array of exercises. Some you will like and some you won't. Don't be afraid to try new ways of gaining insight, developing your instincts, or solving problems.

Getting Started

|||||||||| The exercises from the book are summarized in Appendix A. There are exercises, such as meditation or concentration exercises, which must be done every day and require an investment of time to do. There are also exercises and

techniques which are incorporated as part of your day-to-day activities, such as Breath Awareness and the RARE technique for conflict management. These do not require any separate time to do. Then there are exercises which take some time to do, but can be done whenever you have the need, such as the Insight Exercise from Chapter 8.

The absolutely essential techniques are:

- Diaphragmatic Breathing
- Relaxation, particularly Deep-State Breath Relaxation and "61 Points"
- Breath Awareness
- Concentration (such as the Candle Gaze Exercise)
- Meditation

You will find that your ability to work successfully with any mind technique will depend on your ability to concentrate. Of course, the more you use any technique, the more skilled you become.

The Essential Elements

||||||||||| *Make a Commitment:* Set aside one period of time during the day which you dedicate to developing self-mastery skills. Pick a time when you can leave all other concerns and duties behind. This time should become sacred to you, and don't allow anything to intrude or postpone it. A reasonable beginning time is fifteen minutes. Once you make the commitment, always find a time to fulfill it. It's best if that time is the same every day, but there may be times when you can't be that consistent. Then be practical, and take the time when you can.

Different exercises are best done at different times. It might be best to practice relaxation right after you come home from work. But after you are skilled in relaxation, that fifteen minutes should be given over to concentration and meditation exercises. These are often best done in the early morning before your mind is distracted and disturbed by the day's events.

||||||||||| *Build the Foundation:* The first techniques should be focused on diaphragmatic breathing and relaxation skills. Use the practice period to work on relaxation. Start by learning muscle relaxation. Then shift to the Deep-State Breath Relaxation. After mastering this exercise, move on to the "61 Points" Exercise. Once you are skilled in relaxation, never spend more than five minutes doing deep relaxation unless it is the "61 Points" Exercise. Make sure you don't

allow yourself to fall asleep during relaxation training. Go back periodically and do a long relaxation just to maintain a high degree of skill.

At the same time, reestablish diaphragmatic breathing as your moment-to-moment breathing pattern. Establish a habit of practicing for at least ten minutes right before falling asleep. Focus on even breathing for the first five to eight minutes, then switch over to 2:1 Breathing to create a deeper state of rest. Practice diaphragmatic breathing during the day as often as you can remember to do so. The more you practice, the stronger your habit becomes. Continue to practice even after diaphragmatic breathing becomes your habit. After twenty-five years, I still practice diaphragmatic breathing right before falling asleep.

|||||||||| *Incorporate Breath Awareness into Your Day-to-Day Activities:* Breath Awareness is a key skill. It can be done anywhere, anytime. All you have to do is remember to do it. Leave notes for yourself, use the alarm on your wristwatch to remind you to practice, do whatever you need to do to remember to practice Breath Awareness. This exercise is the most practical and important mind-management technique you have available to you. Use it, use it, use it, every chance you have.

Taking two minutes to clear your mind with Breath Awareness minimizes chronic stress and fatigue and clears your mind for the next task you face. Using Breath Awareness during traffic keeps you free from traffic stress. Whenever I travel on a plane, I spend at least part of the time focusing on Breath Awareness. This minimizes travel fatigue and leaves me ready to work when I arrive at my destination.

|||||||||| *Develop Concentration Skills:* Once you are skilled at relaxation, use the fifteen-minute period to practice concentration exercises. When you practice concentration and meditation exercises, sit in an erect, relaxed posture with your head, neck, and trunk properly aligned. This allows your mind to come to a deep state of focus and your body to be very relaxed without falling asleep. Continue to practice deep relaxation once or twice a week, but use breathing techniques or the "61 Points" Exercise.

|||||||||| *Build a Solid, Consistent Meditation Practice:* After six to eight weeks, you should be sitting at least once a day to train your mind in concentration and meditation. Try to maintain at least a fifteen-minute period, but don't force your mind. On days when your mind won't focus on the meditation technique, switch to Breath Awareness for that period of time. But gradually, train your mind to stay focused on the image of a flame or the *So/Hum* of the Meditation Exercise. This will refine your power of concentration, develop your intuition, and gently lead to the mystical experience that has so much power. Once you

establish a meditation exercise, don't keep switching the focus point. Maintain a consistent practice so the concentration becomes refined.

|||||||||| *Incorporate Techniques into Your Day-to-Day Activities:* Develop the habit of using mind exercises and techniques whenever you have the opportunity. It takes very little time to use the Centering Exercise for creative problem solving or to minimize an emotional reaction. By using different techniques, you build powerful habits for problem solving in the mind. You will find that even a short five-minute meditation or concentration practice during a hectic day will pay large dividends in your ability to maintain a calm mind and solve problems in a creative way.

|||||||||| *Find Time to Stay Flexible:* Stretching exercises are best done in the morning for general health, and in the evening to increase flexibility. It is often very useful to spend a few minutes stretching in the morning before practicing meditation. You will find the Sun Salutation to be very helpful in the morning for taking the kinks out of the body and energizing your mind. Do a minimum of six every morning for the best effect.

A Personal Self-Training Program

|||||||||| This section includes a suggested daily schedule for a self-training program. Use it as a guide to help you establish your own unique program based on your schedule, needs, and goals. Remember, you have to fit your needs and goals into your own program.

You can also establish your own unique program. Grab a pencil and a piece of paper, and let's outline a program. This will help clarify your goals and what steps you need to take in order to accomplish them. We will look at four areas: goals, steps to accomplish your goals, possible interference, and specific steps to take.

1. *Goals:* Decide what you would like to accomplish in the next month, six months from now, one year from now. Write out your goals. You can project as far as you want, but keep it practical.

2. *What will help me accomplish my goals:* List the specific things that you must do to accomplish your goals. This will include setting up a time to practice the exercises, noting changes in your diet, setting up reminders in your computer or on your desk, and so on.

3. *Interference and countermeasures:* We all have habits and patterns that

Addendum Table A.1
Suggested Daily Schedule for
Relaxation/Meditation Techniques

Morning:

Practice 10–15 minutes of diaphragmatic breathing immediately upon awakening. Use an 8- to 10-pound pliable weight to strengthen the diaphragm.

Shower or bath: loosens up the muscles, clears the mind.

5 minutes of stretching exercises.

5–10 Sun Salutations; begin with 2 or 3, gradually increasing the number over a period of weeks until doing 12 or more.

Sit quietly for 10 minutes of Breath Awareness; gradually increase to 20 minutes.

During the Day:

2-minute breath break or Breath Awareness as often as you can, and particularly between projects. It helps clear the mind and allows you to focus on the new project. (2:1 Breathing can be very helpful.)

Take a 10-minute relaxation (concentration) break in the morning and afternoon; you will be surprised at how it helps clarify your thinking.

After Work:

Relaxation exercise right after you come home from work: this clears your mind of work-related tensions, increases your energy, and facilitates interaction with friends and family.

Evening:

10 minutes of 2:1 diaphragmatic breathing in bed right before going to sleep, using the 8- to 10-pound weight.

Concentration exercise should be done at least once daily; 15 to 20 minutes of concentration is worth 60 minutes of relaxation exercises.

Using the Breath Awareness technique as often as you can during the day will gradually increase your ability to stay calm and relaxed. This schedule is only a guide. Evolve your own schedule and slowly increase the time spent on concentration/meditation exercises. The key is to be consistent!

create resistance. Identify these habits and the steps you can take to minimize their impact on you.

4. *Specific steps:* Decide what practical steps to take in order to reach your goals. Be very specific about how much time you will commit to, when you will do it, and even what exercises you are going to do.

Below is a sample program to give you an idea of what your outline could look like. This program is on concentration.

1. *Goals:* Increase my power of concentration. To accomplish this I first need to lower my stress level and then learn to focus my mind more effectively. So I will need to learn deep relaxation, make sure my breathing is done with the diaphragm, and practice concentration exercises. By the end of:

- First month: I want to establish diaphragmatic breathing as my normal breathing pattern.
- Second month: Become skillful at deep relaxation.
- Third month: Practice Candle Gaze Exercise after doing relaxation.
- Sixth month: Sit comfortably and still for 15 minutes, focusing on Breath Awareness.

2. *What will help me accomplish my goals:* I will do the following to help me achieve my goals:

- Set up a specific time for practice; for the first two months I will take 15 minutes to practice relaxation right when I come home from work.
- Reduce my intake of stimulants (coffee) and depressants (alcohol), particularly at times when they might interfere with my practice.
- Practice being more patient with myself and others; use Breath Awareness to help me be less reactive; set up notes to remind me to use Breath Awareness.
- Take time to read materials that interest and inspire me.

3. *Interference and countermeasures:* Taking the time to do the exercises; I hate to follow a schedule; laziness; not seeing any progress; boredom with the exercise routine. Solutions:

- Set up and commit to a specific time for practice that has minimal chance for interference.
- Don't allow myself to become a fanatic. Be flexible, vary my schedule, and don't be overly restrictive about my diet.

- Reward myself when I feel I have accomplished a certain degree of ability to relax, to stay calm during conflict situations, or to become more focused.
- Keep sight of my goals.
- Add a new exercise when I become bored.

4. *Specific steps:*

- *First step:* Read more about stress, make or buy a relaxation tape; practice Breath Awareness during the day as often as I can remember, work with diaphragmatic breathing for 15 minutes before going to sleep, and as often as I can during the day. Length of time: one month.
- *Second step:* Practice relaxation exercise at least once a day lying in the Relaxation Posture. Be aware of breathing as often as I can during the day; take breath breaks at work. Length of time: one month.
- *Third step:* Begin practicing Candle Gaze after relaxation period. Length of time: one month or until I reach 15 minutes on the gaze.
- *Fourth step:* Begin practicing inner concentration using *So/Hum* for at least 15 minutes every day. Begin to work with the Centering Exercise to solve problems and use the Insight Exercise to help me make decisions.

Don't be discouraged if you aren't enlightened after five days, or five weeks, or five months, or even five years. Self-mastery is a lifetime of exploration, experimentation, and expression. With honest and consistent effort, you cannot fail. After all, you already are the power, you already are the spiritual Self. The only thing left is discovery.

APPENDIX A
SUMMARY OF EXERCISES

||||||||| *Awareness Exercises:* These exercises are designed to increase self-awareness and our sensitivity to the events and relationships within the different dimensions of the personality.

EXERCISE	CHAPTER	PAGE	PURPOSE AND VALUE
Traveling Exercise	2	33	To become aware of the different levels of the personality and the power functions operating at each level.
Mind/Body Awareness	3	92	Develops sensitivity to the impact of our thoughts on the body.
Butterfly Image	3	64	To gain awareness of how images in the mind can control a physical event in the body.
Green Frog	3	72	Develops awareness of how language can provide invalid information; helps gain objectivity toward our thoughts and images.

||||||||| *Desk Exercises:* Simple stretching exercises for the head, neck, and shoulders to help minimize and eliminate chronic stress in these areas. These exercises are easily done while sitting at your desk, or at any time during the day.

EXERCISE	CHAPTER	PAGE	PURPOSE AND VALUE
Shoulder Rotations	5	122	Loosens shoulder muscles.
Neck Rotations	5	123	Loosens neck muscles
Forehead and Sinus Massage	5	123	Reduces tension in face and eye muscles.

|||||||||| *Balancing Exercises:* Simple, easy-to-do exercises to increase the coordination between the left and right hemispheres of the brain.

EXERCISE	CHAPTER	PAGE	PURPOSE AND VALUE
Hand-to-Knee	5	126	Mental and physical balance, increased alertness.
Elbow-to-Knee	5	126	Mental and physical balance, increased alertness.
Elbow-to-Knee Front to Back	5	126	Mental and physical balance, increased alertness.

|||||||||| *Relaxation Exercises:* Designed to help create deep relaxation, to reduce chronic levels of tension, stress, and emotional reactivity, and to systematically build skills in deep relaxation.

EXERCISE	CHAPTER	PAGE	PURPOSE AND VALUE
Relaxation Posture	5	106	A posture that allows all the muscles of the body to achieve a state of relaxation; helpful in learning deep relaxation.
Muscle Relaxation	Appendix B	273	Systematic exercise to learn deep relaxation on the structural level.
Sweeping Breath	6	167	A simple, easy-to-use relaxation exercise often used as a preliminary relaxation exercise for other relaxation techniques or concentration exercises.
Deep-State Breath Relaxation	6 & Appendix C	166 275	A sophisticated breathing exercise that creates a deep state of relaxation by manipulating the autonomic nervous system.
61 Points	8 & Appendix D	200 278	A sophisticated concentration/relaxation exercise which provides a profound state of relaxation, useful in preventing hypertension.

|||||||||| *Stretching Exercises:* A series of stretching exercises based on hatha yoga designed to improve flexibility, enhance glandular and neurological activity, and calm the mind.

EXERCISE	CHAPTER	PAGE	PURPOSE AND VALUE
Side Stretch	5	127	These exercises increase circulation and breathing capacity, bring flexibility to the spine and limbs, develop arms and chest, and help reduce abdominal fat.
Simple Back Stretch	5	128	
Angle Posture	5	128	
Torso Twist	5	130	

| Sun Salutation | 5 | 130 | The Sun Salutation is a sophisticated integrated series of 12 spinal positions, each stretching various joints and ligaments and giving different movements to the spinal column. |

|||||||||| *Breathing Exercises:* Designed to develop healthy breathing patterns, increase capacity and energy levels, reduce stress, and stabilize emotional reactivity.

EXERCISE	CHAPTER	PAGE	PURPOSE AND VALUE
Diaphragmatic Breathing	6	147	The natural moment-to-moment breathing pattern; absolutely essential to achieve balance in the body.
2:1 Breathing	6	152	Creates a deeper state of balanced rest in the body by increased stimulation of the parasympathetic nervous system.
Alternate-Nostril Breathing	6	155	Calms and focuses the mind; increases lung capacity and control over autonomic nervous system; can be extended into a sophisticated concentration exercise.
Nasal Wash	6	164	Cleans and rejuvenates the mucus membrane, alleviating congestion and sinus problems; helps eliminate sinus headaches, reduce the symptoms of allergies, prevent colds and sore throats.
Complete Breath	6	166	Increases level of energy, reduces fatigue, and reduces muscle tension.
Sweeping Breath	6	167	A simple, easy-to-use relaxation exercise often used as a preliminary relaxation exercise for other relaxation techniques or concentration exercises.
Deep-State Breath Relaxation	6 & Appendix C	166 275	A sophisticated breathing exercise that creates a deep state of relaxation by manipulating the autonomic nervous system.
Two-Minute Breath Break	6	168	Simple relaxation/mind-clearing exercise to use any time to rebalance, clear the mind, and refocus attention.
Sleep Exercise	6	169	A simple-to-learn and effective sleep exercise that leads to a deep, restful sleep and minimizes, even eliminates, insomnia.

||||||||||| *Mind-Control Techniques:* These techniques are direct methods to strengthen conscious control over the mind and to develop different mind skills.

EXERCISE	CHAPTER	PAGE	PURPOSE AND VALUE
Breath Awareness	7	172	Provides direct control of mind chatter. When used skillfully, provides absolute control over emotional reactions. It is the single most important tool available for taking charge of the mind and creating mental clarity.
RARE Exercise	7	177	A very effective model for conflict management based on self-control and eliminating opposition.
Scanning Exercise	7	178	A technique for a quick check and release of muscle tension.
Three Strategies to Control Fear	7	183	To develop the ability to minimize and eliminate worry and fear.
Four Strategies to End Self-Hatred	7	185	To minimize self-hatred and access inner strength.
"Should" Stopper	7	188	Disrupts the habitual pattern of the mind to rely on "should" and "should not" as a method of self-punishment.
Walking Exercise	7	195	Develops sensitivity to subtle feelings in your body as you react to others. Develops awareness of instincts as well as insights into other people's personalities and your relationship to them.
Creative Thought Exercise	7	192	Demonstrates the creative force of the sensory mind to either help us or create problems for us.

||||||||||| *Concentration and Meditation Exercises:* These exercises are designed to enhance your powers of concentration and lead to the ability to meditate, and to enhance insight and develop self-confidence.

EXERCISE	CHAPTER	PAGE	PURPOSE AND VALUE
61 Points	8 & Appendix D	200 278	A sophisticated concentration/relaxation exercise which provides a profound state of relaxation, useful in preventing hypertension.
Insight Exercise	8	205	An exercise designed to develop insight into which solution or direction is the best one to take to resolve a particular problem or choice point.
Candle Gaze	8	209	An efficient concentration exercise combining an external and internal focus point.
Breath Awareness as Meditation Exercise	8	221	Using Breath Awareness to train concentration and develop meditation skills.
Centering Exercise	8	223	A basic exercise to establish a steady point of internal awareness. Used at the beginning of any meditation exercise, and for exercises involving

other inner skills, such as intuition, imagery work, and conflict resolution.

APPENDIX B
DETAIL OF A MUSCLE-RELAXATION
EXERCISE

||||||||| Begin by lying in the Relaxation Posture. Close your eyes and focus your attention on your breath . . . Breathe easily and gently with the diaphragm, with no jerkiness, stops, or pauses . . . Let your breath be very smooth and even, without any effort on your part . . . Picture yourself breathing in relaxation and exhaling all the tension out of your body . . . Let your breath be very easy and gentle, with no strain or effort . . . You are breathing in peacefulness and quietness, exhaling all thoughts of the past, all concerns for the future . . . Just bring all of your attention to your breath as it flows in and out of your body . . . Now picture your forehead as smooth as a piece of silk . . . as if you are looking into the mirror of your mind and seeing all the bumps and wrinkles melting away in your forehead . . . You can feel the muscles in your forehead relaxing down into your face, relaxing your eyebrows and your eyes . . . relaxing your cheeks . . . the corners of your mouth, your lips, and even your tongue . . . relax your lower jaws and your ears . . . and relax your neck muscles, front and back . . . Picture the muscles in your neck as being very warm, very heavy, and so loose they can't even hold your head up . . .

Again, bring your attention back to your breath, breathing in relaxation and exhaling tension . . . easily, gently, no strain or effort . . . Let your body do all the breathing for you . . . relax your shoulders, letting go of all tension from your shoulders . . . Relax your upper arms and your forearms, picturing the muscles in your arms as being very warm and heavy . . . relax your hands, your fingers, and even your fingertips . . . Again bring your attention back to your breath, and imagine yourself exhaling down to your fingertips and exhaling all the tension out of your arms . . . Very easy, very gentle, no effort . . . letting your body do all the breathing for you . . . Relax your fingertips, fingers, and hands . . . Relax your forearms and your upper arms, picturing the muscles as being very warm and heavy . . . And relax your shoulders . . . Again, bring your attention back to your breath . . . Let the inhalation merge into the exhalation merge into the inhalation . . . smooth and even, the breath is like a large wheel moving effortlessly through the body . . . Relax your chest muscles . . . Relax your stomach and your abdominal muscles . . . Relax your hips . . . Relax your thighs, picturing the muscles as being very warm and heavy . . . Relax your calves . . . your feet, toes, and even the tips of your toes . . .

Again, bring your attention back to your breath . . . Imagine your body to be like a hollow reed, and you are breathing in through your toes, inhaling to the top of your head, filling the body with breath . . . then exhaling from the top of your head to your toes, completely emptying the body of breath . . . all very easily, and gently, and without any effort . . . you are only the witness, allow the body to do all the work . . . In your mind you can feel the entire body breathing in and breathing out . . . expanding on the inhalation and contracting on the exhalation . . .

Relax your toes and your feet . . . relax your calves and thighs, picturing the muscles in your legs as being very warm and heavy . . . Relax your hips . . . Relax your abdominal muscles and your stomach . . . Relax your chest muscles . . . And relax your shoulders . . . Let your whole body become warm and heavy, give up all control over the body, and trust that the floor will support you completely . . . Again, bring your attention back to the breath . . . Let the inhalation merge into the exhalation merge into the inhalation . . . Very easily, very gently . . . breathing in and out very smoothly, without any effort on your part . . .

Relax your neck muscles, front and back . . . Relax your lower jaw and your ears . . . Relax your lips, the corners of your mouth, and even your tongue . . . Relax your cheeks . . . And your eyes . . . Now picture your forehead as smooth as a piece of silk . . . Now right in the center of your mind, where all your thoughts seem to begin, on your next exhalation, relax that mind center . . .

Gently wriggle fingers, toes. Being aware of every movement, slowly raise your arms and hold your hands about four inches in front of your face. Slowly open your eyes to the palms of your hands, then gently lower your hands. Remain as relaxed as you can throughout the day.

During the day, take a few moments to picture your forehead becoming very smooth and even. This will help you stay more relaxed. Don't forget to use diaphragmatic breathing to also keep you more balanced. The greater your skill at muscle relaxation, the more relaxed you stay throughout the day.

APPENDIX C
DETAIL OF DEEP-STATE BREATH
RELAXATION

|||||||||| Lying in the Relaxation Posture with your eyes closed, focus on even, diaphragmatic breathing . . . Let the body do all the breathing for you, you are only the witness to the breathing . . . Let your breath become very smooth and even . . . Breathing in relaxation and exhaling all the tension from your body . . . Breathing in peacefulness and quietness, exhaling all thoughts of the past, and all concerns for the future . . . Now picture your body like a hollow reed, and you are breathing in from your toes, filling your body with breath to the crown of your head, and exhaling back down and out your toes . . . Let your conscious mind travel up the body with the inhalation and back down with the exhalation . . . easily, gently, without any effort and strain, let your body do the breathing for you . . . Inhale from your toes to the crown of your head and exhale down to and out your ankles, then inhale as if you are breathing in through your ankles back to the crown of your head . . . easily, gently, letting your conscious awareness travel between the two points with the inhalation and exhalation . . . Inhale from the ankles to the crown of your head and exhale down and out your knees . . . Inhale through your knees to the crown of your head and exhale down and out the tip of your spine, and inhale from the tip of your spine to the crown of your head, filling only the trunk, neck, and head with breath . . .

Easily and gently, letting your conscious thought travel up and down with the inhalation and exhalation between the two points . . . Inhale from the tip of your spine, up the spine to the crown of your head, and exhale down and out your navel . . . Inhale through your navel to the crown of your head, filling only the stomach, chest, neck, and head with breath . . . easily and gently, without any effort or strain . . . Inhale from the navel to the crown of your head and exhale down and out your heart center, the center of your chest, then inhale from your heart center to the crown of your head, filling only the chest, neck, and head with breath . . . Breathe as quickly as you need to be comfortable, but very easily and gently . . . Without any strain or effort . . . Inhale from your heart center to the crown of your head and exhale down and out the base of your throat, then inhale to the crown of your head filling only your neck and head with breath . . . Notice that your breath is becoming very shallow, hardly any motion of the lungs at all . . . Inhale from the base of your throat to the crown of your head, and exhale down and out the nostrils, then inhale from the opening of the nostrils to the point between the eyes, and exhale back down and out your nostrils, filling only the nose with breath . . . Breathe as quickly as you need to feel comfortable, but very gently, very easily, you shouldn't have to pant . . . Now there is really no breath going at all down into the lungs, just an exchange of air in the nose . . . Your breath will be extremely shallow and light at this point . . .

Now inhale through the tip of your nose to the crown of your head, and exhale from the crown of your head down and out the base of the throat. Then inhale through the base of the throat to the crown of the head, filling the neck and head with breath . . . Let your conscious thought travel up and down between the two points with the inhalation and exhalation, very easily, very gently . . . Inhale from the base of the throat to the crown of the head, and exhale down and out the heart center in the center of the chest, then inhale again from the heart center to the crown of your head, filling the chest, neck, and head with breath . . . Remember, there should be no strain or effort, you are only the witness, letting your body do all the work . . . Inhale from your heart center to the crown of your head and exhale down and out your navel, then inhale from your navel to the crown of your head, filling the stomach, chest, neck, and head with breath . . . easily, gently, without any strain or effort . . . Inhale from your navel to the crown of your head and exhale down your spine and out the tip of your spine, then inhale from the tip of your spine, up the spine to the crown of your head, filling the entire trunk, neck, and head with breath . . . letting your conscious thought travel up and down between the two points . . . Inhale from the tip of your spine, up the spine to the crown of your head and exhale down and out your knees, then inhale through your knees to the crown of your head . . . filling your body from the knees to the crown of your head with breath . . . Easily, gently, let the body do all the work for you . . . Inhale from your knees to the crown of your head and exhale down and out your ankles, then inhale as if breathing through your ankles, filling the body with breath to the crown of your head . . . Let your conscious thought travel up the body with the inhalation and back down with the exhalation, easily, gently . . . Inhale from your ankles to the crown of your head and exhale down and out your toes, completely emptying your body of breath . . . Then inhale, from the toes, filling the body with breath, peacefulness, and quietness to the crown of the head, exhaling from the crown back down and out the toes, completely emptying the body of breath, leaving only the peacefulness and quietness behind . . .

In your mind you can feel your whole body breathing, as if every pore and cell were breathing in and out . . . The entire body expands on the inhalation and contracts on the exhalation . . . very easily, without any effort . . . for a few moments, concentrate on this feeling of expansion and contraction . . .

Gently wriggle fingers, toes. Being aware of every movement, slowly raise your arms and hold your hands about four inches in front of your face. Slowly open your eyes to the palms of your hands, then gently lower your hands. Remain aware of inner calmness and the energy that flows within you, and remain calm and aware throughout the rest of the day.

After you become skillful with this exercise while lying in the Relaxation Posture, you can do it sitting. Our minds have difficulty going around corners, so change the base point from the toes to the tip of the spine. You still begin with a deep and complete gentle breath, but then work your way up the spine. The imagery helps make the exercise effortless so you do not become tense from trying to control your breath. Once you can change the motion without effort or strain, you no longer need to use imagery. At this point, each breath should be either more shallow or deeper than the one before it, depending on which way you are going.

APPENDIX D
DETAIL OF "61 POINTS"
CONCENTRATION EXERCISE

||||||||| Lying in the Relaxation Posture, close your eyes and concentrate on making your breath very even, very steady, and very smooth . . . You are not trying to fill your lungs completely, or trying to empty them. Breathe easily and gently, letting your body do all the work for you. Your breath should be smooth and even, letting your inhalation and exhalation be smooth and even . . . The pressure of the flow of the breath should be even, having the same flow or pressure at the end of the exhalation as at the beginning and in the middle. Don't allow any pauses, jerks, or shakiness in your breath. Even minimize the pause between the inhalation and the exhalation.

Now mentally scan down through the body, checking for any excess muscle tension . . . Wherever you find tension, simply release the tension in the muscles . . . Now using your imagination, picture your body as being a hollow reed. Breathe as if you are breathing through your toes, filling your body with breath to the crown of your head, and exhaling back down and out your toes again. Breathe easily and gently, no strain and no effort . . . Again, you aren't trying to fill your lungs, or empty them completely, just an easy, deep, slow, and gentle breath . . . breathing in through the toes to the crown of your head and exhaling back down and out the toes.

In your mind, you can feel your whole body expanding when you inhale and contracting when you exhale, as if every cell in your body were breathing in and breathing out . . . Easily, gently, no strain, no effort . . .

And now bring your attention to your mind center, the space between your two eyebrows. Picture as clearly as you can a small blue star or blue flame inside the space between the two eyebrows. Let the star or flame be as perfect, as small, and as clear as your mind will allow . . . and now at the base of the throat, the throat center, picture a small blue star or flame . . . in the center of the right shoulder joint . . . in the center of the right elbow joint . . . in the center of the right wrist joint, a small blue star or flame, as clear and as perfect as your mind will allow . . . on the tip of the thumb on the right hand . . . on the tip of the forefinger on the right hand . . . on the tip of the middle finger . . . on the tip of the ring finger on the right hand . . . on the tip of the small finger, a small blue star or flame, as clear and as perfect as your mind will allow . . . again in the center of the right wrist joint . . . in the center of the right elbow joint . . . in the center of the right shoulder joint, a small blue star or flame . . . again, at the base of the throat, the throat center, visualize a small blue star or flame . . .

Now in the center of the left shoulder joint, let the star or flame illuminate the entire center of the joint . . . in the center of the left elbow joint . . . in the center of the left wrist joint . . . now on the tip of the thumb of the left hand . . . on the tip of the forefinger of the left hand . . . on the tip of the middle finger of the left hand . . . on the tip of the ring finger . . . and on the tip of the small finger of the left hand, a small blue star or flame, as perfect and as small as your mind will allow it to be . . . Again, visualize the star or flame in the center of the left wrist joint . . . in the center of the left elbow joint . . . in the center of the left shoulder joint . . . again at the base of the throat, the throat center, a small blue star or flame . . .

Now visualize the star or flame in the center of the chest, between the two breasts, the heart center . . . on the nipple of the right breast, visualize a small blue star or flame . . . back again to the heart center . . . now on the nipple of the left breast . . . back again to the heart center . . . Now visualize the star or flame at the navel center, just behind the navel . . .

Now visualize a small blue star or flame at the pelvic center, in the center between the two hip bones . . . in the center of the right hip joint, let the star or flame illuminate the entire center of the joint . . . in the center of the right knee joint . . . in the center of the right ankle joint . . . at the tip of the large toe on the right foot, a small blue star or flame . . . on the tip of the second toe . . . on the tip of the third or middle toe of the right foot . . . on the tip of the fourth toe . . . and on the tip of the small toe of the right foot, a small blue star or flame as clear and as perfect as your mind will allow it to be . . . Again, in the center of the right ankle joint . . . in the center of the right knee joint . . . in the center of the right hip joint . . .

Now visualize a small blue star or flame at the pelvic center . . . in the center of the left hip joint . . . in the center of the left knee joint, let the star or flame illuminate the entire joint area . . . in the center of the left ankle joint . . . . At the tip of the large toe on the left foot . . . on the tip of the second toe . . . on the tip of the third toe of the left foot . . . on the tip of the fourth toe . . . and on the tip of the small toe, a small blue star or flame, as perfect and as clear as your mind will allow it to be . . . Again, in the center of the left ankle joint . . . in the center of the left knee joint . . . in the center of the left hip joint . . . and again at the pelvic center, a small blue star or flame . . .

At the navel center . . . at the heart center in the middle of the chest . . . at the throat center at the base of the throat . . . and in the mind center, the space between the two eyebrows, let the star or flame be as clear, as perfect, and as small as your mind will allow it to be . . .

Now using your imagination, picture your body as being a hollow reed. Breathe as if you are breathing through your toes, filling your body with breath to the crown of your head, and exhaling back down and out your toes again. Breathe easily and gently, no strain and no effort . . . Again, you aren't trying to fill your lungs, or empty them completely, just an easy, deep, slow, and gentle breath . . . breathing in through the toes to the crown of your head and exhaling back down and out the toes.

In your mind, you can feel your whole mind expanding when you inhale and contracting when you exhale, as if every cell in your body were breathing in and breathing out . . . Easily, gently, no strain, no effort . . .

Gently wriggle fingers, toes. Being aware of every movement, slowly raise your arms and hold your hands about four inches in front of your face. Slowly open your eyes to the palms of your hands, then gently lower your hands. Remain aware of inner calmness and the energy that flows within you, and remain calm and aware throughout the rest of the day.

INDEX

ABOUT THE AUTHOR

PHIL NUERNBERGER, PH.D., is founder and president of Mind Resource Technologies and editor of *Mindscape*, a quarterly newsletter dedicated to the practical investigation of the human mind and its potentials. More than twenty years ago, Dr. Nuernberger initiated one of the earliest clinical biofeedback programs in the U.S.A., teaching patients how to use their minds to solve chronic pain problems, anxiety, and hypertension. At that time he also began one of the first corporate stress-management training programs in America.

Dr. Nuernberger is internationally recognized for his work in leadership training, stress management, and personal effectiveness. Recent corporate clients include Cargill, the Texas State Bar Association, Bank of Nova Scotia, and Unisys. Dr. Nuernberger also trains nursing staff in several large hospitals, serves on the faculty of the Wharton Nursing Supervisors Program sponsored by Johnson and Johnson and serves as a visiting faculty member of The Wharton Arresty Institute of Executive Education. In addition, Dr. Nuernberger has authored two other books, coauthored eight books, and published numerous articles in professional and popular magazines on stress, personal effectiveness, and meditation.

For the past twenty-six years, Dr. Nuernberger has studied and lived with his Tantra Yoga Master both in the United States and in the Himalayan mountains of India and Nepal. For the past seven years, Dr. Nuernberger has also studied karate under the direction of a Japanese Samurai Master and has achieved black-belt ranking. With his lifelong dedication to developing the power of the mind, Dr. Nuernberger combines the knowledge and wisdom of these powerful traditions with his scientific and academic background to create a bridge between East and West.

Dr. Nuernberger is a Selected Honored Member, *National Directory of Who's Who, 1995–96*. He lives with his wife and three children in Honesdale, PA.

Many of the exercises and information discussed in this book are available on audio cassette. For information about audio cassette tape programs in relaxation and meditation, training seminars and key-note engagements, or subscriptions to *Mindscape*, contact:

Mind Resource Technologies
One Rock Ledge Drive
Honesdale, PA 18431
(717) 253-4754